OCR Classical Civilisation

A LEVEL

COMPONENTS 23 AND 24

ALSO AVAILABLE FROM BLOOMSBURY

OCR Classical Civilisation GCSE Route 1: Myth and Religion,
Ben Greenley, Dan Menashe and James Renshaw

OCR Classical Civilisation GCSE Route 2: Women in the Ancient World,
Robert Hancock-Jones, Dan Menashe and James Renshaw

OCR Classical Civilisation AS and A Level Component 11: The World of the Hero,
Sally Knights

OCR Classical Civilisation A Level Components 21 and 22: Greek Theatre and Imperial Image,
Robert Hancock-Jones, James Renshaw and Laura Swift

OCR Classical Civilisation A Level Components 31 and 34: Greek Religion and Democracy and the Athenians,
Athina Mitropoulos, Tim Morrison, James Renshaw and Julietta Steinhauer

OCR Classical Civilisation A Level Components 32 and 33:
Love and Relationships and Politics of the Late Republic,
Matthew Barr, Lucy Cresswell and Alastair Thorley

OCR Ancient History GCSE Component 1: Greece and Persia,
Sam Baddeley, Paul Fowler, Lucy Nicholas and James Renshaw

OCR Ancient History GCSE Component 2: Rome,
Paul Fowler, Christopher Grocock and James Melville

OCR Ancient History AS and A Level Component 1: Greece,
Charlie Cottam, David L. S. Hodgkinson, Steve Matthews, Lucy Nicholas and James Renshaw

OCR Ancient History AS and A Level Component 2: Rome,
Robert Cromarty, James Harrison and Steve Matthews

Books published for the OCR specifications in GCSE and AS / A Level Latin and Classical Greek are also available, including editions of every set text for A Level. Please see our website
www.bloomsbury.com/uk/education/secondary/classics

OCR Classical Civilisation

A LEVEL

COMPONENTS 23 AND 24:
Invention of the Barbarian and Greek Art

ATHINA MITROPOULOS
LAURA SNOOK
ALASTAIR THORLEY

GENERAL EDITOR:
JAMES RENSHAW

Bloomsbury Academic
An imprint of Bloomsbury Publishing Plc

BLOOMSBURY
LONDON · OXFORD · NEW YORK · NEW DELHI · SYDNEY

BLOOMSBURY ACADEMIC
Bloomsbury Publishing Plc
50 Bedford Square, London, WC1B 3DP, UK

BLOOMSBURY, BLOOMSBURY ACADEMIC and the Diana logo are trademarks of
Bloomsbury Publishing Plc

First published 2017
Reprinted 2019

Cover design by Terry Woodley and Olivia D'Cruz
Cover image © Getty/DEA/G. Dagli Orti

A catalogue record for this book is available from the British Library.

A catalog record for this book is available from the Library of Congress.

ISBN: PB: 978-1-3500-2095-5
       ePDF: 978-1-3500-2097-9
       eBook: 978-1-3500-2096-2

Typeset by RefineCatch Limited, Bungay, Suffolk
Printed and bound in India

To find out more about our authors and books visit www.bloomsbury.com
and sign up for our newsletters.

ACKNOWLEDGEMENTS

The authors divided the text between them as follows:

Part 1: Invention of the Barbarian by Alastair Thorley
Part 2: Greek Art by Athina Mitropoulos and Laura Snook.

The authors would like to thank the many anonymous reviewers at universities, schools
and OCR who read and commented on drafts of this text. All errors remain their own.

CONTENTS

INTRODUCTION

Welcome to your textbook for OCR A Level Classical Civilisation.

This book has been created to support two of the components from Component Group 2 Culture and the Arts: Component 23 'Invention of the Barbarian' and Component 24 'Greek Art'.

Through your reading of this textbook and your wider study in class, you will be able to gain a broad knowledge and understanding of a range of literary and cultural materials from the classical world. As well as learning about the culture, history and ideas of the ancient Greeks and Romans, you will read ancient texts in translation and study ancient art and objects from the classical world, together with the surviving remains of religious and domestic architecture.

The specification requires you to respond to the prescribed source material and assess content through analysis and evaluation. The box features (see pp. vii–viii) are designed to build up your skills and knowledge, while exam tips, practice questions, and chapters on assessment will prepare you for taking your final examinations.

A Companion Website, available at www.bloomsbury.com/class-civ-as-a-level, supports this textbook with further information, resources and updates. If you have any suggestions for improvement and additional resources, please get in touch by writing to contact@bloomsbury.com.

We hope you will enjoy this wide-ranging and fascinating course, and that it will inspire you to go on to further study of the ancient world.

HOW TO USE THIS BOOK

The layout and box features of this book are designed to aid your learning.

COLOUR

Box features that focus on assessment preparation and exam skills are coloured in blue.

Box features with Stretch and Challenge material are coloured in yellow.

All other box features are coloured in red.

ICONS

The Prescribed Source icon **PS** flags a quotation or image that is a source prescribed in the specification.

The Stretch and Challenge icon **S&C** indicates that an exercise extends beyond the core content of the specification.

The Companion Website icon **CW** highlights where extra material can be found on the Bloomsbury Companion Website www.bloomsbury.com/class-civ-as-a-level.

BOX FEATURES

In the margins you will find feature boxes giving short factfiles of key events, individuals and places.

Other features either **recommend** teaching material or highlight **prescribed** content and **assessment** tips and information.

Recommended teaching material is found in the following box features:

Activities
Debates
Explore Further
Further Reading
Modern Parallels
Study Questions
Topic Reviews

Prescribed content and assessment-focused tips and information are found in the following box features:

Exam Overviews
Exam Tips
Modern Scholarship
Practice Questions
Prescribed Sources

Material that extends beyond the specification is found in the Stretch and Challenge box features. Remember that the specification requires students to study extra sources and material not listed in the specification, so S&C information and exercises will provide a good place for you to start.

A NOTE ON QUESTIONS

Questions found in Topic Review boxes and Study Question boxes are not worded in the form you will find on the exam papers. They are intended to encourage investigation and revision of the material, but do not reflect the questions you will answer in the exam. Practice Questions at the end of each topic, and the questions found in the 'What to Expect in the Exam' chapters do mirror the format and wording you will encounter in the exam.

GLOSSARY

At the back of the book you will find a full glossary of key words. These words are also defined on pages in margin features.

Spellings of names and texts are formatted in line with the OCR specification.

On the Companion Website you will find a colour-coded glossary that highlights which components the word come from.

IMAGES

Illustrations give you the opportunity to see the ancient visual material you are required to study, flagged with the **PS** icon, but also illustrate other relevant aspects of the ancient world. Often what survives from the ancient world does not provide us with ways to illustrate what we study. Thus, art, drawings and reconstructions from later periods and the modern day may be used to illustrate this book. Don't forget that these are not sources like your prescribed texts and visual material – they are later interpretations of aspects of antiquity and do not represent evidence for analysis.

TRANSLATIONS

Where OCR has commissioned translations of prescribed sources, documents of these are available from the OCR website.

COMPANION WEBSITE

Resources will include:

- links to the text of Prescribed Literary Sources
- further images and information on Prescribed Visual/Material Sources
- annotated further reading
- links to websites that give useful contextual material for study
- quizzes on key topics and themes
- worksheets to supplement Activity box features in the book

DON'T FORGET

Look out for cross references to other pages in the book – this is where you will find further information and be able to link concepts or themes.

PART 1
INVENTION OF THE BARBARIAN

Introduction to Invention of the Barbarian

The invention of the barbarian was a crucial step in the process of defining a Greek identity: through the creation of an 'anti-Greek' barbarian, the Greeks (particularly the Athenians) were able to explore what it meant to be 'Greek'. A variety of 'anti-Greeks' are considered in this topic, ranging from historical Persian kings, such as Xerxes and Cyrus, to mythical barbarian women, such as Medea and the Amazons. The concept of the barbarian was invented from common aspects of the attitudes and behaviour of these 'anti-Greeks'.

The Persian invasions of Greece in the fifth century BC provide an important background to and reason for this invention of the barbarian. Sources considered in this topic include various representations of these battles and their aftermath. The heroic rebuttal of the Persian invasions became, in the hands of Greek writers and artists, a victory of one ideology over another.

The Greeks had their reasons for inventing the barbarian by means of exaggerating stereotypes and polarising differences: the alliance formed between the Greek states in the face of the danger from the Persians was fragile and needed a unifying principle. However, the Greek invention of the barbarian remained distinct from the reality of Persia. The kings of Persia also used art and architecture to project more positive images of themselves and their power, and this topic includes examples of Persian material culture.

In the first James Bond film ('Dr. No', 1962), Bond says to the eponymous villain, 'With your disregard for human life, you must be working for the East'. Dr. No replies, 'East, West, just points of the compass, each as stupid as the other'. This topic examines the root of such prejudices and, inevitably, learners will consider whether, in the modern world, the East and West continue to invent barbarian versions of one another.

General bibliography

Allen, W. (2013) *Euripides' Medea*. London: Duckworth

Hall, E. (1989) *Inventing the Barbarian*. Oxford: Oxford University Press

Harrison, T. (ed.) (2001) *Greeks and Barbarians*. Edinburgh: Edinburgh University Press

Morkot, R. (1996) *Penguin Historical Atlas of Ancient Greece*. London: Penguin

Osborne, R. (2014) *Greek History: The Basics*. London: Routledge

Waters, M. (2014) *Ancient Persia: A Concise History of the Achaemenid Empire*. Cambridge: Cambridge University Press

EXAM OVERVIEW: A LEVEL   H408/23

Your assessment is a written examination testing AO1 and AO2. It is:

30% of the A Level   1 hr 45 mins   75 marks

35 marks will test AO1: demonstrate knowledge and understanding of:

- literature, visual/material culture and classical thought
- how sources and ideas reflect, and influence, their cultural contexts
- possible interpretations of sources, perspectives and ideas by different audiences and individuals

40 marks will test AO2: critically analyse, interpret and evaluate literature, visual/material culture, and classical thought, using evidence to make substantiated judgements and produce coherent and reasoned arguments.

The examination will consist of two sections.

All questions in **Section A** are compulsory. There are three question types:

- short-answer questions
- 10-mark stimulus question using the prescribed sources
- 20-mark essay

Section B has one question type:

- 30-mark essay

There is a choice of one from two essays. In these essays, learners will be expected to make use of secondary sources and academic views to support their argument.

TIMELINE

All dates BC

c. 650	Black Sea colonisation
559–530	Rule of Cyrus the Great
550	Cyrus conquers Media
547–546	Cyrus conquers Lydia
539	Cyrus conquers Babylon
530–522	Rule of Cambyses
525	Persian conquest of Egypt
525	Birth of Aeschylus (dies 456)
522–486	Rule of Darius I
510	The tyrant Hippias is exiled from Athens with Spartan help
508–507	Spartan attempt to halt emerging Athenian democracy fails.
506	A Spartan, Peloponnesian and Theban army invades Attica but does not attack Athens
c. 500	Construction of Persian Royal Road from Sardis to Susa
c. 500–300	Creation of Oxus treasure
499–494	Ionian Revolt
494	Burning of Sardis by the Ionians and Athenians
490–479	Greco-Persian Wars
490	Battle of Marathon
487	Athens is defeated by Aegina
486–465	Rule of Xerxes
c. 484	Birth of Herodotus (dies in *c.* 425)
480	Battles of Thermopylae and Salamis
479	Battle of Plataea
478	Creation of 'Delian League'
472	Aeschylus' Persians
454	Treasury of Delian League is moved from Delos to Athens
432	Completion of Parthenon
431	Beginning of Peloponnesian War pitching Athens and her allies against Sparta and the Peloponnesian League
431	Euripides' Medea

Sources

A varied approach will be necessary when analysing the different types of sources outlined below. It is always important to determine who the intended audience of each source was. Some of the sources were intended for the wider public, whereas some, such as the Greek vases, were for a more select audience. Some of the sources show Greek depictions of Persians, whereas in others the Persians depict themselves. A varied approach will help you to work out what the intended message of the source was, and to evaluate how effective it was at conveying this message.

GREEK HISTORY: HERODOTUS' *HISTORIES*

Herodotus describes his *Histories* as researches into the causes of the Greco-Persian Wars. However, he also includes digressions, which are sometimes very long. These digressions may offer ethnographic information about the different races of the ancient world. For instance in Book 2 (168–181), Herodotus describes the customs of the different tribes of Libya. He also tells stories that offer a moral. Unlike modern historians, Herodotus writes speeches for his characters. Although Herodotus researched his work widely, he will not have had verbatim transcripts of discussions that took place in closed councils from which he copied these speeches. It is not necessary or advisable, however, to disregard everything said in them. They all give readers a lively insight into the characters of the *Histories*, or at least a view of how Herodotus wanted to present them.

It is necessary to take all of the above into account when analysing Herodotus. Historians sift his account for facts which can be verified by other sources. They also ask the question of whether or not Herodotus might be lying and if so why he might be lying. Both of these questions are very difficult to answer. Some historians have seen evidence of a pro-Athenian bias in his work and others have felt that he is pro-Persian; there are still others who see evidence of neither.

GREEK TRAGEDY: *PERSIANS* BY AESCHYLUS, *MEDEA* BY EURIPIDES

Both *Persians* and *Medea* were drama productions known as tragedies. Tragedies were performed in a large open-air theatre built into the slope of the Acropolis in Athens (see Figure 1.1) every year as part of a religious festival in honour of Dionysus. The actors

Part One Invention of the Barbarian

FIGURE 1.1
Theatre of Dionysus in
Athens.

would perform on a low stage and would wear masks, which would help to project their voices to the back of the seating area. The actors would all be male. The flat circular area in front of the stage, known as the *orchestra*, would be occupied by a chorus who would sing and dance at intervals during the play. Although much of the language and style, and many of the references, may be unfamiliar, modern audiences still enjoy productions of Greek tragedies today. Many of the issues raised and discussed in the plays are still relevant. The following suggestions may help you to enjoy *Persians* and *Medea*.

1. Read through the whole play yourself first. Aim to get a sense of the pace of the play and a feel for the different characters. Write down your first impressions of the characters and the themes. Consider which parts of the play were the most memorable.
2. Note the differences in style between the episodes (involving the actors) and the odes (involving the chorus).
3. Consider the main themes of the play – is the playwright trying to put across a 'message' to the audience?
4. Try to put yourself in the position of the original audience – what do you think they would have thought or felt about the characters? How and why would their views and feelings differ from yours?
5. Go back through the play, looking for particular lines and phrases that support your views on the characters and themes of the play.
6. Consider why this play has been included as a source for this topic. Try to identify links between the play and the other sources.
7. Compare the play to other literary and visual sources you have studied. Consider how the play fits with events in Greece at the time it was performed.

8. Performing the play out loud can often give a good idea of how the lines would come across 'off the page'.

9. Watching a performance of a Greek tragedy (even if it is not one of the plays you are studying) is a valuable experience. Productions take place frequently and there are clips online that you can watch. Many modern productions adapt tragedies to reflect concerns or issues in today's society. Considering how you might adapt either *Persians* or *Medea* for a modern production can often help you to identify key themes or spot aspects of the play to which a modern audience would respond most.

This process should help you to formulate your own ideas, which you can back-up by referring to the play itself. When writing your own analysis, don't forget to explain how the play supports your ideas – you must not just let quotes speak for themselves.

A Greek tragedy is usually divided into the following structure:

- Prologue – the introduction to the play and the plot
- Parodos – the entrance of the chorus into the orchestra
- Episodes – scenes when the actors interact with the chorus or each other
- Odes – scenes between the episodes when the chorus perform in the orchestra
- Exodos – the final scene of the play.

GREEK VASE-PAINTING

FIGURE 1.2
Greek **kylix** (drinking cup) depicting a **symposium**.

---

kylix (pl. **kylikes**) a drinking cup used at a symposium

symposium (pl. **symposia**) a Greek drinking party

The prescribed sources are:

- Red-figure kylix, Persian and a Greek fighting, in the manner of the Triptolemos Painter
- Attic red-figure kylix depicting Achilles and Penthesilea, by the Penthesilea Painter
- The battle of Achilles and Penthesilea. Lucanian red-figure bell-krater
- Attic red-figure **krater** depicting Herakles and the Amazon warriors, attributed to Euphronios.

> **krater** (pl. **kratera**) a large bowl used for mixing wine and water

All four vases are 'red-figure': a painter would paint in the black background to the scene, leaving the figures the natural colour of the clay. Details would then be painted on to the blank spaces to create the figures. Painters would decorate the outside of the vases but also the inside. Giving the names of vase-painters is very difficult. Some are attributed to different painters because the style of the painting is similar to the style of a vase that a painter has signed (this is the case for the krater depicting Herakles and the Amazons, attributed to Euphronios). Other painters are named after a character they have painted on one of their vases (this is the case for the Triptolemos and Penthesilea Painters).

When analysing these four vases, it may help to consider the following questions:

- What conversations at an ancient symposium might have been inspired by the scene shown on the vase?
- How do the poses of the figures help to tell the story?
- What do the poses of the figures suggest about their character?
- What similarities are shown between the Persians and the Amazons?
- Is the vase-painter using the image to make a statement about any or all of the Greeks, Persians, Amazons or barbarians?
- How does this visual source compare with the written sources you have studied?
- When was the vase painted?
- What are the limitations of using a Greek vase as an historical source?

GREEK ARCHITECTURAL SCULPTURE

The prescribed sources are:

> **frieze** (pl. **friezes**) a rectangular band of sculptural decoration that wraps around all four sides of a temple

- South **frieze** of the Temple of Athena Nike from the Acropolis, Athens, depicting the Greeks fighting the Persians
- Frieze of Temple of Apollo at Bassae (British Museum), showing Amazons.

Unlike Greek vases, friezes were intended to be viewed by a wide public audience. It is also important to consider that they were used in the decoration of religious buildings. The examples in the prescribed sources show the Greeks and the barbarians in conflict.

When analysing the friezes, it may help to consider the following questions:

- What conversations might have been inspired by the scenes shown on the frieze?
- How do the poses of the figures help to tell the story?
- What do the poses and expressions of the figures suggest about their character?
- Is the sculptor using the image to make a statement about any or all of the Greeks, Persians, Amazons or barbarians?
- How does this visual source compare with the written sources you have studied?
- When was the frieze carved?
- What are the limitations of using Greek sculpture as an historical source?

PERSIAN ART AND ARCHITECTURE

- The site of Persepolis, including the Gate of All Nations and the **Apadana** (including the relief on the eastern staircase showing delegations from the different peoples of the empire)
- Gold armlets with griffins from the Oxus Treasure
- Statuette of a naked youth from the Oxus Treasure
- The Tomb of Cyrus the Great, Pasargadae
- The Cyrus cylinder
- Statue of Darius I from Susa
- Rock relief at Bisitun, showing Darius the Great after his victory over Gaumata and other rebel kings
- Head of a young Persian prince in lapis lazuli, from the Apadana at Persepolis
- Silver **rhyton** ending in a griffin.

> **Apadana** (pl. **Apadanas**) large columned entrance hall where the king would receive his subjects. It featured porticoes (covered colonnades on two, three or four sides). There were towers on some or all of the corners

> **rhyton** (Gk pl. **rhyta**) a cone shaped drinking vessel

The Persian kings used art and architecture to project an image of their power:

- Consider the importance of the size and beauty of the monuments in demonstrating the power of the kings.
- Look closely at the relief sculptures on the Apadana staircase, which give a visual representation of the Persian Empire: each nation group is depicted bringing a different offering to the king.
- Look carefully at the language used on the 'Cyrus cylinder': Cyrus appears powerful but he also seems keen to win over the Babylonians.

'The Oxus Treasure' is made up of a number of beautiful individual items, which showcase the great skill of Persian artists.

- The examples included show the skill of Persian goldsmiths and silversmiths.
- It is possible to note similarities between these examples and Greek vase shapes and sculpture.
- Consider the use of precious materials – gold, silver and lapis lazuli.
- Persian, Greek and Egyptian sculptures show similarities in the design of the face and the hair, and in the pose and anatomy of the figures.

1.1 Greek Identity

TOPIC OVERVIEW

- The geographical extent of the Greek world and the range of cultures it encompassed
- The autonomy of the *poleis* (cities) and relations between them
- The extent to which a 'Greek' cultural identity could be said to exist

There are no prescribed sources for this topic, but students are encouraged to draw on any other appropriate sources and evidence they have studied in the extended-response exam questions. Here are some suggestions:

- The pediments on the Temple of Aphaia on the island of Aegina: these were carved towards the end of the sixth century and depict the Trojan War (one of the figures is shown in Figure 1.12). Although the Aeginetans and Athenians were rivalling powers in the sixth century, they clearly shared a mythologised history.
- Herodotus' *Histories*, 1.59–68: this section contains useful information about the Athenians and the Spartans in the sixth century.

This topic questions whether a 'Greek' identity existed before the Persian invasions of the fifth century BC. It is important to understand first that the Greek world was not limited to the borders of the country we now know as Greece. Colonisation spread the Greek world across the Mediterranean. This world comprised a wide range of ever-changing cultures, each of which had, at its centre, a **polis**. However, the Greeks were united, at least, by their mythology, their gods and their heroes. Herakles and Achilles recur in Greek literature and art, fighting foreign threats.

> **polis** (pl. **poleis**) an independent state with a city at its heart. Each polis had an army made up of its own citizens and its own political system; in the 7th and 6th centuries BC, the governments in the Greek poleis varied between **aristocracies**, **oligarchies** and **tyrannies**. Each polis varied in size: Athens was the largest by population, Sparta became the largest by territory

THE GEOGRAPHICAL EXTENT OF THE GREEK WORLD AND THE RANGE OF CULTURES IT ENCOMPASSED

In the eighth century BC, there was a sharp rise in population as society began to stabilise and larger communities began to develop across mainland Greece. The larger population needed to be fed and housed, and this led to a pressure on the restricted areas of fertile land in Greece. Greece is a mountainous country and so the population was concentrated into many narrow valleys and around the coast. The necessary expansion was easiest over the sea, rather than across the mountain ranges dividing the country. The Greeks had always been an outward-looking people and many of the cities on the mainland already had foreign trading interests. Colonisation was also an answer to the political turmoil in many mainland Greek cities.

Throughout the seventh and sixth centuries BC, therefore, the Greek world spread eastwards from the mainland to the islands of the Aegean Sea, the shores of the Black Sea and the coast of Asia Minor, and westwards to Italy, Sicily and the Mediterranean coasts of Spain and Africa. The foundation of trading colonies at Al-Mina near Phoenicia and Naucratis in Egypt during the seventh century BC is evidence of the importance of trade across the Mediterranean. However, the inhabitants of the new cities did not extend their interests far inland and there was no attempt to join up the separate settlements into regions.

THE AUTONOMY OF THE *POLEIS* (CITIES) AND RELATIONS BETWEEN THEM

The increase in trade across the Greek world meant that agriculture was replaced as the path to wealth by industries such as pottery and olive oil production. This had a number of effects on the atmosphere in the cities of Greece:

- There was not enough free labour to support the new industries, so slaves began to be imported from Asia Minor and Thrace.
- Land-owning became less important and the aristocratic land-owners no longer had a monopoly on power.
- Political power now became more about wealth than ancestry.

The relationship between the poleis would largely be governed by whether their trading interests clashed or were mutually beneficial. In Attica, rivalries over trading interests developed between Athens and Corinth, and later Athens and Aegina. Argos and Sparta vied to be the strongest power in the Peloponnese. The power balance in Greece was very delicate, as each polis was mindful of its rivals.

aristocracy (pl. **aristocracies**) formed from 'aristos' meaning 'the best' and 'kratos' meaning 'power'. A system of government where the noble families in the city have the power. Their power is handed down through their families. In the Greek poleis, power was connected with ownerships of land

oligarchy (pl. **oligarchies**) formed from 'oligos' meaning 'few' and 'archo' meaning 'rule'. It is a system of government where a small group of wealthy people rule the city

tyranny (pl. **tyrannies**) formed from 'tyrannos' meaning 'ruler'. It is a system of government where one person has overall control. Although it later came to be associated with cruelty, many Greek tyrants came to power after a revolt by the people of the city against wealthy land-owners

EXPLORE FURTHER

Using Naucratis as a focus, consider how the Egyptians shaped Greek culture. Consider also the presence and influence of Phoenicians, Cypriots and Persians.

S & C
The foundation of Poseidonia on the coast of Italy was described by Strabo (*Geography*, 6.1.1). Greeks fleeing from the city of Sybaris founded the city. The site, now known as Paestum, is famous for three magnificent Greek temples, which are still largely intact.

Study question
Why and where did the Greeks found colonies?

EXPLORE FURTHER

In Search of the Greeks by James Renshaw (Bloomsbury Academic, 2015) offers a very useful overview of Greek history.

KEY PLACES

Athens the most important polis in the region of Attica. At the heart of the city on a high plateau was the Acropolis, the ancient citadel of the city

Corinth (including Corcyra) an important trading city in Greece, with easy access to the sea on both sides of the Isthmus of Corinth. The Corinthians founded a colony at Corcyra partly as a solution to political turmoil in the city. A war later followed between Corinth and Corcyra in 664 BC

Sparta the most important polis in the region of Laconia. The Spartans were famous for their selfless patriotism. They had expanded their territory by subjugating the surrounding area

Argos the most important polis in the region of the Argolid. Argos was the chief rival to Sparta in the Peloponnese.

Study questions

1 How did the poleis differ from each other?

2 How might the history of Greece have developed differently if one polis had grown more powerful than all the others in the sixth century BC?

THE EXTENT TO WHICH A 'GREEK' CULTURAL IDENTITY COULD BE SAID TO EXIST

The words 'Greek' and 'Hellenes' were descriptions of Greeks by non-Greeks. So, initially, it was not by themselves but by others that the Greeks were defined as a people. Although they expressed similar views earlier (sharing twelve Olympian gods and competing in the Olympic Games from the eighth century BC), Greeks would only come to define themselves by their shared values and characteristics in the fifth century BC. Homer refers to the united Greek army that fought at Troy as 'Achaians' after Achaia, an area in the Peloponnese. These Greeks are represented as having a common descent from their gods, through their heroes.

The Greeks shared the same religion and mythology, although each polis had its own cult and principal god or goddess. Athens considered itself the city of Athene and the goddess was given ten different descriptions to identify her with different areas of Athenian life (e.g. *parthenos* meaning 'the maiden', *nike* meaning 'victory'). The Argives worshipped Hera as the patron deity of Argos and the Spartans celebrated an annual festival every year in honour of Apollo (the 'Hyakinthia'). Each polis also had its own 'heroes' who were each celebrated with a cult. Theseus was one of the Athenian heroes and the Spartans had a cult to Castor and Polydeuces, the sons of Zeus who were known as the Dioscuri.

The Greeks claimed different descent from different races: the most important of these were the Dorians and the Ionians. The Spartans believed that they were from the Dorian race, which had immigrated into Greece. The Athenians considered themselves to be Ionians, who were an autochthonous (native to the area) people. Each of the races had its own dialect, calendar and festivals.

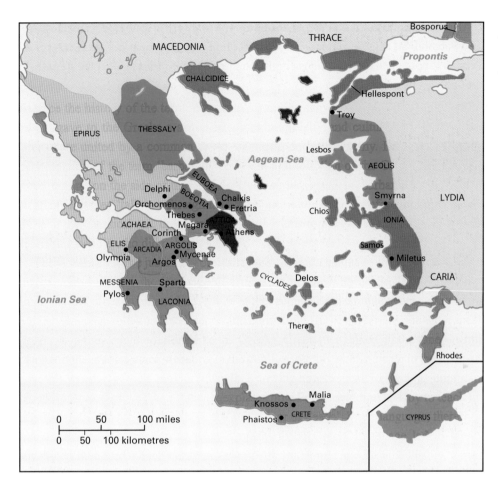

FIGURE 1.3
The regions and cities of
Greece.

There were some shared cultural experiences that brought the Greeks together. Regular athletic festivals brought the poleis together in relatively friendly competition. The Olympic Games, which began in the eighth century, were celebrated with a truce across Greece for their duration. The Greeks also all recognised the importance of the oracle at Delphi, and every polis would respect the advice of the Pythia, the priestess of Apollo who would deliver the oracles. However, the main shared cultural influence for all the Greeks was Homer. In the *Iliad*, the Greek generals come together to bring back a Greek woman abducted by a foreigner and taken across the sea to Troy. In the *Odyssey*, a Greek general rejects immortality and perseveres for ten years to return to Greece. These poems also encouraged an intellectual approach to life – key questions about the gods and fate, about virtue, about restraint and about responsibility are raised. Homer defined and described the gods of the Greeks (who are also the gods of the Trojans), and although they are occasionally frivolous, their power is indisputable. For generations, Greeks and their children were raised on these powerful and wonderful poems. Their overriding message is that to be Greek was worth defending and worth fighting for, but also that to be Greek was to be endlessly inquisitive. Many Greeks lived and worked away from mainland Greece and the Greek colonies. There is evidence of Greek craftsmen working within the Persian Empire. Greeks were also valued as mercenaries. The Babylonians had used Greek mercenaries against the Assyrians before the rise of the Persian Empire, and the Egyptians employed Greek mercenaries against the Persians in the sixth century BC.

MODERN SCHOLARSHIP

'Greekness', that is to say, had at least enough purchase on reality to allow of a definition that was not purely wishful thinking.

Cartledge, *The Greeks* (OUP 2002), p. 3

Cartledge identifies problems with applying the term 'Greekness', as the Greek peoples were so different from one another, but he still feels as though the term is valid. Consider whether or not you agree with him.

TOPIC REVIEW

These questions should draw on your knowledge of the whole topic, so think carefully about the different things you have learned (check the Topic Overview on p. 10).

1. What was the 'Greek world' and where, how and why did it spread?
2. What was a polis?
3. What did the Greeks have in common?

Further Reading

Cartledge, P. (ed.) (1998) *Ancient Greece*. Cambridge: Cambridge University Press
Hansen, M. H. (2006) *Polis*. Oxford: Oxford University Press
Lane Fox, R. (2005) *The Classical World*. London: Penguin

PRACTICE QUESTIONS

1. Describe what is meant by a polis.	[3]
2. Why did Greek cities found colonies?	[3]

1.2 The Persian Wars and Greek (Dis)Unity

TOPIC OVERVIEW

- Relations between Greek poleis (cities) and attempts to unify the Greeks during this period of conflict
- The divisions and unity of the Greeks as reflected in Herodotus' narrative of key events
- Varying responses to the Persian threat; poleis (cities) which medised, and those which did not

There are no prescribed sources for this topic, but students are encouraged to draw on any other appropriate sources and evidence they have studied in the extended-response exam questions. Here are some suggestions:

- Herodotus, Histories, 6.103–120; 7.201–238; 9.40; 9.59–64; 9.71; 9.98–106

The alliance of Greek states at the start of the fifth century BC was based on mutual self-preservation. However, Herodotus' *Histories* relates the ongoing disputes between the Greek poleis about the best way to defend themselves. Any unified action was compromised by deep-seated resentments between the poleis and by fear of the mighty Persian force. The Athenians often seem to be isolated during this period and their admiral, Themistocles, emerges as a memorable character.

RELATIONS BETWEEN THE GREEK POLEIS (CITIES)

They speak the same language and should settle their differences with heralds and messengers rather than always resorting to war.

Herodotus, *Histories*, 7.9

Herodotus creates speeches for his characters (both Greeks and Persians) in his *Histories*. This quote is taken from one such speech delivered to the Persian king Xerxes by one of his generals, Mardonius, during a discussion before the second Persian invasion in 480 BC. He refers to the shared language of the Greeks and to their reputation for fighting each other. Before the Greeks were forced to come together to face their common enemy,

KEY INDIVIDUAL

Mardonius

General of Xerxes' army when he invaded Greece in 480 BC. Herodotus portrays him as a man who had great influence over Xerxes. Mardonius had also been a general under Darius, Xerxes' father and the previous king of Persia.

KEY INDIVIDUAL

Xerxes

Date: King of Persia between 486 BC and 465 BC

The portrayal of Xerxes by both Herodotus and Aeschylus is a very important part of this topic.

hoplite (pl. **hoplites**) a Greek soldier armed with a long spear and a large circular shield. They fought in a tight formation called a phalanx. Hoplite tactics were particularly effective against the Persians at Marathon in 490 BC

democracy (pl. **democracies**) formed from 'demos' meaning 'people' and 'kratos' meaning 'power'. It is a system of government where the freeborn men of the city voted on issues and elected officials

there had been many wars between the different poleis. The two most important poleis were Athens and Sparta.

Sparta was the head of the Peloponnesian League, which developed over the sixth century BC. This League included all the poleis of the Peloponnese apart from Achaea and Argos. Apart from Sparta, the two most important cities in the Peloponnesian League were Corinth and Elis. Sparta and Argos both saw themselves as the principal polis in the Peloponnese and there was an extended rivalry between them.

Figure 1.4 shows Greek **hoplites** fighting against each other. Such scenes would have been repeated across Greece throughout the century preceding the Persian invasions.

Sparta had intervened in Athenian affairs towards the end of the sixth century BC. First, they had helped get rid of the tyrant Hippias in 510 BC. In 508–507 BC, they had intervened again to prevent the emergence of a **democracy** in Athens. However, on this occasion, their attempt failed and a Spartan contingent, including the Spartan king Cleomenes, was captured in Athens. Although the Spartan soldiers were freed by the Athenians, they returned home in shame.

The Spartans invaded Attica, the region of which Athens was the key polis, again in 506 BC. They were helped by the Thebans who were angry with the Athenians for supporting Plataea against them in 510–509 BC. The Corinthians, whose dominance of trade in the Aegean was being threatened by the Athenians, were also initially interested in joining the Spartans and the Thebans against the Athenians. However, they pulled out of the alliance; it suited their interests for the Athenians to remain as strong rivals to the Aeginetans, who were also their trading rivals. Herodotus also explains that they mistrusted the Spartans. Aegina defeated Athens in a sea battle in 487 and the Athenians justified their increased spending on their navy by focusing on the threat of this island, which lay only twenty miles from Piraeus, the port of Athens. The situation in Greece in the sixth century was complicated.

These and other long-standing resentments and uneasy alliances would all be evident in the attempts to create unity among the Greeks in the face of the Persian invasion. The notion of 'Greekness' and the 'Greek way of life' that they were defending would become very important when trying to overcome the narrow self-interest of the independent poleis. It was also important that the Persian Empire was seen as the direct opposite of these principles.

EXPLORE FURTHER

Themistocles used the threat of Aegina to persuade the Athenians that they should invest in their navy (Herodotus describes this in *Histories*, 7.144). Consider how the Athenians also used the Persian invasion to further their own interests.

ATTEMPTS TO UNIFY THE GREEKS DURING THIS PERIOD OF CONFLICT

In 490 the Persian king Darius began to plan an expedition against Greece. According to Herodotus, his main purpose was to get revenge on the Athenians for their part in the burning of Sardis. The Athenians shared Ionian descent with those who lived along the Aegean coast of the Persian Empire and had sent ships to help their revolt.

The Persian fleet, led by Datis and Artaphernes, was accompanied by Hippias. Darius also sent envoys to Greece to demand earth and water as tokens of their submission. Some islands, including Aegina, which was very close to Athens, gave in, but Sparta and Athens both refused and executed the envoys, despite religious conventions that protected their safety.

The unlikely Athenian victory was a significant success for the new democracy. One interpretation of the frieze of the Parthenon is that it commemorates the 192 who died at Marathon as horsemen in order to acknowledge the role the victory played in the development of the Athenian identity in the fifth century BC.

The Persians continued to sail south and rounded Cape Sounion, but the Athenians had been alerted by a runner and were able to prepare. Like the 192 who died in the battle, the story of this runner also passed into the city's mythology. Pheidippides' heroic 26-mile run from Marathon to Athens is now the distance for all modern marathons.

After the death of Darius in 486 BC, Xerxes succeeded him as King of Persia. He was keen to finish his father's work in Greece and exact revenge on Athens. After he had dealt with rebellions in Egypt and Phoenicia, he gathered his army at Sardis in 481 BC and then began the second Persian invasion of Greece. The march passed easily until they

Study question
What resentments existed between the Greeks before the Persian invasions in the fifth century BC?

KEY INDIVIDUALS

Darius

Date: King of Persia between 522 BC and 486 BC

Darius probably usurped the Persian throne after killing Bardiya, the brother of Cambyses. He appears as a ghost in Aeschylus' *Persians*, and Herodotus describes his failed invasion of Greece in 490 BC in Book 6 of his *Histories*.

Hippias

Date: Athenian tyrant from *c.* 528/7–510 BC

Hippias was exiled from the city in 510 BC and fled to Persia.

EXPLORE FURTHER

Read Herodotus' account of the Ionian Revolt in Book 5 and consider why he attaches so much importance to the burning of Sardis as a motivating factor for the Persian invasion.

FIGURE 1.5
The battles of the Greco-Persian Wars 490–479 BC.

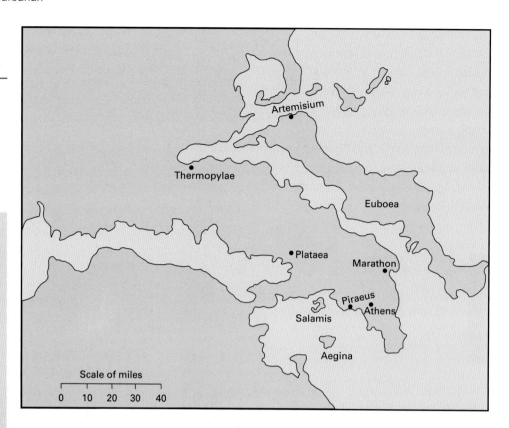

KEY EVENT

The burning of Sardis

Date: 494 BC

The Ionians who lived along the west coast of Asia Minor revolted from the Persians in 499 BC. They approached the Spartans and the Athenians for help, but only the Athenians sent a fleet. The revolt had its greatest success when Sardis, the capital of the Lydian Empire before it was conquered by the Persians, was burnt. The revolt was put down by the Persians in the same year. Herodotus describes the Ionian Revolt in Book 5.

KEY INDIVIDUAL

Miltiades

Date: Athenian general at the battle of Marathon in 490 BC.

Historians have pointed to his inventive use of tactics as one of the reasons for the Athenian victory. After a failed naval expedition in 489 BC, Miltiades was put on trial and fined. He died in the same year.

KEY EVENT   The Battle of Marathon

Date: 490 BC

When the Persian army arrived at Marathon, the Athenians sent a message to the Spartans to ask for their help. However, the Spartans were unwilling to march in a month when there was a full moon. The Plataeans did, however, join the Athenians. The Athenians delayed the battle, hoping that the Spartans would join them but eventually decided to march out to meet the Persians, although they were heavily outnumbered. Miltiades, the Athenian general, had deliberately weakened the centre of their battle line. The Persians broke through but were wrapped up by the flanks of the Athenian army and defeated. Herodotus describes the battle of Marathon in Book 6.

reached the Hellespont, the narrow neck of water that formed a symbolic border between Persia and Greece, and is now the border between Europe and Asia. Two bridges had been constructed but both had been destroyed in a storm. Xerxes was furious at this disaster and gave orders for the sea to be given 300 lashes. He then constructed two more bridges and the army crossed. He led contingents from across the vast Persian Empire; Herodotus suggests five million marched with Xerxes, but 200,000 is a far more likely estimate.

When news of the muster of the Persian army at Sardis reached Greece, the poleis decided to meet at the Isthmus of Corinth in order to discuss how they might best protect themselves. The congress sought to move past old resentments between the Greek states,

FIGURE 1.6
Section of the frieze of the Parthenon.

particularly between Athens and Aegina (the island of Aegina had joined the Persian side in the previous invasion) and between Sparta and Argos (no delegate from Argos attended the congress). The congress also aimed to establish which polis would take overall control of the Greek force. The leadership of the land army by Sparta was agreed by all and, after Athens yielded her claim, Sparta was also given control of the navy. Athens had a strong argument to be in control of the navy as she was providing the majority of the ships. However, the other poleis were not in favour of the Athenians being in charge. Herodotus suggests that the other states were jealous of Athens, and it is certainly the case that the largest navy in Greece was as much a threat to the other Greek poleis, their colonies and trading interests, as it was to Persia. Stiff penalties were agreed for any poleis that decided to **medise**. Many of the northern poleis in Greece, including cities in Thessaly and Boeotia, were not confident that the Greek defence would be mounted north of the Isthmus and decided that they would therefore be foolish to resist the Persians openly.

Following the congress, 10,000 hoplites were sent to guard the Vale of Tempe, which was a narrow pass through which it was presumed that the Persians would pass. However, when the Greeks realised that there were alternative routes through Thessaly, they decided to abandon their defence of northern Greece and withdraw further south. Now that the northern passes were left undefended, the poleis in Thessaly decided to medise.

After withdrawing south, the Greeks decided to defend the pass of Thermopylae. This was a narrow area with a cliff wall on one side and the sea on the other. The Spartan king Leonidas was in command of the army. He had a force of around 7,000 men but only 300 of these were Spartan. The rest of the Spartans were unwilling to defend northern Greece as they were celebrating a religious festival and so could not march. Other Peloponnesian states did not join up because they were attending the Olympic Games.

medise a verb that means 'to go over to the Persian side'. The Persians are often called Medes in Herodotus. In every polis there will have been elements in the city who would have been keen to medise, particularly those who were not keen on popular democracies. The success of the Greeks against the Persians may have seemed unlikely to some

Study question
Why did some Greek states choose to medise?

KEY INDIVIDUAL

Leonidas

The king of Sparta who led the Greek army at the Battle of Thermopylae in 480 BC.

KEY EVENT The Battle of Thermopylae

Date: 480 BC

The narrow pass of Thermopylae was relatively easy for a small force to hold against a much larger one. However, a treacherous Greek, Ephialtes, revealed to Xerxes the path that went over the mountains to the rear of the pass, and the Persians could now surround the Greeks. Xerxes sent his **Immortals** over the path to the rear of the pass. When the Greeks realised what had happened, Leonidas and his 300 Spartans remained in the pass but the rest of the army withdrew. Leonidas and the 300 Spartans heroically attacked the advancing Persians and all but two were killed. The defence of the pass of Thermopylae had failed.

Immortals the name of the personal guard of the king, which was always made up to 1,000 soldiers. They were the elite soldiers of the Persian army and are represented on the walls of the royal palaces (see Figure 1.7)

MODERN SCHOLARSHIP

The Battle of Thermopylae, in short, was a turning-point not only in the history of Classical Greece, but in all the world's history, eastern as well as western.

Cartledge, *Thermopylae* (Macmillan, 2006), p. xii

To what extent do you agree with Cartledge's description of the Battle of Thermopylae?

EXPLORE FURTHER

Persian Fire by Tom Holland (Abacus, 2006) and *Thermopylae* by Paul Cartledge (Macmillan, 2006) are both excellent accounts of the battles of and background to the Persian war. Compare their accounts of the battle with Herodotus'.

Luck Bringer (New Generation Publishing, 2013) and *The Wooden Walls of Thermopylae* (Clink Street, 2014) by Nick Brown are both very readable fictionalised accounts of the important events surrounding the battles. The playwright Aeschylus also features as a central character.

ACTIVITY

Debate

Which do you think was the most important battle of the Persian Wars? Why?

Study question

How important were the battles of the Greco-Persian Wars between 490 and 479 BC in creating a Greek identity?

The crews and ships in the Persian fleet came from all the coastal regions of the Persian Empire – the three largest contingents sailing from Phoenicia, Egypt and Cyprus. This fleet was accompanied by the land army and so it was also necessary for the Greeks to defend the narrow strait between Euboea and the mainland. The Greek fleet, which was made up mostly of Athenian ships, took up their position at Artemisium. The Persian fleet was so large that it could not fit along the shore and so the ships were moored alongside each other at Cape Sepias. They were hit by a storm there and suffered heavy losses. There were some minor engagements between the fleets at Artemisium but once the Persian land army had progressed through the pass of Thermopylae, both fleets sailed south.

FIGURE 1.7
Immortal Persian guard, low relief of the Apadana.

THE DIVISIONS AND UNITY OF THE GREEKS AS REFLECTED IN HERODOTUS' NARRATIVE OF KEY EVENTS

Herodotus gives his readers dramatised versions of the discussions that took place between the Greeks and Persians. Some have also suggested that Herodotus' account of the war recasts the Greek victory over the Persians as an ideological victory of democracy over tyranny.

Herodotus claims that the Persian invasion was mostly directed at Athens and then goes on to divide the Greek poleis into the following groups:

> Those who gave earth and water to the Persian king had confidence that they would not suffer any hardship from the barbarians. Those who had not given earth and water lived in great fear since there were not enough ships in Greece to match the invader in battle, most of these did not want to fight against the Persians and were keener on siding with them.

Herodotus, *Histories*, 7.138

FIGURE 1.8
Marble bust of Herodotus.

Herodotus has here suggested that all of the Greek states apart from the Athenians have either surrendered, or are considering surrendering to the Persians. However, he then acknowledges that a positive view of Athens would be even more unpopular with his readers than the previous accusation of a lack of spirit:

> At this point I am forced to give an opinion which may offend many people, but it seems to me that this is the truth. If the Athenians had been struck with panic by the imminent danger and had abandoned their city, or if they had not left and, instead, stayed there and surrendered themselves to Xerxes, no one else would have stayed to resist the king on the sea. And if no one had resisted Xerxes on the sea, then the following would have happened on the land.
>
> Herodotus, *Histories*, 7.138

Herodotus explains that a defence of the Isthmus would have been in vain and continues his line of argument:

> . . . to call the Athenians the saviours of Greece is the truth. For whoever's side they fought on, this was the side most likely to prevail. They chose Greece and, as a result, Greece remained and remained free, and they inspired the rest of the Greeks, who had not already gone over to the Persian side, to defend themselves, alongside their gods, against the Persian king. Even the terrifying oracles, which came out of Delphi, shocked them but did not convince them to abandon Greece. They stayed firm and withstood the invader of their country.
>
> Herodotus, *Histories*, 7.138

Herodotus goes on to describe the 'terrifying oracles' from Delphi and the Athenian response, which was to demand another oracle. In response to the second, gentler, oracle the Athenians then chose to evacuate the city and put their trust in their navy. The Athenians even set aside their resentment towards the Aeginetans for the sake of the greater good. Although Herodotus praises the Athenians for their 'inspiration' of Greece, the Athenians themselves may already have been looking ahead to a time after the Persian Wars when they could assert themselves over the rest of the Greek poleis.

This is followed soon after by the totally opposite reaction of the Argives to a similarly unfavourable oracle, which was to make an unrealistic demand of their old enemies, the Spartans, and then withdraw from the fighting altogether. Herodotus adds that the Argives may have already secretly medised before this time.

Herodotus therefore makes a clear contrast: while the rest of the Greeks medised, panicked or nursed resentments, the Athenians made plans to defend their way of life even if they would have to make compromises. Herodotus describes a further compromise at the start of Book 8 (1–5) before the battle of Artemisium, when the Athenians cede overall command of the fleet to the Spartans, even though the Athenians provided the majority of the ships. Herodotus explains that this gesture was necessary because the rest of the Greeks refused to fight under Athenian command. Even after this, the Greeks panic when they see the Persian fleet. Herodotus explains how the Athenian admiral Themistocles needed to bribe the Spartan admiral Eurybiades, who was in overall control of the fleet, to make him stay at Artemisium. Themistocles then also bribes the Corinthian

KEY INDIVIDUAL

Eurybiades

Spartan who replaced Leonidas in overall control of the Greek army and navy in 480 BC.

admiral Adeimantus, yet is clever enough still to make himself some money out of the arrangement. Themistocles is not only a reliable defender but also cunning enough to outsmart those who would betray the defence of Greece.

In 480 BC, following the defeat at Thermopylae and the inconclusive naval engagement at Artemisium, the Greeks needed to decide where they would next make a stand against the Persians. The fleet assembled at Salamis, an island off the coast of Athens opposite the port of Piraeus. Themistocles thought that they should make a stand there but the Peloponnesians felt that they should move further south and make their defence at the Isthmus of Corinth. Herodotus represents the Peloponnesians as expecting to lose the battle; they discuss the most preferable site for a defeat. This is how he describes their reasoning:

> Most of those who spoke urged sailing to the Isthmus and fighting a sea battle there in defence of the Peloponnese, offering the following as proof: if they were defeated at Salamis, they would be besieged on an island where no help would come to them, whereas from the Isthmus, they might be able to escape to their own territories.
>
> Herodotus, *Histories*, 8.49

By contrast, Herodotus gives a speech to Themistocles in which he presumes victory and the successful defence of Greece. Themistocles argues skilfully; realising that the points he has made to Eurybiades would be offensive to the rest of the Greeks, he uses different arguments. He also wittily dismisses Adeimantus, the Corinthian admiral, who then resorts to cheap insults. Themistocles' impassioned plea reaches a climax with an emotional threat to lead the Athenians away to Italy to found a new city there. Herodotus says that it was this possibility that convinced Eurybiades more than anything else Themistocles said.

The Greeks initially agreed to follow Themistocles' advice and stay at Salamis. However, their resolve began to waver. When Themistocles realised that they were on the point of changing their mind, he resorted to desperate measures. In order to force the issue, he sent his slave with a secret message to Xerxes. In this message, the Greeks' plans to withdraw were laid before the Persian king. Xerxes was determined not to let the Greeks escape the certain defeat that he had in mind for them. He sent his Egyptian contingent to block the other end of the strait between the island of Salamis and the mainland. Now the Greeks were trapped at Salamis and Themistocles would get his battle.

During the battle that followed (some have suggested that the date of the battle was 20th September 480 BC, which has also been offered as a possible birth date of Euripides),

---

KEY INDIVIDUAL

Adeimantus

Leader of the Corinthian navy at the battle of Salamis in 480 BC.

KEY INDIVIDUAL Themistocles

Date: *c.* 524–459 BC

Athenian admiral and politician.

He is credited with persuading his fellow citizens to invest in the naval power of the city. He was ostracised (exiled after a vote) from the city in 472 or 471 BC and eventually ended up in Persia, where he lived until his death in 459 BC. Herodotus portrays him as a cunning and resourceful leader who shows great foresight.

Herodotus reports that the Corinthians fled. However, he does acknowledge that this is an Athenian story, with which the rest of the Greeks disagree. The Aeginetans boast of their loyalty to the Greek cause as they pass Themistocles' ship during the fighting and are later given an award for bravery. Following the Greek victory at Salamis, each Greek admiral voted for himself in the individual awards but all put Themistocles in second place.

After his defeat, Xerxes headed back to the Hellespont. He left Mardonius and the land army of 60,000 men behind. These men spent the winter in Thessaly and planned to invade the Peloponnese in the following spring. When the spring of 479 BC arrived, the army was reinforced by the 60,000 who had escorted Xerxes back to Persia and Greece was again threatened. Mardonius sent Alexander, the king of Macedonia, to make an offer of an alliance with the Athenians. The Athenians knew that the Spartans would come to them to offer a counter-proposal and they waited for them to arrive before giving their response to the Persians.

> We are well aware the Mede is far more powerful than us, you do not need to try and scare us with this fact. Nevertheless, as lovers of freedom, we will defend ourselves as best we can. You should not try to persuade us to make pacts with the barbarian, we will not agree. Now report to Mardonius that this is the answer of the Athenians: as long as the sun travels across the same path as it does now, we will never make any pact with Xerxes. Trusting in our allies we will fight him without end, defended by those gods and heroes for whom he showed little regard when he burned their homes and gifts.
>
> Herodotus, *Histories*, 8.143

The Athenian message to the Persians is clear: they are willing to risk their lives for their freedom and are not willing to make pacts with barbarians who burned their temples. To the Spartans, they say the following:

> . . . we are Greek, we share the same blood, the same language, the same shrines of the gods and methods of sacrifice, the same customs; it would not be right for the Athenians to betray all of this.
>
> Herodotus, *Histories*, 8.144

Study question

How does Herodotus stress the importance of the Athenians in ensuring that the Greeks remained united before Salamis?

MODERN SCHOLARSHIP

In cold historical fact the defeat had been effected by a shaky and improvised coalition of a mere thirty to forty Greek states – out of more than seven hundred in the Aegean world alone; and the Athenians' alliance was not as Hellenic as Athenian propaganda maintained.

Cartledge, *The Greeks* (OUP, 2002), p. 54

To what extent would you agree with Cartledge's analysis of the Greek victory over the Persians?

S & C The film *300*, directed by Zack Snyder, was released in 2006. It represents a fantasised version of the battle of Thermopylae. On its release it caused much offence in Iran because of its depiction of the Persians. The film was adapted from a graphic novel by Frank Miller, also called *300*. Read the graphic novel and/or watch the film and consider how both the Persians and the Greeks are represented. Compare the ancient sources you have studied with Miller's portrayal.

Once the Persians had finally returned home after defeat at the battle of Plataea in 479 BC, the Athenians set about both rebuilding their city and recasting the Greek victory over the Persians as a victory for Athens over barbarian ideology.

VARYING RESPONSES TO THE PERSIAN THREAT: POLEIS (CITIES) WHICH MEDISED, AND THOSE WHICH DID NOT

The Plataeans were the only Greeks who supported the Athenians at the battle of Marathon. Herodotus describes in Book 6 of the *Histories* that the Plataeans had earlier 'surrendered' to the Athenians so that Athens would defend Plataea against Thebes, the most powerful city in Boeotia.

Herodotus gives the following list of poleis that medised by sending tokens of submission when Xerxes invaded Greece in 480 BC: Thessalians, Dolopes, Aenianes, Perhaebi, Locrians, Magnetes, Malians, Achaeans of Phthiotis, Thebans and all the Boeotians except for the Plataea and Thespiae.

He also lists the Greeks who provided troops to Xerxes, these are: Thracians, Paeonians, Eordi, Bottiaei, Chalcidians, Brygi, Pierians, Macedonians, Perrhoebians, Enionians, Dolopes, Magnetes, Achaeans and the coastal settlements of Thrace.

Most of these tribes lived in Northern Greece in the regions of Thessaly and Macedonia, through which the Persians would be marching. The neighbouring region of Thrace was already under Persian control at the time of the invasion. Unless the Athenians and the Greeks of the Peloponnese committed to defend the northern borders of Thessaly, it would have seemed foolish for these states to appear openly hostile to the Persians. Thebes, the principal polis in Boeotia, was already hostile towards the Athenians and may have seen the Persian invasion as a way to increase its prominence in Greece.

Herodotus reports that the Thessalians only made terms with the Persians after the Greeks had withdrawn from the Vale of Tempe. He also suggests that Argos, a city in the Peloponnese, medised, although he does not have compelling evidence for this.

The Greeks who fought at Thermopylae, he lists as: Sparta, Tegea, Mantinea, Orchomenus, Arcadia, Corinth, Phlius and Mycenae, Thespiae, Phocis and Thebes (Thebes is also listed among the states who had made terms with the Persians).

Herodotus suggests that Thebes had secretly medised and that the Spartan king, Leonidas, specifically requested troops from the city so that they would have to come out on one side or the other.

At the start of Book 8, Herodotus gives us the contingents in the Greek fleet who fought at Artemisium and Salamis: Athens, Corinth, Megara, Chalcis, Aegina, Sicyon, Sparta, Epidaurus, Eretria, Troezen, Styra, Ceos and Opus.

In addition to those who fought at Thermopylae, Herodotus gives the following list of Greek contingents at the battle of Plataea in 479 BC: Potidaea, Sicyon, Epidaurus, Troezen, Lepreum, Tiryns, Hermion, Eretria, Styra, Chalcis, Ambraciots, Anactorians, Leucadians, Paleans, Aeginetans, Athens, Plataea and Megara.

Boeotia, Locris, Malis and Thessaly and some of the Phocians fought on the side of the Persians at Plataea.

These extensive lists prove that Greece was not united in the defence of Persia. For all the Athenian talk of 'Greekness' against the barbarian threat, many poleis, including Athens, sought to use the Persian invasion as a way to improve their own standing. All were confident that the localised resentments that had mostly been paused in the face of the Persian threat would soon begin again after they left.

TOPIC REVIEW

These questions should draw on your knowledge of the whole topic, so think carefully about the different things you have learned (check the Topic Overview on p. 15).

1. What were the main rivalries between the Greek poleis and how did they affect the response to the Persian invasion?
2. What were the principal battles of the two Persian invasions and how were they decided?
3. Who were the main personalities on both sides?
4. To what extent is Herodotus a reliable source?

Further Reading

Bradley, P. (1988) *Ancient Greece*. Melbourne: Edward Arnold Australia

Bury, J. B. and Meiggs, R. (1975) *History of Greece*. London: Macmillan

Green, P. (1996) *The Greco-Persian Wars*. Oakland, CA: University of California Press

Source A: *Herodotus, Histories, 8.60*

For the time being, he answered the Corinthian gently then, turning towards Eurybiades, he said none of what he had said before, namely that they would disband if they left Salamis, for it would have done him no good whatsoever to suggest, in their presence, that the allies would behave in a cowardly fashion. He had another idea and said the following, "It is your responsibility to save Greece, if you listen to me and stay here and do not follow the advice of others to retreat to the Isthmus. Listen to me and then make your decision. Joining battle off the Isthmus, you will be fighting in open water where we will be at a disadvantage as our ships are heavier and fewer in number. You will also lose Salamis, Megara and Aegina, even if we win the rest. And their land army will follow their fleet. And so you will lead them into the Peloponnese and you will endanger all of Greece."

Source B: *Herodotus, Histories, 8.49*

Most of those who spoke urged sailing to the Isthmus and fighting a sea battle there in defence of the Peloponnese, offering the following as proof: if they were defeated at Salamis, they would be besieged on an island where no help would come to them, whereas from the Isthmus, they might be able to escape to their own territories.

Study **Sources A** and **B**.

1. Explain how Herodotus highlights the skills of Themistocles in **Source A**? [10]
2. How much evidence is there of Greek unity during the Greco-Persian Wars? You may use **Sources A** and **B** as a starting point, and should justify your response. [20]

1.3 Greeks and Barbarians

TOPIC OVERVIEW

- Pre-Classical ideas of the 'barbarian' including the origin of the term and its original connotations
- The role of binary oppositions (for example Greek/foreigner; man/woman; slave/free) in the Greek world view
- The typical depiction of barbarians in classical Greek sources, including:
  - the standard visual depiction of 'barbarians' in Greek art
  - their way of life and customs
  - their character
  - politics and hierarchy
  - their religion and rituals
- The role of the historical context in this 'invention' of the barbarian, including:
  - the role of the Persian wars in crystallising images of foreign peoples

The following prescribed sources are covered in this topic:

- Red-figure kylix, Persian and a Greek fighting, in the manner of the Triptolemos Painter
- South frieze of the Temple of Athena Nike from the Acropolis, Athens, depicting the Greeks fighting the Persians

Don't forget that you will be given credit in the exam if you study extra sources and make relevant use of them in your answers.

The invention of the barbarian may have begun before the Persian wars, but the concept of 'Greekness' was never more important than at the start of the fifth century BC. Art and drama were flourishing, particularly in the city of Athens, and barbarians, both real and imagined, became popular subjects. Herodotus seems keener on representing the barbarians than inventing them, and gives his readers plenty of information about the customs of the Persians.

PRE-CLASSICAL IDEAS OF THE 'BARBARIAN', INCLUDING THE ORIGIN OF THE TERM AND ITS ORIGINAL CONNOTATIONS

To trace the history of the term 'barbarian', it makes sense to go back to Homer, as his poetry gave to the Greeks a sense of common ancestry and culture. In the *Iliad*, the Greeks are united by a common cause, against a common enemy. However, Homer's only mention of the term 'barbarian' comes in a description of the Carian people, who were fighting on the side of the Trojans. He describes them as 'barbarophonoi' (2.867) meaning that they 'talk in a foreign language', i.e. not in Greek. Before the fifth century BC and the Classical era, the term 'barbarian' seems to have been primarily linguistic, describing people who did not speak Greek.

The Greeks could be justifiably proud of their common language and its effect on their shared culture. It was the language of a thinking people who needed words to define emotions and other complex ideas. Much of the technical and complex vocabulary of the English language relies on Greek terms and derivations. If the barbarians could not speak Greek, then they could not think like the Greeks. Greek men talked all the time – while trading in the market-place, debating in the public assembly or exercising in the gymnasium; this was part of their outdoor lifestyle. Knowing how to speak well was an important virtue: in Book 9 of the *Iliad*, Phoenix explains how Peleus sent him to Troy to teach his son, Achilles, to be 'a speaker of words and a doer of deeds'. Their language, therefore, was an essential expression of what it meant to be Greek. Language led to highly developed literature, which began as epic poetry by Homer and became history, drama and philosophy.

However, it is also true that the Greeks were influenced by barbarian cultures. Herodotus explains the Egyptian origins of most of the Greek gods in Book 2 (48–58). Poseidon, the god of the sea, was not originally Egyptian but he was, according to Herodotus, from Libya. The Greek poets Hesiod (in the *Theogony*) and Homer (in the *Iliad* and the *Odyssey*) developed the ideas of the gods and gave them their form and character. The 'hero-cults' that were important in the Greek poleis were a Greek invention.

Such development of a barbarian idea is also evident in Greek Art. The Greeks took the idea and the technique of monumental figure sculpture from the Egyptians but then developed both. Greek statues were nude where the Egyptian figures were clothed. The Greeks also moved on from blocky figures, which had four successful viewpoints, to figures that were conceived 'in the round'. When the Greeks began to replace their wooden temples with stone structures they also, like the Persians, took their stone-working techniques from the Egyptians.

FIGURE 1.9
Greek sculpture of a standing youth (the New York Kouros) from the late seventh century BC.

FIGURE 1.10
Egyptian sculpture of a standing youth c. 2500 BC.

barbaros (pl. **barbaroi**) Greek word referring to someone who makes the unintelligible sounds of a foreign language – 'bar-bar-bar'. The English language contains some comparable terms: 'jabber', 'mumble' or 'babble'

EXPLORE FURTHER

The Greeks by Paul Cartledge (OUP, 2002) is an excellent examination of Greek self-evaluation.

KEY INDIVIDUAL

Demaratus

Date: King of Sparta in the late 5th century BC.

After an argument with his fellow king, Cleomenes, Demaratus left Sparta in 491 BC. He fled to Persia, where he was welcomed by Darius. He later accompanied Xerxes in his invasion of Greece in 480 BC.

THE ROLE OF BINARY OPPOSITIONS IN THE GREEK WORLD VIEW

Over the sixth and fifth centuries BC, the word **barbaros** became more than just a rather blunt expression of frustration that all the ancient world was not Greek speaking. The more the Greeks began to develop their own identity, the more they began to distinguish themselves from 'non-Greeks'; to be 'Greek' was to be 'not barbarian'. Therefore, as they developed the idea of being Greek, they would also create, by directly inverting Greek values, the idea of what it meant to be barbarian. Herodotus uses the term throughout his *Histories* to describe the Persians but, although he considers the Persians capable of great deeds, he is keen to point out that they have a very different character from the Greeks. 'Barbarian' now becomes a term that indicates more than linguistic differences.

A key difference was the professed attitude towards slavery. The Greeks had slaves; although some were also Greeks (particularly from Thrace in northern Greece), the majority were barbarian. The Greeks therefore created an association between the barbarians and slavery, and the idea of 'natural slavishness' grew. The barbarians were represented as slaves by nature and, therefore, inferior to the Greeks. This extended to other areas of their character. As they were slaves to their king, they could also be slaves to their impulses and desires. By contrast, the Greeks loved their freedom and took pride in their ability to master their passions.

In the fifth century BC, the Greeks, in particular the Athenians, were increasingly interested in defining themselves as humans, as mortals and, above all, as Greeks, and the question of 'What does it mean to be Greek?' was perhaps easiest answered by 'To be not barbarian'.

Politically in the sixth century the Greek states were moving from tyrannies to democracies, and this interest in their own self-government also defined them. The English word 'idiot' comes from a Greek word used to describe an individual with no interest in the affairs of the state. Just as people were, and are, described as 'barbarian', we can understand why both terms developed a negative connotation. Democracy was born of a love of discussion and debate, which was born of an expressive and complex language. Those who were content to be ruled must have little interest in politics, which was the opposite of the Greeks.

Freedom became a defining characteristic of the Greeks. The rhetoric of the Persian Wars, particularly in the discussions before the battle of Salamis (Herodotus, *Histories*, 8.56–65), employs ideals of freedom. In his discussion with Xerxes in Book 7, Demaratus also explains to Xerxes that the Spartans are braver than the Persians because they fight, freely, with respect for a law, not out of fear for a king.

The inversion of Greek thought also applies to their understanding of gender. As barbarians were defined by being 'not Greek', women were defined by being 'not men'. Similarly, the Greeks defined Greek as superior to barbarian, and also men as superior to women. Men would spend the majority of their lives outside the home, women would spend the majority of their lives inside the home.

Greek women were therefore precluded from exerting any influence on matters relating to the city. Women are also represented as being more emotional, whereas men show calm logic. However, there are strong Persian women in all three literary sources, each of whom emerge from or reject the domestic sphere. In the *Persians*, Atossa takes control of the Persian court as the male chorus hesitate and worry. In *Medea*, Medea dramatically takes control of her predicament. In Herodotus (8.68), Artemisia is the only one of Xerxes' admirals to advise him against fighting the Greeks at Salamis, she then distinguishes herself in the battle (although she does so with deceit and luck, not bravery). After seeing Artemisia sink what he thinks is an enemy ship, Xerxes says of her:

> My men have become women and my women men.
>
> Herodotus, *Histories*, 8.88

In 7.99, Herodotus describes Artemisia's involvement in Xerxes' expedition as 'strange' and 'interesting'.

THE DEPICTION OF BARBARIANS IN CLASSICAL GREEK SOURCES

The standard visual depiction of 'barbarians' in Greek art

When Persians are painted on Greek vases, they wear flamboyant, heavily patterned costumes. Greek males on vases tend to be shown in heroic nudity; it is Greek women who wear patterned dresses. Persians are often shown as archers, either firing a bow or wearing a quiver. When they are shown in a combat situation with a Greek, they are usually either being killed or running away.

PRESCRIBED SOURCE

Red-figure kylix of a Persian and a Greek fighting, by the Triptolemos Painter

Date: 5th century BC

Material: earthenware

Original location: Athens

Current location: National Museum of Scotland

Significance: depiction of Persian warrior by a Greek vase-painter.

FIGURE 1.11 **PS**
Red-figure kylix of a Persian and a Greek fighting, painted in the manner of the Triptolemos Painter.

tondo (pl. **tondos**) a circular image painted on the inside of a kylix

The **tondo** of the red-figure kylix shown in Figure 1.11 depicts a Greek fighting a Persian. The Greek is clearly dominant; he occupies the centre of the image and overlays the Persian. The Greek raises his sword over his head, suggesting that he is about to administer the final blow. The Persian cowers before him, his head bowed in a submissive gesture. The Persian is wearing a distinctive hat and patterned costume. Persians were famed archers and are therefore usually shown with a bow and a quiver. This Persian is forced to use his sword but he holds his bow behind him.

The image in Figure 1.12 shows a cast of a Trojan archer from the sculpture on the Temple of Aphaia at Aegina. He is dressed in a similar way to the Persian warrior on the vase in Figure 1.11, with a heavily-patterned, tight-fitting outfit and a quiver. The cast has been painted to give an idea of how it would have looked when it was first created. The bright colours would have clearly distinguished the archer from the Greek warriors around him. This was also an attempt to identify the Trojans, another race that a united Greek army had defeated, as Persians.

In Greek sculpture, barbarians are shown more as the equals of the Greeks. The Trojan War is a familiar theme and, as every viewer would have known that the Greeks were victorious, their success over worthy enemies is more notable. On the pediments (the sculptures fitted into the triangular shape formed by the end of a gabled roof) of the Temple of Aphaia at Aegina, carved at the beginning of the fifth century, the Greeks and Trojans are grouped into warring pairs of marble figures. The suggestion is that the battle for civilisation over barbarism is not only never-ending, it is also

FIGURE 1.12

Paris as an archer, Temple of Aphaia on Aegina, Greece.

FIGURE 1.13
Sections of the South frieze from the Temple of Athena Nike in Athens.

PRESCRIBED SOURCE

Frieze from the Temple of Athena Nike in Athens

Date: 5th century BC

Material: Pentelic marble

Original location: Athens Acropolis

Current location: sections of the South frieze are in the British Museum

Significance: depiction of a battle between the Greeks and the Persians by a Greek sculptor

one in which each individual must take part. Decorations in Athens in the mid-fifth century BC began to mythologise the Persian Wars. A mural in the Stoa Poikile by the famous painter Polygnotus showed Marathon next to victories of Theseus and Herakles over monsters. A frieze on the Temple of Athena Nike may show the battle of Plataea.

The Temple of Athena Nike was part of the building programme on the Acropolis that took place in the second half of the fifth century BC. It was completed *c.* 420 BC. It is a small Ionic temple, which sits on an artificial plateau on the south-west corner of the Acropolis. In the sections of the south frieze shown in Figure 1.13, the Greeks are generally nude, wearing only cloaks and holding swords and shields. The Persians, by contrast, are heavily draped. Two Persians in submissive positions can be seen in the left corners of these sections. The bodies of dead Persians are also shown slumped at the bottom of the frieze.

Their way of life and customs

In Book 1 (131–140) of his *Histories*, Herodotus gives us an outline of the customs of the Persians. As with his descriptions of other races, it is likely that he concentrates on those customs that are most unlike Greek ways and therefore most likely to intrigue his readers. Here are a few of the customs he mentions:

- The Persians do not build temples or erect statues because they do not have anthropomorphic (having human form: from the Greek 'Anthropos' meaning 'man' and 'morphe' meaning 'form') gods.
- They do not make offerings on an altar.
- They celebrate their birthdays lavishly and eat a whole animal – ox, horse, camel or donkey. This is followed by a variety of desserts.
- They are not allowed to vomit or relieve themselves in front of another.
- They discuss important decisions twice, once drunk and once sober before they come to a decision.
- They kiss equals on the mouth, those close in rank on the cheek but prostrate themselves before one of higher rank.
- They consider themselves superior to every other race but are keen to take on other customs – they have adopted their style of dress from the Medes and the practice of pederasty (sexual relationships between men and boys) from the Greeks.

Study question
Which aspects of barbarian and Greek character are stressed in Greek visual depictions?

EXAM TIP

In the exam you will need to be able to cross-reference different sources. Compare the visual depictions of the Persians with the descriptions in the literary sources.

- They are polygamous but also have mistresses.
- They gain respect by having many sons.
- A boy is educated between the ages of five and twenty and he is taught only three things: riding, archery and telling the truth.
- A boy does not see his father until he is five years old.
- They show reverence for rivers.

Herodotus confirms that he has personal knowledge of each of these examples of their behaviour.

Their character

In the fifth century, however, barbarians became symbolic of all those excesses a Greek must resist or avoid – lust, anger and greed for luxury/decadence. Barbarians were shown as slavish – slaves to a master, slaves to their impulses. The impression therefore is that there is a 'barbarian' in all humans and that the Greeks used the laws and customs of their civilisation to control these impulses. A barbarian, therefore, is a Greek without civilisation.

Politics and hierarchy

ACTIVITY

Consider the reaction of a Persian to the way in which Persian character, culture and military strength are portrayed in Herodotus, Greek art and on the tragic stage. Do they think that they would have been offended?

The king is at the head of the Persian Empire. In Herodotus his advisers are older and more experienced (Mardonius and Artabanus). Xerxes displays bouts of extreme cruelty (after the first bridge over the Hellespont is destroyed, he beheads the builders) but he also listens to, and occasionally accepts, advice. He is, however, frequently caught between opposing influences and, on these occasions, he must make a decision. Mardonius

MODERN SCHOLARSHIP

In *Inventing the Barbarian* (OUP, 1989, p. 17) Edith Hall explains that, although there are notable exceptions, barbarians in tragedy are 'emotional, stupid, cruel, subservient or cowardly'.

Evidence can be found for Hall's view in Aeschylus' *Persians*:

- Xerxes displays excessive grief over the defeat at Salamis, although he never shows any recognition of his own part in the downfall of the Persians.
- Due to his over-confidence, Xerxes is easily tricked by the Greeks at Salamis.
- The Chorus in the Persians seem cowardly and are unwilling to give their opinions. They refuse to speak at all in the presence of the ghost of Darius.
- The Messenger describes the abrupt flight of the Persians at Salamis.

EXAM TIP

It is always important to consider the reliability of Herodotus as a source. If his information is incorrect, it may be because he is biased but he also may have been misinformed by his own sources.

is keen to take chances, but Artabanus is more conservative. At the start of Book 7 (1–20), the expedition to Greece is being discussed. Mardonius is dismissive of the Greeks' fighting ability and urges an invasion but Artabanus remembers Darius' failed expedition to Scythia and advises Xerxes to abandon his plans. Xerxes is also swayed by what he sees as his responsibility to his ancestors to extend the Persian Empire. Later in Book 7 (44–50), Xerxes and Artabanus have a more philosophical discussion on taking risks, and at this point Herodotus' audience perhaps glimpse another side to the king.

Many of Xerxes' staff are eunuchs (men who have been castrated). In the anecdote of Hermotimus in Book 8 (105–106), it is explained that eunuchs were valued highly amongst the barbarians because they were considered more trustworthy. Hermotimus' speech illustrates the cruel practice of castration and would also suggest Herodotus' disapproval. However, he does not find fault with every Persian practice and singles out some for praise. In the list of Persian customs in Book 1 (131–140), Herodotus praises the principle that not even the Persian king can put a man to death because of one act. However, this principle does not appear to be followed by any of the Persian kings he includes. Throughout his account, Herodotus consistently points out that the subjects of the Persian king were punished or rewarded in line with their service.

> Whenever Xerxes saw any conspicuous act of bravery from his own sailors, as he
> sat watching the battle on a hill called Aegaleos which faced Salamis, he found out
> the name of the captain and his scribes also wrote down the name of his father and
> of his city.
>
> Herodotus, *Histories*, 8.90

Herodotus often shows Xerxes' warped applications of justice. Pythius, a rich Lydian, is initially rewarded for his show of generosity towards Xerxes (7.28–29). However, when he asks Xerxes for a further favour (to release the oldest of his five sons from the army), Xerxes is furious and gives orders for Pythius' oldest son to be cut in half and placed on either side of the army's route (7.39). A similarly 'double-edged' approach is seen on Xerxes' voyage back to the Hellespont after the defeat at Salamis. When the ship is caught in a storm, the captain advises Xerxes that they need to reduce the weight of the ship by getting rid of some of the sailors. Xerxes puts this suggestion to his soldiers who dutifully throw themselves into the sea and the ship reaches the Hellespont. Herodotus then describes Xerxes' treatment of the captain.

> As soon as Xerxes had disembarked onto the land, he did the following: first he
> gave a golden crown to the captain, for saving the life of his king, then he gave orders
> for his head to be cut off as he had been responsible for the death of so many
> Persian men.
>
> Herodotus, *Histories*, 8.118

Their religion and rituals

In Aeschylus' *Persians*, the ghost of Darius is summoned from Hades, and speaks with Atossa and the Chorus after the Chorus sing a chant to him. However, there are other

---

KEY INDIVIDUAL

Artabanus

Date: Adviser to Xerxes and Darius in their expeditions to Greece in the fifth century BC.

In Artabanus' discussions with Xerxes, Herodotus represents him as an overly cautious, risk-averse figure.

examples of such necromancy (the practice of summoning up the dead) in Greek tragedy, so this cannot be labelled as a purely Persian ritual. Similarly, there are examples of Greeks making human sacrifices in tragedy, although this only occurs in desperate situations, whereas there is a suggestion that it is carried out more regularly by the Persians.

However, barbarian religion is sometimes represented as more spiritual and, therefore, closer to the gods. Dionysus, the god of tragedy, was supposed to have come from the East (Herodotus explains that the idea of Dionysus was brought to Greece from Egypt (2.48)). Such rituals were, however, a risk, as they offered liberation.

Herodotus gives a speech to Xerxes in which Xerxes explains that the Persians have won their Empire due to a god's guidance and approval. The winged disc image appears on Persian Art from the rule of Darius onwards and some believe that it signifies the Persian god Ahuramazda protecting and guiding the king.

A god has brought us this far and we continue to benefit from taking on challenges.

Herodotus, *Histories*, 7.8

FIGURE 1.14
Relief detail depicting the Zoroastrian god Ahuramazda.

THE ROLE OF THE HISTORICAL CONTEXT IN THIS 'INVENTION' OF THE BARBARIAN

The role of the Persian Wars in crystallising images of foreign peoples

Of all the Greek city-states in the fifth century BC, Athens was best placed to benefit from the victories over the barbarians, and was very interested in representing how these victories had been achieved. The city was home to magnificent sculptors and painters, progressive politicians, inventive dramatists and inquisitive philosophers. The most noticeable development in the city was the rebuilding of the temples on the Acropolis.

The Parthenon, a magnificent new temple to the goddess Athene, was completed by 431 BC. The new building more than adequately replaced the one destroyed by the Persians, the foundations of which were left as a reminder of Persian aggression. In the sculptures which decorate the temple, the Greeks and their gods triumph over various versions of 'barbarians': Trojans, Amazons, Giants and Centaurs. The Centaurs are truly barbarous beings; half man, half horse, they are slaves to their desires, drunkenly and lustfully attempting to carry off maidens who are defended by gallant Greek youths.

In the Theatre of Dionysus on the southern slope of the Acropolis, Aeschylus' *Persians* won first prize in the drama festival of 472 BC. The audience sat with the burnt Acropolis behind them. Some have also suggested that they sat on wood taken from the wreckage

Study question
How did the Persian Wars change Greek attitudes towards barbarians?

MODERN SCHOLARSHIP

The battle was for Greek freedom, but the contrasts of justice and luxury were woven into memories of it.

Lane Fox, *The Classical World* (Allen Lane, 2005), p. 107

What does Lane Fox mean by 'woven into memories'?

TOPIC REVIEW

These questions should draw on your knowledge of the whole topic, so think carefully about the different things you have learned (check the Topic Overview on p. 28).

1. In very simple terms, what did 'barbarian' mean before the fifth century BC?
2. How and why did this meaning change?
3. How were the Persians represented in Greek art and literature of the fifth century BC?
4. How much was defining the Persians really about defining the Greeks themselves?

of Persian ships. In this play, the Persian defeat at Salamis becomes a punishment from the gods for their barbarian arrogance. On the plain of Marathon, in the straits of Salamis, on the four facades of the Parthenon and on the Athenian stage, the barbarian was created and vanquished over and over again.

Further Reading

Beard, M. (2010) *The Parthenon*. London: Profile Books
Cartledge, P. (2002) *The Greeks: A Portrait of Self and Others*. Oxford: Oxford University Press
Vlassopoulos, K. (2013) *Greeks and Barbarians*. Cambridge: Cambridge University Press
Woodford, S. (1997) *An Introduction to Greek Art*. London: Duckworth

PRACTICE QUESTIONS

Source A

1. What is the Greek name for this type of vase? [1]
2. Explain how this source illustrates the different ways in which Greeks and Barbarians are depicted in Greek art. [10]

1.4 Depictions and Portrayals: Mythical Barbarians

TOPIC OVERVIEW

- The Amazons, including:
  - their appearance and behaviour
  - how their behaviour and values set them apart from the Greeks

- Medea, with study of Euripides' *Medea,* including:
  - the plot, structure, characterisation and themes
  - the context in which the play was produced
  - how the plot and Medea's character is formed by her status as a barbarian
  - how Medea's actions may have been viewed by the audience
- How gender is linked to the sense of 'other' and danger associated with barbarian characters

The following prescribed sources are covered in this topic:

- Euripides' *Medea*
- Attic red-figure krater depicting Herakles and the Amazons, attributed to Euphronios
- Frieze of Temple of Apollo at Bassae (British Museum), showing Amazons
- Attic red-figure kylix depicting Achilles and Penthesilea, by the Penthesilea Painter
- The battle of Achilles and Penthesilea. Lucanian red-figure bell-krater
- Herodotus' *Histories*, 4.110–117

Don't forget that you will be given credit in the exam if you study extra sources and make relevant use of them in your answers.

This topic focuses on barbarian women. The Amazons are briefly described as an historical Scythian tribe in Herodotus' *Histories* (4.110–117), but also feature as mythical opponents of Theseus, Herakles and Achilles. The Amazonian Princess Diana, better known as the DC Comics superhero Wonder Woman, confirms our continuing fascination with these warrior women. Euripides' *Medea* remains one of the most popular Greek tragedies and still has much to tell us about relationships between men and women.

PRESCRIBED SOURCE

Medea

Date: 431 BC

Author: Euripides

Genre: tragedy

Collection: 19 of his plays still survive

Plot: Medea gains a terrible revenge on Jason, the husband who abandoned her

Significance: *Medea* is one of Euripides' earliest plays. He was particularly interested in showing the internal motivations and thought processes of his characters. Many of his plays feature very dominant female characters.

Read it here: *Euripides: Medea (Cambridge Translations from Greek Drama)*, transl. J. Harrison (CUP, 1999)

THE AMAZONS

Their appearance and behaviour

The Amazons are frequently depicted by the Greeks both on vases and in sculpture. This was particularly the case in the fifth century following the Persian Wars. They are frequently shown armed for war, although there is a great variety of different scenes: on some vases they are dancing and one even shows them swimming nude. They generally dress for the cold steppes in Scythia (an area to the north of the Black Sea), where they lived a nomadic lifestyle. They wear pointed caps with patterned tunics and trousers. Occasionally, they are shown wearing leopard skins. Sometimes they are barefoot but in most images they wear boots: boots and trousers were more appropriate for horse-riding. Amazons sometimes have tattoos on their arms or legs; these tattoos can be patterns or even small pictures of animals.

They are most often shown with a bow and accompanying quiver (a case for arrows). However, they use a variety of weapons, including a battle axe with a blade on one side and a lethal-looking spike on the other. Amazons also fought with spears and swords and defended themselves with a small, light, half-moon shaped shield. They are also shown using a sling or a lasso.

The Amazons were respected as warriors; the Greeks are shown defeating them but their victories are hard-won. They are described in Homer as 'the equals of men'.

In mythology, the Amazons went up against the two mightiest Greek heroes: Herakles and Achilles. Scenes of single combat between the two heroes and Amazon queens are popular on Greek vases. Amazons are also shown fighting the Greeks in pitched battles. These scenes could be from the Trojan War but there is a myth that the Amazons also attacked Athens. One of Herakles' labours was to recover the girdle of Hippolyte, queen

KEY INDIVIDUALS

The Amazons a tribe of female warriors. They fight under their queen, Penthesilea, in the Trojan War. Herodotus describes them (4.110–117) as a race from Scythia.

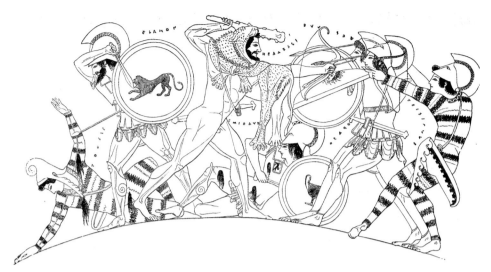

FIGURE 1.15
Drawing (on left) taken from an early fifth-century BC Attic red-figure krater (below) depicting Herakles and the Amazons, attributed to Euphronios.

PS

PRESCRIBED SOURCE

Attic red-figure krater depicting Herakles and the Amazons, attributed to Euphronios

Date: 6th century BC

Material: earthenware

Original location: Etruria (Southern Italy)

Current location: Museo Civico, Arezzo

Significance: depiction of Amazons by a Greek vase-painter

of the Amazons. Theseus accompanied Herakles on his mission and as Herakles brought back Hippolyte's girdle, Theseus brought back Hippolyte's sister, Antiope. Theseus and Antiope had a son who was named Hippolytus. The Amazons attacked Athens to try to recover Antiope, who was killed by mistake in the attack. As with many Greek myths, there are different versions of the story.

The image in Figure 1.15 shows Herakles (accompanied by his friend Telamon) fighting the Amazons. Some are armed as Greek warriors but the two Amazons at the extreme ends of the image are dressed in patterned tunics. A frieze featuring images of revellers also decorates this vase, which would have been used for mixing wine and water. The connection of the two scenes is interesting. It is clear from the number of images produced of Amazons that the Greeks held a fascination for them. Amazons often feature on vases that, like the mixing bowl shown, would have been used in symposia (drinking parties).

Figure 1.16 shows a Greek warrior struggling to defend himself against the onslaught of an Amazon warrior. She wears a pointed Scythian cap and has a half-moon shaped shield. Her thin drapery clings to her body revealing the outline of her breasts.

In Figure 1.17, Penthesilea is shown reaching for Achilles' chin to supplicate him, her toes flex to grip the rim of the tondo. She is depicted wearing a tunic. Her fellow Amazon on the right of the picture wears the distinctive patterned costume and, unusually for figures on Greek vases, she is represented facing outwards. The viewer will have initially viewed this scene through the wine in the cup and the gaze of this Amazon will have emerged slowly as the wine was drained.

Figure 1.18 shows Achilles chasing Penthesilea, the Amazon queen, during the Trojan War. Achilles is nude. He is armed with a spear and a shield and wears a helmet, although his spear is pointed towards the ground rather than at Penthesilea. Penthesilea wears a heavily patterned tunic and an elaborate headdress. She is armed with an axe and a shield, but neither is held in an offensive position as she flees before the onrushing hero. Her dress swishes with her movement. She turns back to look at Achilles and their eyes meet. Their poses also match and this gives the vase a repetitive rhythm as both characters run from left to right.

FIGURE 1.16
Scene from the frieze of the Temple of Apollo at Bassae in Greece.

PRESCRIBED SOURCE
Frieze of the Temple of Apollo at Bassae
Date: 5th century BC
Material: marble
Original location: Bassae (central Peloponnese)
Current location: British Museum
Significance: depiction of Greeks fighting Amazons by a Greek sculptor

FIGURE 1.17
Attic red-figure kylix depicting Achilles and Penthesilea, by the Penthesilea Painter.

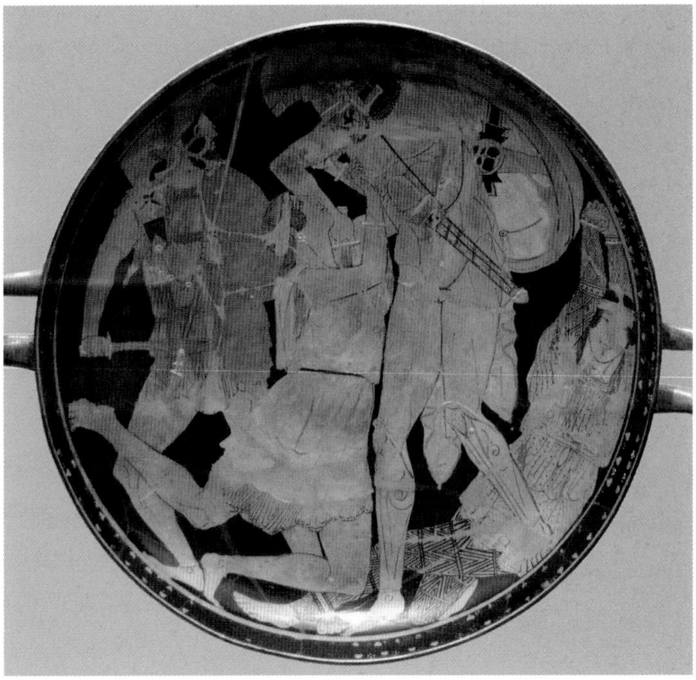

FIGURE 1.18

The battle of Achilles and Penthesilea, Lucanian red-figure bell-krater, late fifth century BC.

Study questions

1 What similarities
between the various
depictions of
Amazons on Greek
vases have you
noticed?

2 Why do you think the
Amazons appear so
frequently in Greek
myths?

ACTIVITY

Find some different
images of Amazons on
Greek vases and from
Greek sculptures, and
consider how each
emphasises the
barbarian nature of
the women.

S
&
C
Read more about
attitudes to women in
fifth-century BC Athens
in *Women's Life in
Greece and Rome* by
Lefkowitz and Fant
(Duckworth, 1992) to
see how different the
Amazons were.

Some of the fascination of Greek men for the Amazons could have been an erotic fantasy. Amazons are athletic and desirable young maidens, who are often shown with either or both breasts revealed. However, Amazons also appeared on perfume containers for women, showing that they had universal appeal. Greek girls had Amazon dolls, which they would surrender when they were married. Amazons offered an image of freedom and gender-equality, unbound by the demands and expectations of society. They were supposed to have lived on the Scythian steppes, hunting with dogs, riding or fighting mythical griffins.

Two of the most famous myths about the Amazons are probably even less reliable than the rest of the guesses made about them:

- They did not cut off one of their breasts to help them fire arrows. One ancient historian interpreted the name 'Amazon' as a derivation from the Greek a-mastos, meaning 'without a breast', but there is no other evidence for this bizarre practice and, in depictions on Greek vases, Amazons are always shown with both breasts intact.
- They did not maim male babies to prevent them from taking over once they grew up. Herodotus, who certainly would have described this behaviour if it were true, makes no mention of it.

How their behaviour and values set them apart from the Greeks

Amazons were the opposite of Greek women: they were nomads, they lived outdoor life-styles, they had sexual freedom and they fought. Amazons are described as virgins but this meant, more accurately, unmarried. Herodotus tells a story (4.110–117) explaining how the Scythians and Amazons first began to intermingle. This story stresses the Amazons' sexual freedom, since they choose to have sex with the Scythian men in the open air and in groups. They are then reluctant to live the indoor lifestyle of a Scythian woman. The Amazons are clearly desirable: the Scythians end up leaving their families

EXPLORE FURTHER

The Amazons by Mayor
(Princeton University
Press, 2014) is a
fascinating and
complete account.

MODERN SCHOLARSHIP

. . . any Greek with a knowledge of Herodotus's histories would be justified in imagining euphoric, naked, glistening Amazons inside their steamy sauna tents, inhaling billowing clouds of hemp smoke, and then languorously applying lotion redolent of cedar and frankincense before retiring to their beds of soft fur.

Mayor, *The Amazons* (Princeton University Press, 2014), p. 151

Do you agree with Mayor's conclusions about Herodotus' description of the Amazons in 4.110–117?

and lands to be with them. Herodotus also mentions their marriage law, which stated that a girl must kill an enemy in battle before she was able to marry.

MEDEA, WITH STUDY OF EURIPIDES' *MEDEA*

The plot

Pelias had stolen the throne of Iolcus from Jason. In order to get Jason out of the city, hopefully forever, Pelias sent him to the Black Sea to win the Golden Fleece, a legendary treasure guarded by a dragon. After many adventures on his ship, the Argo, with his crew known as the Argonauts, Jason arrived in Colchis to complete his quest. In the palace, he was seen by Medea, the daughter of the king. Medea immediately fell in love with Jason and resolved to do whatever she could to help him win the fleece and return safely to Greece. Medea was the granddaughter of the Sun and had magical powers. She was therefore able to help Jason conquer the challenges that her father set for him. After Medea had put the guarding dragon to sleep, Jason was able to steal the fleece and escape back to Greece. To slow her father's pursuit, Medea was even prepared to murder her brother, so great was her desire to escape with Jason. After they came to Iolcus, Jason's ancestral home, Medea tricked the daughters of Pelias into killing their father. They were required to flee from Iolcus and came, as exiles, to Corinth.

Structure

Prologue (lines 1–120)

The Nurse explains that her mistress, Medea, is in pain; she is not eating and she weeps all the time, lying on the ground. She had come from Colchis because of her intense love for Jason and he has betrayed the oaths he made to her. Jason has married the daughter of the king of Corinth and abandoned Medea and their two sons. The Nurse mentions that Medea seems to hate her sons and is concerned about what Medea might be planning.

The Tutor enters with the two boys. He brings the news that King Creon is planning to exile Medea and her sons. The Nurse is angry that Jason will allow this to happen but the Tutor encourages her not to tell Medea yet. The Nurse repeats her concerns about Medea's plans and, as Medea begins to speak from within, she hurries the children into the house. The Nurse preaches moderation as the best way to avoid the anger of the gods.

Parodos (lines 121–202)

The entry speech by the Chorus of Corinthian women is split by Medea's cries from within the palace. Medea shouts out that she wants to die and the Chorus are surprised by her extreme reaction to her betrayal. The Chorus and the Nurse both wish that they could soothe Medea's grief and anger. Medea wishes death on Jason and his new bride, and regrets betraying her father and her country when she murdered her brother.

Study question

How differently do you think a modern and an ancient audience would respond to Medea's speech on the plight of women in the ancient world at 203–254?

First Episode (lines 203–398)

Medea enters, coming out of house to secure the good will of the Chorus. She is aware that, as a foreigner, she must conform. She mourns her betrayal by Jason and passes on to mourning the vulnerability of women. She points out that women have to buy a husband, taking their chances on what sort of man they end up with. They may then have to put up with a bad marriage without the sexual freedom enjoyed by men. She also explains that a woman's life is dangerous, particularly childbirth. Medea reminds the Chorus that she cannot return to her family and asks for the Chorus not to say anything about any plans she might make to gain her revenge, however murderous these might be.

The Chorus support her right to take revenge on Jason and then Creon, the king of Corinth, enters. Creon explains to Medea that he has decided that she should be exiled immediately. He fears her anger, her magical powers and the rumours of the threats that she has made.

Medea explains to Creon that he has nothing to fear from her and that her anger is exclusively aimed at Jason. She explains to him that the rumours have arisen from her reputation for cleverness, which is resented by others. Creon replies that he fears her even-tempered words more than her passionate anger, and repeats his decision that she should leave. Medea pleads for one day to make preparations for her exile and Creon agrees. He says that one day is not long enough for Medea to create any disasters and then he leaves, acknowledging that his reluctance to see through his decision is a mistake.

Medea explains to the Chorus that she has tricked Creon by 'fawning' on him. She is still planning trouble for Jason, his new bride and for Creon himself. She mocks Creon for changing his mind and goes on to talk through various brutal ways in which she might gain her revenge. She finally decides on poison and resolves to bide her time.

First Ode (399–424)

The Chorus speak of upheaval in the world: men break their oaths and women gain honour. They describe Medea's plight as a foreign exile who left her land, stricken with love, but now has no husband.

Second Episode (425–608)

Jason enters. He blames Medea's exile on the foolish threats she has made against the royal family. However, he is still willing to help her by offering money, despite her insults towards him. Medea is furious with Jason. She reminds him of how she helped him win the Golden Fleece and then brought about the death of Pelias. Because of his lust for a new woman, Jason has now abandoned her after she bore him sons. She has nowhere to turn as she now cannot return home or to Iolcus. It is a disgrace to Jason that his wife and sons will be cast out.

Jason explains to Medea that she helped him because she was under the influence of Aphrodite. She did not act out of loyalty. Jason points out to Medea the advantages she gained by accompanying him to Greece: she now lives in a land of justice and law, where her talents are famous. Jason goes on to explain that he has married the king's daughter to ensure security for them all in Corinth; he was not motivated by sexual desire, nor by having more children. He finishes by claiming that women only think about their sex life.

The Chorus admire Jason's speech but still feel that he has behaved wrongly.

Medea takes issue with Jason's speech and says that she is not convinced by his clever explanations. Jason continues to try unsuccessfully to encourage Medea to accept the situation. He offers to help her once she leaves the city but Medea returns to the subject of his betrayal and refuses his offer of assistance.

Second Ode (609–639)

The Chorus discuss the problem of love without moderation and express their fear of the power of Aphrodite. They also wish never to be struck by adulterous love. They mourn the plight of an exile and say that they would rather die than live having lost their country. The Chorus pity Medea in her suffering.

Third Episode (640–802)

Aegeus, the king of Athens, enters. He is on his way back from the oracle at Delphi where he has been to inquire about how he might have children. Medea expresses surprise that he has not yet had a child and then proceeds to tell Aegeus about Jason's betrayal. Aegeus is appalled by Jason's behaviour but, nevertheless, encourages Medea to move on. She tells him that she is banished and pleads with him to offer her refuge in his city, promising in return that she will cure his childlessness. Aegeus promises to receive Medea in Athens if she can make her own way there. Medea encourages him to swear an oath promising that he will protect her in Athens. Aegeus agrees and leaves.

Medea is delighted that she now has a place of refuge and proceeds to lay out her plan. She will pretend to Jason that she agrees with his arrangements and that she will be compliant, and then use her children to take a poisoned robe to Jason's new bride. After this, she will have to kill her children. She acknowledges the enormity of this crime. However, Medea will not be thought weak, or mocked by her enemies. The Chorus cannot agree with Medea's plan but they are reminded of their promise of silence.

Third Ode (803–836)

The Chorus sing about the purity of Athens. They claim that Aphrodite once visited the city and inspired its culture. They express surprise that Athens will offer sanctuary to a woman who has murdered her own children, and plead with Medea to think again. They encourage her to think through the deed itself.

Fourth Episode (837–944)

Jason enters and Medea asks him to forgive her changeable moods. She says that she has come around to his way of thinking and is now convinced that it will be in her best interests to go along with his plans. She calls for the children to come out of the house and embrace their father. Jason is pleased (and convinced) that Medea has changed her mind. He is certain that his sons will grow up to be great men in the city. Medea begins to cry at this mention of her sons' future. She asks Jason to try to persuade Creon not to send the boys into exile. Jason says that he will speak to the king but thinks that his new bride might better persuade her father.

Medea promises to send the boys with a dress and a crown for Jason's new bride. This dress had come to Medea from her grandfather, the god of the Sun and was made from woven gold. Jason says that she can keep the gift as the palace is already full of dresses. Medea says that the gifts are to encourage the princess to allow the boys to stay in the city.

Fourth Ode (945–968)

The Chorus now give up hope that Medea will change her plans, now that the poisoned dress and crown are on their way to the palace. They mention the grief which Jason will soon suffer and the actions that led to this disaster.

Fifth Episode (969–1050)

The Tutor enters with the boys. He tells Medea that the boys have delivered the presents to the princess and suggests that they have won her over. However, Medea is upset by the news and this surprises the Tutor.

The Tutor goes into the house, leaving Medea alone with the boys. Medea mourns the fact that she will soon be parted from her children and will never see them grow up and marry. They will also not be there to look after her in her old age. Medea then suggests to the Chorus that she will give up her plan to kill the children and will instead take them away to Corinth.

She abruptly changes back to her former intention and chastises herself for weakness. Then, just as abruptly, she changes back to her original idea and then back the other way again, suggesting this time that they will go to Athens instead. She reminds herself that the fate of the princess is sealed and she cannot, therefore, leave her children at the mercy of her enemies. She embraces the boys and sends them inside the house. She now understands the horror of what she is about to do and blames the passion that is driving her on.

Choral Interlude (1051–1086)

This is a lyrical section and so it is more correct to call it an 'interlude' than a full ode. It is possible that this indicates a form of debate between the members of the Chorus.

The Chorus begin by reflecting on the passions of women. They then move on to the trials of being a parent and how children can be a constant source of anxiety. The greatest grief for a parent is the death of their child.

Sixth Episode (1087–1225)

The Messenger enters, bringing news to Medea about the death of the princess and her father. Medea expresses joy at the news and is keen to hear the details of the event.

The Messenger begins his report by saying that there was great joy in the palace at the reconciliation between Medea and Jason. The princess was initially unhappy at seeing Jason's sons but was delighted with the crown and the dress. Jason and the boys left the palace and the princess put on the dress and admired herself in the mirror. Then the poison began to take effect and the Messenger describes dramatic physical changes. The whole palace was then in uproar: some rushed to tell the king, others ran to Jason. The princess screamed and began to run through the palace, desperately trying to tear off the crown. Finally, her body, burned and bloody, fell to the floor. Creon found his daughter and immediately knelt beside her and embraced and kissed his daughter. Then, the poison began to affect him also: he could not tear himself away from the body and died beside the princess.

The Chorus suggest that Jason has deserved this and they pity the princess.

Medea now seems convinced that the boys will die, and that she will kill them rather than allow them to be murdered by another in vengeance for her actions. She still wavers and steels herself to the completion of the horrifying task.

Fifth Ode (1226–1271)

The Chorus plead with the Sun to stop the act from taking place. The boys are descended from the god. They are appalled at what Medea is about to do. During this ode, screams are heard from inside the palace and the Chorus consider breaking into the house to stop Medea. They compare Medea to Ino who was driven mad by the gods and killed her children but then threw herself into the sea and drowned.

Exodos (1272–1396)

Jason enters, hoping to save his sons from their mother. The Chorus tell him that he is already too late and that Medea has killed the boys. As Jason tries to get into the house, Medea appears above the stage in the chariot of the Sun. Jason says that he was wrong to have brought Medea to Greece: she had already shown herself to be a traitor to her own family by betraying her father and murdering her brother.

Medea explains that she will not give a long reply. She reminds Jason that he did not treat her fairly after she helped him. She adds that she was not prepared to be laughed at by her enemies. Jason and Medea both then blame each other for the deaths of the children.

Medea refuses to give Jason the bodies of the children for burial and says that she will take them with her to Athens. She foretells that Jason will die after he is hit on the head by timber from his ship, the Argo. Jason finishes by cursing Medea to Zeus.

The Chorus close the play by explaining that life holds many shocks and surprises.

> **Study question**
> What is the Chorus' opinion of the different characters of the play and how does it change?

Characterisation

Jason

To a modern audience, Jason can often seem smug and unsympathetic; an ancient audience, however, might have been less damning of him. His family have arrived in Corinth in exile, due to Medea's actions, and he says that, in marrying the princess, he is doing what is best for all of them. Medea feels that this is the shameful justification of a man who just wants a younger, Greek wife. Medea cannot understand his logic, just as Jason cannot understand her emotional response. Throughout the play, he is dismissive of all women: it is clear that he uses sexual relationships as a way to further his own ends and displays little emotional involvement. He is easily tricked by Medea and is represented as quite foolish in his second scene with her, since the Chorus and the audience both know that he is being flattered and deceived by Medea at this point. He blames himself for the deaths which come at the end of the play, saying that he should never have brought Medea to Greece. The Chorus waver in their support for Jason: they understand that he was acting in the best interests of his family but still blame the deaths of the children on his betrayal.

Creon

Creon is also deceived by Medea, although he seems more perceptive than Jason and continues to express his concerns about her. He loses his authority during his scene with Medea: although he attempts to be decisive, he does not want to appear to be a tyrant and is willing to compromise. He underestimates Medea when he feels that a day will not be long enough for her. His death is poignant: he does not understand that poison has been used and dies trying to help his daughter.

Aegeus

Aegeus arrives on the stage after Medea has won an extra day from Creon and then had her memorable argument with Jason. She manages to persuade him to offer her sanctuary in the city of Athens. The Chorus later express surprise that Athens would be willing to take in a child-killer who would pollute the city. Aegeus explains his sexual difficulties (he and his wife have not yet been able to have a child) to Medea and, keen for Medea's help, he is sympathetic towards her plight. Unlike other men in the play, he is able to empathise with Medea's side of her argument with Jason.

Themes

There are a number of interesting themes in Medea, many of which contribute to the enduring popularity of the play.

The family

Family relationships are very important. The Choral Interlude (1051–1086) concentrates on the anguish for parents but, despite this, Aegeus is dismayed by his childlessness. Medea's love for her children almost causes her to waver in her purpose and the effect that the children have on the servants in the play is clear.

Men and women

Medea and Jason have clashing ideas on their marriage (this is memorably and succinctly expressed at 1346–1348). Medea memorably describes the 'plight' of marriage in the ancient world at 219–240. Medea expresses wider ideas of how women are regarded more generally. She complains to Creon in the First Episode that her cleverness means that she is not trusted.

Gods

Both Jason and Medea appeal to the gods to avenge their treatment. There is an argument that, in appearing in a dragon-powered chariot above the stage, endowed with the gift of prophecy, Medea becomes a goddess at the end of the play. The apparent divine sanction for the murder of the children is disquieting.

The context in which the play was performed

Medea was performed in 431 BC and is one of Euripides' earliest plays. This was the first year of the Peloponnesian War between Athens and Sparta. At this time, Athens was at the head of a large maritime empire, which spread across the Aegean Sea. Nearly fifty years had passed since the Persians had been defeated in the sea battle off Salamis; however, there would still have been a fascination for seeing a barbarian represented on stage.

The Athenians were proud of their democratic government and, therefore, the kings in the play, Creon and Aegeus, are anxious to appear sympathetic but are also weak and both put their states in a worse position. However, the Athenians were also aware that a democracy was vulnerable to a demagogue (a skilled orator who could whip the people up into a frenzy). Jason is represented as a clever speaker but the fact that we hear his thought processes before he makes his speech is, perhaps, an indication that is not easy for him to talk in a clever way. Medea, however, is comfortable with deception and is able to convince those around her. Allied with her evil intent, this makes her appear even more dangerous to a democratic Athenian audience. Creon says as much; he trusts a cold, clever person much less than a passionate one. Medea expresses regret at being thought clever, as this means that people trust her less.

Women in Athens did not have a vote and could not be elected. They were also unable to divorce their husband; Medea comments on the inequality between the sexes. Her famous comparison between fighting in the front line of battle and bearing children still resonates today. There is some debate over whether Athenian women would have attended the theatre, but non-Athenian women may have been present. However, the audience will certainly have been predominantly male. However, the audience would not have been surprised to see a powerful female figure on the stage, many had preceded Medea in the plays of the two other great Athenian playwrights, Aeschylus and Sophocles. The audience would have been even less surprised to see a powerful female figure causing disaster and distress by her actions.

> **Study question**
> Why do you think *Medea* is one of the most popular ancient tragedies to perform today?

How the plot and Medea's character is formed by her status as a barbarian

Jason stresses to Medea that he did her a great service by bringing her to Greece. He describes the country from which she came as 'primitive'. Jason describes Greece as a land of justice and the rule of law. It is also a place where Medea has become known. As a hero, Jason sees renown as a good thing (his status as a hero probably secured his new marriage). Medea's reputation, however, has not been entirely positive for her: although Aegeus values her intelligence, Creon mistrusts her. By the end of the play, all Jason's promises about the glory of Greece have become hollow. Jason and two Greek kings have been deceived by Medea and her advanced knowledge of poison has given her a power none of the Greeks in the play expected. Medea escapes at the end of the play untouched by Greek justice, despite murdering her two children and causing many more deaths both before and during the play.

At the start and the end of the play, Jason is blamed for bringing his barbarian wife to Greece. Medea's name suggests 'Mede', a familiar Greek name for Persians and, throughout the play, we are reminded that Medea is foreign. The frequent references to the sea and sea-faring by the Chorus stress the distance between Greece and Medea's homeland. Medea has found it hard to conform as a foreigner and as a woman. She uses her loneliness as an exile and as a woman without a husband to win over the Chorus. Medea also refers to her status as a foreigner in Greece to Jason later in the play. She claims that he has left her for a new wife because it did not look right for him to be married to a foreigner. Jason disagrees with this and there is no indication elsewhere in the play that their marriage was thought to be wrong.

Creon fears Medea's intelligence more than her foreign birth, to which he makes no reference. Similarly her magic is not described as 'foreign', nor is it explained as coming from barbarian lands. Jason puts her emotional and, to his mind, irrational behaviour all down to the fact that she is a woman. He will also show frustration later in the play towards his new wife when she becomes upset that his sons enter the palace. However, towards the end of the play, Jason will say that no Greek woman could have brought herself to kill her own children: his suggestion is that Medea's evil act is particularly foreign.

How Medea's actions may have been viewed by the audience

The myth on which Euripides bases his play was already well-known in Athens. However, in the myth, the Corinthians kill Medea and Jason's children in revenge for her murder of the princess. In Euripides' play, Medea's plan to kill her children seems clear and obvious from the start and any audience finds it difficult, if not impossible, to overlook this act. The Nurse and Medea both mention her hatred for the children. Medea is immoderate in her anger and will inevitably be punished for this. Within the Nurse's speech, she switches from immoderate love to immoderate grief (the Nurse, Tutor and Chorus all express surprise at the length of her grief) to immoderate hate (for Jason and the children).

In one respect, at least, she behaves as a tragic hero: her passion is driving her to act regardless of the advice of the other characters in the play. However, Medea is a unique character who threatens the conventions of tragedy itself. She intrudes into the Nurse's speech at the start of the play, the Chorus consider entering the house to stop her from

The conventional plot typology can be formulated as follows: women in Athenian tragedy only become transgressive in the physical absence of a legitimate husband with whom they are having regular sexual intercourse.

Hall, *Greek Tragedy* (OUP, 2010), p. 128

What differing attitudes towards sex and/or marriage are displayed by Jason and Medea in the play?

S & C

In Euripides' *Helen*, a Greek woman is alone in a foreign country, Egypt; this is a reversal of Medea's situation. However, like Medea, Helen also outsmarts those who underestimate her during the play and manages the escape plan for both her and Menelaus, her husband. Read the play and consider the differences and similarities between Euripides' portrayals of Helen and Medea.

murdering the children, and in the *exodos* she appears in a chariot above the stage. She bares her soul to the audience who are as unable as the other characters in the play to affect her thoughts and actions.

Medea challenges so many of the conventions important to society. After Medea has explained to them her plan to kill Creon, Jason and the princess, the Chorus talk about the upheaval of society and the liberation of women. Medea chose her husband and openly expressed her attitude to sex, she betrayed her father, murdered her brother, persuaded girls to kill their father, murdered her own children and cheated both divine and mortal justice. She also sees child-bearing as a bargain rather than a duty: she expresses the joy of seeing her children married and their care for her in old age as an exchange for giving birth to them.

The end of the *Medea* is unsettling: the mechane is more frequently used for the arrival of a god to bring resolution but, in this play, Medea herself appears in the chariot of the Sun above the stage. The play has been set up for Medea to head off to Athens but the Sun clearly colludes in the dramatic and unjust escape of a murderess.

How gender is linked to the sense of 'other' and danger associated with barbarian characters

The audience would have been made up, mostly, if not entirely, of adult Athenian males; Medea was a young, intelligent foreign woman, who was also an exile within Greece. Medea was clearly 'other' than the audience watching the play. The comparison she makes between fighting in battle and giving birth is striking – for her, standing in the front line is three times more preferable. The men in the audience would certainly disagree. The Nurse expresses the attitude of a traditional Greek woman: she should not cross her husband.

It is possible to suggest that Medea's status as a foreigner enables Euripides to give her a more objective view on Greek marriage customs. She complains that a woman is powerless: her husband is bought for her, at great expense, and then she cannot leave him. Women are then expected to go through the difficult and dangerous process of having children. Medea, however, has chosen and bought her own husband and has developed a strong sexual attachment to him. There are references to her bed and to their sexual relationship throughout the play. Medea, at least, feels that she is speaking for all women, Greek and barbarian, when she complains at Jason's lack of understanding.

Medea's anger is heroic and male: in a simile typical for epic heroes, she is compared to a wild bull in the Prologue. However, her response to this anger is not male, physical and predictable. Medea herself says that she cannot act in this way as a woman and must instead use the skills that she has: seduction, manipulation and deceit. As part of this deceit, she skilfully emphasises her vulnerability in front of Creon and, in their second scene, with Jason. She shows understanding and displays empathy when faced with Aegeus' potential embarrassment. Creon voices the concern of all males when he says that he fears such a cold and calculating woman and yet, for all his anxiety, he still under-estimates her. This ability to persuade men is not confined just to Medea; Jason says that the princess is more likely to persuade Creon to let the boys stay in the city because she is a woman.

Her murder of the princess with poison is typically feminine. Before settling on poison, Medea has considered a number of possibilities, including setting fire to the palace and creeping into the palace and stabbing her. Medea's later use of a sword to kill her children suggests a more masculine approach to murder.

In the play, Medea is dangerous because she is unpredictable, and unpredictable because she is a barbarian woman. She is feared because, in addition to the danger she poses, she is also a mystery; as a barbarian woman, she is as different as it is possible to be from a Greek man.

TOPIC REVIEW

These questions should draw on your knowledge of the whole topic, so think carefully about the different things you have learned (check the Topic Overview on p. 39).

1. How do the Greeks portray Amazons?
2. Why were the Greeks so fascinated by the Amazons?
3. Can you summarise Euripides' *Medea* confidently?
4. What are the most important themes of Euripides' *Medea*?

Further Reading

Hall, E. (2010) *Greek Tragedy*. Oxford: Oxford University Press
Harrison, J. (1999) *Medea*. Cambridge: Cambridge University Press
Mossman, J. (2008) *Euripides: Medea*. Warminster: Aris and Phillips

PRACTICE QUESTIONS

Source A: Euripides, *Medea*, lines 1316–1348

Medea: Why do you rattle and batter the doors here? Are you looking for the corpses
and me, who did it?
Stop it. If you want me, say what you wish. You will never lay hands on me again.
This chariot the Sun has given to me, my father's father, to save me from the
hands of enemies.   5

Jason: Hateful creature!
O most detestable of women to the gods and me and all the human race!
You could bring yourself to put to the sword the children of your womb.
You have taken my sons and destroyed me.   10
And can you still face the Sun and this Earth, guilty of the most unholy crime?
Curses on you!
Now I am sane.
But I was mad to bring you from your home, from your savage land to a Greek
family: a mighty trouble, already a traitor to your father and the country that had   15
nurtured you.
The avenging spirit meant for you the Gods have visited on me: you killed your
brother at the family hearth and came on board the Argo, my fair-faced ship.
That's how you began! You became my bride.
You bore my children, and because of your feelings about our marriage bed, you   20
killed them.
No Greek woman could ever have brought herself to do that.
Yet I rejected them, to marry you, a wife who brought me enmity and death, a
lioness, not human, wilder than Tyrrhenian Scylla.

Study **Source A**.

1. In what city do the events of the play take place?   [1]
2. How does Euripides emphasise Jason's shock at Medea's actions in this passage?   [10]

1.5 Depictions and Portrayals: Historical Barbarians

TOPIC OVERVIEW

- Aeschylus' portrayal of the Persians in the *Persians*, including:
  - the plot, structure, characterisation (including chorus) and themes
  - the context in which the play was produced
  - characteristics and 'un-Greek' nature of the Persians
  - the behaviour and characterisation of Xerxes

- Herodotus' portrayal of the Persians, including:
  - the characteristics and 'un-Greek' nature of the Persians
  - the behaviour and characterisation of Xerxes
  - Herodotus' accounts of the supernatural (including oracles)
  - Herodotus' narrative and literary devices

- Comparison of Aeschylus' and Herodotus' depictions of the Greeks, Persians and the Greek victory

The following prescribed sources are covered in this topic:

- Aeschylus' *Persians*
- Herodotus' *Histories*, 1.1, 131–140; 2.48–58; 4.168–181; 7.8–19, 33–37, 100–105, 145–152; 8.49–63, 67–69, 70–103, 108–110, 117–120, 140–144

Don't forget that you will be given credit in the exam if you study extra sources and make relevant use of them in your answers.

Aeschylus and Herodotus both consider the Greeks as naturally superior to the Persians. They give this superiority as the primary reason for the failure of the Persian expedition. Both represent Xerxes as a hubristic tyrant, and therefore a clear villain, to their Greek audience. This audience is given privileged access not only to the Persian court in the immediate aftermath of the battle of Salamis, but also to the inner motivations and private doubts of Xerxes.

AESCHYLUS' PORTRAYAL OF THE PERSIANS IN *PERSIANS*

The plot

The play is set in Susa in 480 BC, in the immediate aftermath of the battle of Salamis. The Persians have been beaten in the battle but the news of their defeat has not yet reached the Persian court. Atossa, the mother of the Persian king Xerxes, anxiously awaits news of the battle and confirmation of her son's safety. She is accompanied by a Chorus of Persian elders, counsellors of the Persian king.

Structure

Parodos (1–158)

The Chorus enters. They are waiting for the Persian army to return and list the names of all the commanders of the host. These men crossed the Hellespont over a bridge made of boats on an expedition to enslave Greece. The Chorus are concerned that they have not heard any news, and also speak of a prophecy that the Persians should seek victory on land and not on sea. They hail the entrance of Atossa.

First Episode (159–531)

Atossa shares the concerns of the Chorus. In a dream, she has seen Xerxes attempt to yoke two women to his chariot (one Greek, the other Persian). One of the women threw off the bridle and Xerxes was thrown from the chariot. Darius, the previous king of Persia and Atossa's husband before he died, appeared and looked down on him. Atossa then explains how, when she went to the altar the following morning, she saw a falcon tear at an eagle, which offered no resistance.

The Chorus encourage her to pour libations for Darius and to ask for his help. Atossa asks the Chorus a number of questions about Athens. The Chorus explain why Xerxes has begun an expedition against Athens and they describe the city and its men. They remind the queen that the Greeks once defeated her husband Darius. Atossa now becomes more concerned.

A messenger enters and reports the defeat of the Persians at Salamis. Athens is credited with the victory and the Chorus recall Marathon. Atossa asks for the names of the Persian generals who have died. The messenger gives short descriptions of the deaths of a number of Persian generals. Atossa now asks for more specific details about the battle. The messenger explains that there were 1,000 Persian ships (including 207 fast ships) to 300 Greek. The messenger blames the gods for the Persian defeat and says that a fury started the battle. A Greek had told Xerxes that the Greeks were planning to escape and Xerxes believed him. He moved the Persian ships under darkness and they patrolled all night; Xerxes threatened death to any Persian who let the Greeks escape. However, the Greeks did not attempt to flee. At dawn the Greeks attack: the Persian ships cannot move in the narrow confines and are surrounded. The Persian fleet is quickly destroyed.

PRESCRIBED SOURCE

Persians

Date: 472 BC

Author: Aeschylus

Genre: tragedy

Collection: seven of his plays still survive

Plot: news of the defeat of the fleet at Salamis reaches the Persian court

Significance: *Persians* is the earliest of Aeschylus' surviving plays and is the only surviving Greek tragedy that deals with a contemporary event

Read it here: *Prometheus Bound and Other Plays*, transl. P. Vellacott (Penguin, 1961)

The messenger then describes the slaughter of the Persian land forces. Before the battle, Xerxes had sent troops to an island to kill any Greeks or rescue any Persians who landed there. Xerxes himself has watched the whole disaster, sitting on a hill opposite the battle. The Persians set off back through Greece, suffering greatly on the way from hunger, thirst and cold. Many Persians were lost when they were crossing the frozen River Strymon and the ice gave way. Atossa and the Chorus express their grief and Atossa thinks back to her dream. The queen says that she will leave to make an offering to the dead.

First Ode (532–597)

The Chorus explain how the women will mourn the deaths and hear that the people are now blaming Xerxes for the loss of men. They claim that the Persians were wrong to put their faith in their ships and then give a description of the dead bodies floating. Xerxes' empire will now fall: the people will no longer pay tribute and will not fear to speak openly.

Second Episode (598–622)

Atossa considers good and bad fortune. She describes her elaborate offerings and then explains her plan to summon the shade of Darius.

Second Ode (623–680)

The Chorus call upon Darius as their beloved king. They praise him as a good king who never led the Persians to a calamitous defeat in war.

Third Episode (681–851)

The ghost of Darius appears and he asks them why there is such mourning and why he has been summoned. The Chorus cannot address him directly out of fear and respect. Darius asks Atossa to speak instead of them. Atossa explains that Xerxes has campaigned against Greece and been defeated. Darius is dismayed by Xerxes' rashness in invading Greece by land and sea and he also says that Xerxes was tricked by a god into crossing the Bosporus. Atossa says to him that the whole army has been destroyed but that Xerxes escaped safely from the battle.

Darius says that oracles have been fulfilled and that Xerxes should not have built his bridge of boats across the Hellespont, turning sea into land. Atossa claims that Xerxes was talked into this by bad advice. Darius lists all the previous Persian kings and their successes and blames Xerxes' youthful impetuosity for his defeat. He advises the Chorus that the Persians should never again attack Greece; the land cannot support a large army. He says that it is a mistake that Persians have been left behind in Greece. Those who have been left behind will be punished on the plains of Plataea by the Dorians for desecrating the temples of Greece. Xerxes should not have wanted more; Zeus punishes such arrogance. Atossa should prepare for Xerxes' return by getting clothes for him.

The Chorus express concern that future disasters still await the Persians in Greece.

Third Ode (852–908)

The Chorus talk about what a good and successful ruler Darius was. They list the territories he conquered including Ionia and the Aegean islands.

Exodos (909–1076)

Xerxes enters, grieving for his fate. The Chorus mourn the men whom Xerxes has lost. The Chorus make Xerxes repeat how the admirals have died. The Chorus and Xerxes exchange their sorrowful thoughts on the Persian defeat.

Characterisation

Atossa

Although she never shares the stage with Xerxes, her son, the language she uses to describe the king stresses her dependence on him. In her first scene with the Chorus, she is fearful. By the time the Messenger enters, this fear turns to panic and she decides to summon her dead husband, Darius. Particularly in this scene, Atossa is represented as having wisdom and perception: she makes thoughtful comments on both wealth and

FIGURE 1.19
Atossa in a production of Aeschylus' *Persians* at Stockport Grammar School.

fortune and on the misguided influences of the Persian court. She is aware of the power of the gods and of the importance of correct religious observance.

Although the Chorus look to her to take control of the situation, seemingly nothing Atossa is involved with comes to fruition. The Chorus gather at the altar to ask their questions, but Atossa interrupts their discussions. The Queen later intends to make a sacrifice but is interrupted by the entrance of the Messenger. She summons Darius but her dead husband promises only that the situation will get worse. Darius leaves her with instructions to go and meet Xerxes with new clothes but Atossa is too late and Xerxes enters in rags.

Darius

Darius' power still intimidates the Chorus. He is amazed at Xerxes' expedition to Greece and by his bridging of the Hellespont. Like the other characters in the play, he expresses sorrow at the deaths of so many Persians and recognises that the gods are partly responsible. He also blames the youth and greed of Xerxes. He is able to predict the Persian defeat at the battle of Plataea in 479 BC. His gentle advice to Atossa on how she should receive their son Xerxes (he will need to be calmed down and given fresh clothes) creates a picture of a family unit.

Xerxes

Xerxes only appears at the end of the play and then his lines fit into a formulaic exchange with the Chorus. He expresses his grief and shame at the loss of life; such mourning of the dead is an act the Greek audience would have more naturally expected of women. Xerxes blames the hatred of the gods but does not suggest that he might have caused their disfavour, so there is no sense of any recognition of his failings earlier identified by both Atossa and Darius.

Chorus

The Chorus describe events and offer answers but they are unwilling to give opinions. They are intimidated, first by Atossa and then by Darius. In addition to their grief, the Chorus also express great anxiety about the safety of the Persian Empire, which seems to depend on the prestige of Xerxes.

Themes

In the play, Aeschylus represents the Greeks through the eyes of the Persians. This is not reliable as evidence but it is interesting as an indication of how the Greeks might imagine that the Persians see them. In Atossa's dream, the Greeks and Persians are represented by two stunningly beautiful girls. Interestingly, these girls are described as 'sisters from the same race'. However, one is prepared to accept the yoke of Xerxes' chariot and the other is not. The Greek girl responds violently and Xerxes is thrown to the ground. The Greek love of freedom is also mentioned by the Chorus when they explain to Atossa that the

Greeks fight under no master. Atossa is surprised by this, and then expresses her fear for the Persians who have gone to fight them. The Messenger describes the two sides in his description of the battle: the Persians are forced to patrol the straits on pain of death; the Greeks charge joyfully into battle chanting slogans of freedom.

The Chorus anticipate, incorrectly, that freedom will now break out across the Persian Empire, following the defeat at Salamis. They are perhaps overreacting to the events at Salamis, but their expression of freedom is interesting. Now that the king's 'strength' has gone, his subjects will no longer pay tribute and bow down before him, and they will also no longer be fearful of speaking out. The Chorus themselves are unable to speak their minds in front of Darius, despite their status as trusted advisors and his as a ghost. When Xerxes returns, they express little of the resentment towards him that has been evident earlier in the play. However, there is a sense that they feel able to apportion some of the blame for the disaster to him.

The differences between the Persians and Greeks are also stressed every time there is a list of Persian names. These names will have sounded outlandish to the Greeks and, despite the shared experience of war, this will have reminded the audience that the Persians were different from them. A list of Persian admirals is repeated by the Chorus at the beginning and then at the end of the play. By contrast, no Greek is mentioned in the play; the emphasis is therefore placed on the collective success of the Greek/Athenian community.

Persia has been unmanned by the war. In the *parodos*, the Chorus describe how young Persian brides have been abandoned. The Chorus are depicted as servile and sycophantic and Atossa appears unable to take charge of the situation. The Empire is lost without its figurehead. When this figurehead returns, he is consumed with grief and publicly embarrasses himself by wearing torn clothing.

Some think that the play is too triumphalist to be truly tragic. The play commemorates, even celebrates, a Greek victory in a battle only eight years earlier. The Athenians who played the chief role in the battle sat watching the play on wreckage recovered from Persian ships. The play shows disarray in the once luxuriant and mighty Persian Empire, whose king is reduced to a ragged mourner. According to the Chorus, this disarray will

MODERN SCHOLARSHIP

'. . . it is beyond all doubt an absolutely truthful record of the ways in which the Athenians liked to think about their great enemy, and a monument to Aeschylus' poetic inventiveness, however 'racist' it may now seem, in his evocation of Persia.

Hall, *Persians* (Aris and Phillips, 1996), p. 5

Do you think that all Athenians would have felt the same way about the Persians in 472 BC?

MODERN SCHOLARSHIP

In this play at least, the argument runs, Aeschylus implies not that all men are subject to the same laws, but that the barbarian character, *in contrast* with the free and disciplined Hellene, is luxuriant and materialistic, emotional, impulsive, and despotic, and therefore especially liable to excess and its consequences.

Hall, *Inventing the Barbarian* (OUP, 1989), p. 71

Is it hard to feel sympathy for the Persians in Aeschylus' *Persians*?

hubris mortal arrogance or defiance that is offensive to the gods

Delian League alliance of poleis set up in 477 BC. Under the leadership of the Athenians, poleis from the coastal regions and islands of the Aegean Sea joined together for mutual defence against the Persians

S & C *Trojan Women* by Euripides also deals with the horrors of war. Read the play and compare the representation of war in Euripides' play and Aeschylus' *Persians*.

DEBATE

Some scholars feel that *Persians* is triumphalist, whereas others feel that the play is concerned with the universal sadness of war.

lead to widespread freedom; people will no longer have to pay tribute or bow before the Persian king and will be able to give their opinions freely.

However it is also possible to read the play as a lesson to all about the dangers of **hubris**. Human nature will overreach itself if not restrained and this will bring disaster. In 472 BC, when the play was produced, the Athenians were already developing ideas for their own maritime empire. The **'Delian League'**, from which the Athenian Empire would later emerge, had been formed in 477 BC.

War is also a universal theme. Although the Greeks had successfully repelled the Persian invasion, this was not without loss and, even eight years later, the Athenians must have looked back on the battles of 480 BC with more sorrow than joy. As the Messenger recounts the Persian admirals who will not return, it is hard to imagine the Athenian audience not transferring the powerful vignettes he offers to their own dead.

The context in which the play was produced

The play was performed eight years after the battle of Salamis. It is likely that feelings still ran high against the Persians in 472 BC. Before the battle, the Athenians had evacuated their city and the invading Persians had burnt the city's temples. The theatre in which the original audience would have sat watching *Persians* was on the slopes of the Athenian Acropolis, on which were the charred remains of those temples. *Persians* was also performed in smaller theatrical festivals around Greece; the resonance of the play must have been felt most keenly at Eleusis, where the theatre overlooks the island of Salamis itself.

Aeschylus probably fought in the battle of Salamis. The epitaph on Aeschylus' tomb refers to his involvement in the battle of Marathon and, in Book 6, Herodotus says that Aeschylus' brother fought in the battle. The detailed descriptions in the play of dead bodies floating in the sea do suggest the haunted memories of an eye witness. Although the bodies that the Chorus describe in their first ode and the women who mourn them are Persian, the description could also fit the Athenians who died in the battle and their relatives in the audience. The play was a success when it was performed, so it can be assumed that the sympathy expressed for the enemy was not offensive to the Athenians.

The utter dejection depicted in the Persian court suggests that the Persians no longer posed a threat to the Athenians. Salamis is represented as the battle that (as the Messenger tells the audience at 278–279) destroyed the Persian Empire. Darius briefly mentions Plataea and the success there of the Dorian (by which he means Spartan) spear, but the focus is very much on the citizen-rowers of Athens at Salamis. In fact, in the years between 480 and 472 BC, the Athenians had had some further military successes against the Persians. The Battle of Marathon, another notable, principally Athenian, victory is not mentioned and there may have been a political motive for this. Themistocles is not named although, as is shown in Herodotus, Salamis was very much his success. By 472 BC, however, his perceived arrogance had made him unpopular in the city. Some think that *Persians* may have been intended, in part, as a last attempt to push forward his finest moment under the eyes of the Athenians before they voted on whether or not to ostracise him. His chief rival, Cimon, was the son of Miltiades, the victor at Marathon.

The hubris and 'un-Greek' nature of the Persians and Xerxes

The wealth of the Persian Empire is mentioned a number of times in the play. The word 'golden' to describe Persia appears twice in the first nine lines of the play. Atossa also refers to her 'golden-furnished chamber' and the Chorus mention the young Persian wives waiting for news on their 'silken beds'. However, in Atossa's first speech, she is concerned that their vast wealth might overturn peace. Later in the play, Darius blames the disaster at Salamis on Xerxes' greed.

Xerxes' immoderate wealth and power have led to immoderate behaviour: his bridge of boats across the Hellespont is offered as an example of his arrogance. The Chorus describe

OUTLINE OF THE PRESCRIBED SECTIONS OF HERODOTUS

Book 1

| 1 | The purpose of the *Histories* |
| 131–140 | Persian customs and way of life |

Book 2

| 48–58 | Egyptian origins of Greek religion |
| | The oracle at Dodona |

Book 4

| 110–117 | The Amazons |
| 168–181 | The customs of the Libyan tribes |

Book 7

8–19	Persian conference to discuss invasion of Greece
	Xerxes' dreams
33–37	Xerxes whips the Hellespont
100–105	Demaratus praise of the Spartans
145–152	Spies are sent to Persia
	The Spartans and the Argives discuss the overall command of the army

Book 8

49–63	The Persians burn the Acropolis
	Discussion amongst the Greek admirals at Salamis
67–69	Advice of Artemisia before Salamis
70–103	Battle of Salamis
108–110	Greek discussions following Salamis
	Themistocles' message to Xerxes
117–120	Xerxes' voyage home
140–144	Xerxes' offer to the Athenians and their reply

PRESCRIBED SOURCE

Histories

Date: 5th century BC

Author: Herodotus

Genre: history

Significance: Herodotus has been accused of pro-Athenian and/or pro-Persian bias. It has also been suggested that he made up some of his account, leading to him being known as the 'Father of Lies'. However, he is also, more plausibly, called the 'Father of History', such is his influence on the process of recording the past. He is the best source for both Persian and Greek history of this period.

Read it here: OCR source booklet

him putting a 'yoke' on the sea but Darius goes further. He talks of Xerxes' attempt to defy nature and enslave the sea. Such an unnatural act inevitably incurs the wrath of the gods. Towards the end of the scene, Darius mentions that Zeus punishes arrogant men.

The eventual disaster at Salamis is foreshadowed by many prophecies and portents, which urged the Persians, specifically, not to fight at sea. The Messenger explains that a fury started the battle and, throughout the play, the hatred of the gods is blamed for the defeat. Darius also refers to the desecration of the Greek temples as an explanation for the gods' support of the Greeks.

HERODOTUS' PORTRAYAL OF THE PERSIANS IN THE PRESCRIBED SECTIONS

Herodotus was born in *c.* 484 BC in Halicarnassus, a city in Caria, which was part of the Persian Empire. He travelled all over the Ancient World, spending time in Egypt, Persia and Athens. He describes his work as 'researches', the purpose of which is as follows:

> This is the account of the researches of Herodotus of Halicarnassus, written so that, as time passes, events may not fade from the memory of mankind and so that the great and wonderful achievements both of Greeks and barbarians might be remembered, most especially the reason why they came into conflict with each other.
>
> Herodotus, *Histories*, 1.1

Characteristics and 'un-Greek' nature of the Persians

When the Spartan commander, Pausanias, enters the tent of Mardonius after his victory at the battle of Plataea in 479 BC, he is taken aback by the riches on show. He looks at the embroidered hangings and the gold and silver decorations. Pausanias then orders Mardonius' cooks to prepare a Persian meal and his own cooks to prepare a Spartan meal. He shows both meals to the other Greek commanders, to point out the absurdity that the

MODERN SCHOLARSHIP

If despotic power has *hubris* as its mainspring and **eros** as its vocation, it should be added that transgression and repetition are its law, that it operates in secret, manifests itself through physical marks and mutilation, and is doomed to ultimate failure.

Hartog, *The Mirror of Herodotus* (University of California Press, 1988), p. 130

Both Herodotus and Aeschylus suggest that Xerxes' failure to conquer Greece was down to hubris. To what extent do you feel that the influence of hubris explained by Hartog is evident in Xerxes' behaviour?

Persians mounted an expedition to Greece despite having all their apparent wealth. The Persian luxuries are given as further indication of their hubris in attacking Greece.

In Book 7 (6–8), Herodotus explains and dramatises Xerxes' intention to invade Greece. Initially, Xerxes is persuaded into taking action against Greece by the Persian general Mardonius. He had been the leader of Darius' army, which was defeated at Marathon in 490 BC. Xerxes, however, describes the invasion to his closest advisers as his idea:

> Since I came to this throne, I have considered how best to match the accomplishments of my ancestors by increasing the power of the Persians by as much as they did.
>
> Herodotus, *Histories*, 8.8

Xerxes goes on to describe the conquest of Greece as a mission of vengeance for the burning of the Lydian city of Sardis in 499 BC. However, as the speech progresses, Xerxes turns his attention to global conquest. The final line of the following section reads as a chilling indication of Xerxes' incipient hubris:

> The sun will not look down on any country which borders our own, I will turn all of their country into one of ours, as I cross through the whole of Europe. For, as I have discovered, there will be no city, nor race left which might be able to stand against us in battle, once these Greeks are out of the way. Both the guilty and the innocent will wear the yoke of slavery.
>
> Herodotus, *Histories*, 7.8

Once Xerxes is resolved to invade Greece, his hubris is accompanied by the references to his desire and passion. He aggressively rejects the advice of Artabanus, which is based on the negative experience of Darius' campaign against the Scythians. Xerxes is so enraged by Artabanus words that he tells him that only their family relationship has saved him. He then plans to send Artabanus from the army in disgrace. After a night-time vision has caused Xerxes to change his mind, he is more receptive to advice, and Artabanus refers to the dangers of insatiable desire for conquest:

> As much as any man, I have seen how often the mighty have been laid low by the blows of lesser races. I did not want you to be carried away by your youthful impulses, knowing how dangerous it is always to desire more . . .
>
> Herodotus, *Histories*, 7.18

However, unlike others in the grip of hubris, Xerxes is more circumspect at other points in Book 7, particularly when he becomes thoughtful as he watches his army cross the Hellespont (7.47). However, his hubris returns when he addresses Demaratus (7.100–105); he shows little understanding of bravery, freedom or tactics. Xerxes also allows three Greek spies captured in the camp to go back to Greece, confident that their report of his strength will cause the Greeks to surrender (7.146–148).

Once Xerxes invades Attica, he burns down the temples of the gods on the Athenian Acropolis (8.50). Herodotus has Themistocles suggest that the defeat at Salamis should be regarded as divine punishment for the hubris that Xerxes had displayed when burning the temples:

KEY PEOPLE

The Scythians a tribe who lived to the north of the Black Sea. Herodotus describes them in detail in Book 4. The story of the meeting between the Scythians and the Amazons is described in 4.110–117

> For we did not bring this about, our gods and heroes did, they refused to allow one man to rule over both Asia and Europe, especially a man who made no distinction between houses and temples, a man who burned and hurled down statues of the gods, a man who whipped the sea and threw fetters into the waves.
>
> Herodotus, *Histories*, 8.109

Study question
How does Herodotus show the different approaches of the Greeks and the Persians to discussing strategy?

The behaviour and characterisation of Xerxes

The behaviour of Xerxes at the Hellespont is offered by Themistocles as another example of him offending the gods. When a storm destroys the bridge he has had built over the Hellespont, Xerxes is furious. Herodotus (7.33–37) describes him giving the water 300 lashes and also throwing fetters (iron handcuffs) into the sea. Xerxes also orders the men who had built the bridge to be beheaded.

The behaviour of his troops at Athens is particularly offensive:

> The first Persians to climb up made for the gates, opened them and then killed those who had sought sanctuary. When they had killed all the Athenians, they plundered the temple and set fire to the whole Acropolis.
>
> Herodotus, *Histories*, 8.53

Xerxes is driven by impulse and is frequently described with passionate vocabulary. He changes his mind abruptly and dramatically before the invasion (7.1–20). Such great power in the hands of someone so unpredictable and volatile is made to seem dangerous by Herodotus.

Like a god from epic, Xerxes sits on high watching his army crossing the Hellespont and then as they fight at Salamis. Herodotus explains that this position does allow him to intimidate his troops:

> Even so, they fought much better on that day than they had at Euboea; fearing Xerxes, every man fought with more determination as each man thought that the king might be watching him.
>
> Herodotus, *Histories*, 8.68

However, his lofty and detached vantage point also causes him to make mistakes. When Artemisia sinks one of the ships on her own side to escape from the Greeks, Xerxes presumes that she has, in fact, sunk a Greek ship and praises her valour (8.87–88).

Herodotus' accounts of the supernatural (including oracles)

There are dreams, visions and oracles throughout Herodotus' description of the Persian invasions. Generally, the Greeks succeed because they interpret the signs correctly, whereas the Persians are usually misled.

However, in his dream following the discussions about the invasion of Greece, Xerxes appears to be deliberately misled by the vision that appears. He had been on the point of changing his decision about the invasion when the vision tells him that he must proceed.

As Xerxes wavers in his purpose, Artabanus provides the following explanation for visions and dreams:

> This is not a message from god, o child. As I am many years older than you,
> I will explain the nature of wandering dreams which appear to men; those visions
> which appear to us in dreams are manifestations of our daily concerns. Over the
> last few days we have had our minds full with thoughts of the imminent
> expedition.
>
> Herodotus, Histories, 7.16

However, when Artabanus sees the vision, he is also convinced that it is divine and therefore, apparently, trustworthy. The vision is then followed by another dream:

> Even now that Xerxes was intent on the expedition, a third vision came to him in his
> sleep, the Magi listened to him and then interpreted the dream to mean that he would
> enslave the whole world and all races. The vision was this: Xerxes saw himself
> crowned with an olive wreath, the shoots from which spread over the whole world,
> then the crown vanished from his head.
>
> Herodotus, Histories, 7.19

The interpretation of the Magi seems to overlook the conclusion of the dream. This might suggest that they are telling Xerxes what he wants to hear at this point, rather than giving a correct interpretation.

Herodotus leaves his readers to draw this conclusion. The Magi give a similarly favourable interpretation of the eclipse which follows Xerxes' extreme behaviour at the Hellespont.

However, when the Athenians receive oracles from Delphi, they discuss interpretations:

> When the envoys had left Delphi and reported back to the people, there were many
> interpretations about the meaning of the oracle; two in particular were favoured.
>
> Herodotus, Histories, 7.142

KEY INDIVIDUALS

The Magi Persian wise men or priests who served as trusted advisers to the king

This open approach enables Themistocles to come up with the correct interpretation of the oracle's reference to a 'wooden wall', which is preferred over the answers of the professional interpreters. The Athenians are persuaded to build ships and also to fight at Salamis, both of which are proved to be successful decisions.

This is followed by another oracle, which Herodotus includes in full:

> I have no way of proving that oracles are not true, their messages are clear and I have
> no desire to speak against them when researching such events as these.
> > "When they bridge the holy coast of Artemis of the golden sword
> > And sea-washed Cynosura with ships,
> > With raging expectation, having destroyed glorious Athens.
> > Divine justice will quench mighty insatiability, the son of arrogance
> > Raging terribly, intending to drink in everything.
> > Bronze will clash on bronze, Ares will turn the sea red with blood.
> > Then far-seeing Zeus and queen Victory will bring the day of freedom to Greece."

> Considering what followed and seeing how clear this oracle of Bacis is, I do not intend to speak against this nor will I listen to others who do so.
>
> Herodotus, *Histories*, 8.77

Herodotus' approval of this oracle is clear; he sees that the precise terms have been fulfilled by the events of the battle. The explanation that defeat at Salamis was divine retribution for Xerxes' hubris seems justified to him.

Herodotus' narrative and literary devices

The clear purpose of Herodotus' introduction reminds the reader of epic poetry:

> This is the account of the researches of Herodotus of Halicarnassus, written so that, as time passes, events may not fade from the memory of mankind and so that the great and wonderful achievements both of Greeks and barbarians might be remembered, most especially the reason why they came into conflict with each other.
>
> Herodotus, *Histories*, 1.1

topos (pl. **topoi**) a recurring feature of a writer's style

However, Herodotus is interested in so much more than just an explanation of the causes of the war. He employs various **topoi** (distinctive features of his writing style):

- Speeches – Herodotus dramatises conversations between his characters. His sources cannot have given him verbatim accounts.
- Thoughts – Herodotus frequently describes the inner thoughts of his characters, particularly Xerxes. This is not reliable information.
- Assessment of sources – Herodotus will include information but will also tell his readers whether or not he believes it. He also gives the reader an idea of how common a particular idea or interpretation is.
- Herodotus also includes different explanations and alternative versions of stories.
- What I have seen/what I have heard – Herodotus will grade his information. He is particularly keen to endorse facts with personal experience but will also explain if information has come to him directly or if it has been passed on.

logos (pl. **logoi**) 'tale' or 'story'. Herodotus includes logoi in his *Histories* to describe people, places and events. Words such as 'biology' and 'prologue' are derived from 'logos'

thoma (pl. **thomata**) a wonder. Herodotus is particularly interested in the surprises offered both by nature and by different cultures.

Two of Herodotus' **logoi** concern the course of the River Nile (2.31–35) and the tribes of the Scythians (4.168–181). Hecataeus, an earlier writer, was a key source for and inspiration behind Herodotus' passages on the different races of the ancient world. Herodotus' description of the course of the Nile shows some important and recurrent features of his writing:

- He describes Egyptian customs as the reverse of the Greeks: women trade in the market place, men weave; women urinate standing up, men urinate sitting down. These **'thomata'** would have intrigued his readers, although they are not offered to suggest that the Egyptian ways are inferior.
- He bases his guess on the course of the River Nile on what he knows about the River Danube. This shows his lack of understanding of geography.

His description of Libya and its tribes shows the following features:

- He is interested in the flora and fauna of the regions he describes.
- He again shows interest in the customs of Scythian women and also describes the sexual practices of the different tribes. However, as with the Egyptian logos, there is no inference that their approach is less civilised.
- Scythia also features in Hippocratic medical theories as a particularly healthy place to live, some commentators have suggested that Herodotus includes most detail on the healthiest places to live. Scythia, an area on which there is a logos in Book 2, also features in these theories.

COMPARISON OF AESCHYLUS' AND HERODOTUS' DEPICTIONS OF THE GREEKS, PERSIANS AND THE GREEK VICTORY

The Greeks

Aeschylus does not mention any Greek by name in the Persians. They are represented as having a united purpose. In lines 392–405, the Messenger describes the Greeks rowing together into battle, shouting slogans of freedom for their families and gods.

In Herodotus, the Greeks can barely remain united in the lead-up to the battle. Themistocles has to use another man's arguments (which he represents as his own view) (8.57–58) and an outrageous gambit in which he sends a false message to Xerxes, telling him that the Greeks intend to flee (8.75). Then finally the Greeks fight. Even then there is bitterness between them shown during the battle when the Aeginetans shout out to Themistocles (8.92) and the Corinthians supposedly abandon the battle (8.94).

The Persians

Themistocles uses the language of Greek tragedy to explain Xerxes' defeat at Salamis at 8.109 – Xerxes' arrogance has offended the gods. At other points, Herodotus also draws attention to the **ate** that has stemmed from Xerxes' hubris. He places too much confidence in his superior numbers in conversations with Artabanus (7.48) and the Spartan Demaratus (7.103). Herodotus has Artabanus say to Xerxes that the very size of the Persian Empire puts it at risk (7.49).

> **ate** blindness that pushes those who display hubris into making poor decisions

Both Aeschylus and Herodotus focus on Xerxes' whipping of the Hellespont as an example of his hubristic behaviour. Herodotus embellishes the whipping with other acts of cruelty. The men who built the bridges are decapitated and the eldest son of Pythius is cut in half. Aeschylus is keener to cast Xerxes' attempt to shackle the sea as a crime against nature.

In the parodos of *Persians*, the Chorus list the nations that form the Persian army and comment on the size of the force (particularly at 73–76). Like Xerxes, Atossa is also guilty of underestimating the Greek resistance (243). Darius lists the Persian kings, including himself, who have managed to conquer without incurring the wrath of the gods and so Xerxes' hubris is 'un-Persian'. Xerxes is named as responsible for the defeat by Atossa (718), Darius (782) and the Chorus. Xerxes is described at numerous points in the play as being deceived by the god (107, 353–368, 472, 724).

EXPLORE FURTHER

Inventing the Barbarian by Edith Hall (OUP, 1989) goes into great detail on Aeschylus' *Persians* and gives plenty of comparisons with other tragedies.

The battle

Herodotus gives much more detail about the Battle of Salamis itself. He describes the tactics of both the Greeks and the Persians and also the topography of the immediate area. In Herodotus, the skill of the Greek rowers is evident, but in Aeschylus there is just a charge at the enemy.

MODERN SCHOLARSHIP

This dichotomy between free and manly Greek/Athenian and servile and effeminate barbarian/Persian may be valid for some texts, such as Aeschylus' *Persians*, but it does not correspond to the way that Persians are depicted in Herodotus.

Flower, *Herodotus and Persia* (CUP, 2006), p. 275

How do you respond to Flower's conclusions about both Herodotus' and Aeschylus' depictions of the Persians?

TOPIC REVIEW

These questions should draw on your knowledge of the whole topic, so think carefully about the different things you have learned (check the Topic Overview on p. 56).

1. How does Herodotus represent the Persians?
2. How does Aeschylus represent the Persians?
3. How do Herodotus and Aeschylus suggest the idea that the Persian defeat at Salamis was divine punishment?
4. Can you summarise Aeschylus' *Persians* confidently?

Further Reading

Rosenbloom, D. (2007) 'Persae'. London: Duckworth
Vellacott, P. (trans) (1961) *Aeschylus: Prometheus Bound and Other Plays*. London: Penguin

PRACTICE QUESTION

'Xerxes is represented in *Persians* as more deserving of his punishment than Jason in *Medea*.'
To what extent do you agree with this statement? [30]

1.6 The Reality of Persia

- The Achaemenid dynasty and the Persian political system, including:
  - the king, his subjects and government of the empire including tributes and satrapies
  - the representation of kings and imperialism in Persian sources

- The artistic and cultural achievements of the Achaemenid dynasty, including:
  - the cultural significance of Persepolis and the Palace of Darius at Susa
  - the relationship between Achaemenid and Greek art, and the influence of each on the other

- The contrast of the 'reality' of Persian culture and society with the Greek view, including:
  - the extent to which Herodotus shows familiarity with the reality of Persia

The following prescribed sources are covered in this topic:

- Statue of Darius I from Susa
- The Cyrus Cylinder
- Rock relief at Bisitun, showing Darius the Great after his victory over Gaumata and other rebel kings
- The Tomb of Cyrus the Great, Pasargadae
- The site of Persepolis, including the Gate of All Nations and the Apadana (including the relief on the eastern staircase showing delegations from the different peoples of the empire)
- Silver rhyton ending in a griffin
- Gold armlets with griffins from the Oxus Treasure
- Statuette of a naked youth from the Oxus Treasure
- Head of a young Persian prince in lapis lazuli, from the Apadana at Persepolis

Don't forget that you will be given credit in the exam if you study extra sources and make relevant use of them in your answers.

The information contained in this topic serves as an important counter-balance to the presentation of the Persians in the Greek sources. The Persian voice is given through their art, architecture and royal proclamations. The Persian invention of the barbarian displays an inventive people governed by a complex and effective bureaucracy. Greater understanding of Persian history, beyond the Greek invention of the barbarian, is important if we are to recognise sufficiently the contribution of the Persians to world culture.

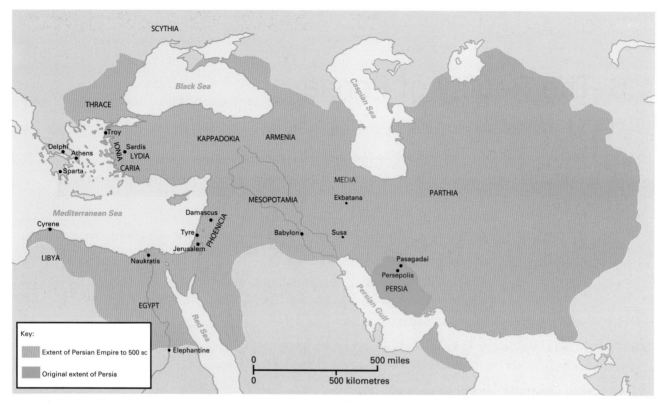

FIGURE 1.20
Map of the Persian Empire.

THE ACHAEMENID DYNASTY

The Persian Empire was created quickly and dramatically in the mid-sixth century by Cyrus the Great. Cyrus came to the throne in 559 and added Media (550), Lydia (547 or 546) and Babylon (539) to the Persian Empire. He transformed Persia from a small kingdom into the Persian Empire. When Cyrus died in 530, he was succeeded by his son Cambyses, who added Egypt to the Empire. Herodotus describes Cambyses as a vicious tyrant, although it is possible that he was influenced by Egyptian temple sources, whose income had been cut by the king.

In 522, Cambyses was accidentally killed on his way to stop a revolt and a man pretending to be Bardiya, the dead brother of the king, took over (Herodotus refers to this man as Smerdis). After a brief civil war, Darius emerged as a figurehead, killed Bardiya and became king. However, it is also thought that this story might be a lie made up by Darius. These historians suggest that Bardiya was, in fact, the brother of Cambyses and that Darius took the throne from the rightful successor. Darius added Cyrenaica to the Empire and campaigned in Scythia and northern Greece in 513. He also pushed out the border of the Persian Empire east towards India. After his death in 486, he was succeeded by Xerxes.

KEY INDIVIDUAL

Cyrus (also called Cyrus the Great)

Date: king of Persia from 559 to 530 BC

Cyrus expanded the Empire greatly during his rule, adding the Median (550 BC), Lydian (547–546 BC) and Babylonian (539 BC) kingdoms. He died in battle in 530 BC

FIGURE 1.21
Statue of Darius I from Susa.

PRESCRIBED SOURCE

Statue of Darius I from Susa

Date: 5th century BC

Material: greywacke sandstone

Original location: first erected in Egypt but then brought to Susa in the 5th century BC

Current location: National Museum, Tehran

Significance: depiction of the Persian king as ruler of Egypt, the only free-standing statue from Ancient Persia

For more information see: http://www.livius.org/su-sz/susa/susa_statue_darius.html

KEY INDIVIDUAL

Cambyses

Date: king of Persia from 530 to 522 BC

Cambyses was the son of Cyrus. During his reign, the Persians conquered Egypt in 525 BC. Herodotus suggests that he died by accident after a wound became infected. Historians have also suggested that he was assassinated by Darius, who may similarly have assassinated his brother Bardiya.

Figure 1.21 is a picture of the statue of Darius at Susa. The king wears a Persian short sword, known as an *akinakes*, in an elaborately embroidered sword belt. The Persian king is usually depicted in sculpture wearing elaborate clothing. Kings are also usually shown with a long, luxuriant beard. More than the Persian kings who had preceded him, Darius exploited the power of image very skilfully. The inscription on the statue is in Egyptian hieroglyphic, with Darius' name in a cartouche (royal names are enclosed in an oval ring on Egyptian inscriptions). The text includes the following proclamation, showing that the statue was being used as a display of authority:

> This is the statue, made of stone, which Darius ordered to be made in Egypt. This is how everyone who will see this in the future will know that the Persian man ruled in Egypt.
>
> DSab

The base of the statue has a list, in hieroglyphic, of those nations that were subject to the Persian king.

ACTIVITY

Role play a discussion of the invasion of Greece in 480 BC between Cyrus, Darius, Xerxes, Herodotus and Aeschylus. How would each differ in the reasons for its failure?

THE PERSIAN POLITICAL SYSTEM

The king, his subjects and government of the empire, including tributes and satrapies

When discussing his plans for the expedition against Greece in 480, Xerxes includes the following in a speech to his closest advisers:

> As I have learned from my ancestors, we have not had a period of rest since we took our dominance of Asia from the Medes, once Cyrus had overthrown Astyages. A god has brought us this far and we continue to benefit from taking on challenges. Cyrus, Cambyses and my father Darius all conquered races and added their territories to our empire, no one needs to remind you of their accomplishments. Since I came to this throne, I have considered how best to match the accomplishments of my ancestors by increasing the power of the Persians by as much as they did.

> Herodotus, *Histories*, 7.8

This passage suggests that Cyrus set an example of ambition and *activity*, which future Persian kings felt obliged to follow. This also explains why Darius and Xerxes would both see Greece as the next logical addition to the Persian Empire. Herodotus focuses the reason for the expedition on gaining revenge on Athens but this is perhaps overstating the importance of one Greek polis to the Persians.

Figure 1.22 is a picture of the so-called 'Cyrus Cylinder': a small, barrel-shaped piece of clay covered in cuneiform writing. On the cylinder, Cyrus states his genealogy and power as king of Persia. The text then describes his liberation and rule over the Babylonians.

The text on the 'Cyrus Cylinder' states that Nabonidus, the previous king of Babylon, had disrespected the Babylonian gods and the religion of the people. Cyrus casts himself

FIGURE 1.22
The 'Cyrus Cylinder'.

PS

PRESCRIBED SOURCE

The 'Cyrus Cylinder'

Date: 6th century BC

Material: baked clay

Original location: Babylon

Current location: British Museum

Significance: foundation deposit describing the conquest of Babylon by Cyrus the king of Persia as a liberator of the Babylonian people from a domineering ruler, rather than their conqueror. The fragmentary text says the following about Nabonidus:

> . . . he brought the daily offerings to a halt; he inter[fered with the rites and] instituted [. . .] within the sanctuaries. In his mind, reverential fear of Marduk, king of the gods, came to an end.
>
> He did yet more evil to his city every day; . . . his [people . . .], he brought ruin on them all by a yoke without relief.

Cyrus Cylinder, lines 7, 8

According to the text, when Cyrus took Babylon, he did so peacefully, with the help of Marduk, the Babylonian god, and with the overwhelming support of the people. The text now refers to Cyrus in the first person:

> As for the population of Babylon [. . ., w]ho as if without div[ine intervention] had endured a yoke not decreed for them, I soothed their weariness; I freed them from their bonds(?). Marduk, the great lord, rejoiced at [my good] deeds . . .

Cyrus Cylinder, lines 25, 26

The text goes on to mention that Cyrus confirmed religious privileges in Babylon. Cyrus claims to have restored the Babylonian gods to their temples and brought peace to the land. This claim of religious tolerance is echoed by passages from the Bible (e.g. in the Old Testament Book of Ezra), where Cyrus is credited with allowing the Jews to rebuild the temple in Jerusalem. Cyrus also returned the Jewish treasures stolen by the Babylonian king, Nebuchadnezzar II. It should also be stated that this religious tolerance could also have been a pragmatic approach to maintaining power as the Babylonians would be less likely to revolt.

Cyrus also divided the Persian Empire into twenty manageable administrative units called **satrapies**. This organisation made it easier to collect taxes in the form of an annual tribute, which the satrapies would pay in return for the security of the Persian Empire.

Xerxes will also have been influenced by the contributions of his father Darius to the Persian Empire. Darius built the Persian Royal Road from Susa, in the heart of Persia, to Sardis, the old Lydian Capital in Asia Minor. He built other roads throughout the Empire and a canal between the Red Sea and the River Nile to assist with trade. He standardised weights and measures and introduced taxation across the Empire. Darius was also the first Persian king to mint coins.

The Persian Empire governed a wide area successfully for over 200 years. The subjects of the Empire spoke a variety of languages, followed a variety of religions and maintained a variety of lifestyles. Some subjects were nomadic peoples, others lived within a democracy. There was no attempt by the king to impose conformity on any aspect of his subjects' lives. Many Persian inscriptions are written in three languages. The Persian administrative system was flexible. The satrapies were each very different and each satrap was given considerable freedom to rule, so long as the annual tribute was

---

KEY INDIVIDUAL

Nebuchadnezzar II

Date: king of the Babylonian Empire from *c.* 605 BC–*c.* 562

He is famed for building his wife the 'Hanging Gardens of Babylon' (one of the Seven Ancient Wonders of the World) and also for destroying the temple in Jerusalem, an act that is described in the Old Testament book of Daniel.

---

satrapy (pl. **satrapies**) an administrative district governed by a satrap (pl. satraps). The satrap controlled only the civil government. As checks on the power of the satrap, the king also appointed a military commander, who was in charge of the army, and a finance officer, who controlled the treasury

paid. This tribute varied; Herodotus records the amounts in Book 3.89–95. Here he states that India contributed nearly a third of the annual tribute.

The Arshama archive is the description for a collection of sources that provide a large amount of information about the daily administrative responsibilities of a satrap in the Persian Empire. Arshama was a satrap of Egypt in the late fifth century. The sources show him organising the collection of the tribute, overseeing the management and transfer of property and even authorising the repair of a boat. Included in the sources are letters that show Arshama's desire to use his position to add to his own possessions.

The Persepolis tablets are another useful collection of sources to explain the system of satrapies. The tablets are evidence for the complex bureaucracy and record-keeping. There are records of state workers involved in farming or building, which describe what their rations were and occasionally what they were paid. A wide range of peoples and occupations are mentioned on the tablets. The tablets also describe the stores of food in warehouses and livestock in the fields.

Communication across the vast expanses of the Persian Empire was enabled by a messenger system. Throughout the Empire, stations were set up a day's ride from each other where fresh horses could be obtained. This enabled messages to travel very quickly. Herodotus explains how the message about the defeat at Salamis was relayed back to Persia:

> There is nothing mortal which moves faster than these Persian messengers; the Persians came up with the following system. It is said that they have as many men and horses lined up as there are days in the journey. Each team of man and horse are set a day's ride apart from each other. Neither snow nor rain nor heat nor darkness checks their speed.

Herodotus, *Histories*, 8.98

The representation of kings and imperialism in Persian sources

In the text of the 'Cyrus Cylinder', Cyrus is described in the following way:

> I am Cyrus, king of the universe, the great king, the powerful king, king of Babylon, king of Sumer and Akkad, king of the four quarters of the world, son of Cambyses, the great king, ki[ng of the ci]ty of Anshan, descendent of Teispes . . .

Cyrus Cylinder, lines 20, 21

This declaration suggests the multiple roles of the King of the Persian Empire as ruler of the various territories but it also stresses the importance of ancestry.

The rock relief at Bisitun (shown in Figure 1.23) has a scene carved in low relief depicting Darius and the rebel kings he defeated. It dates from the sixth century BC and carries cuneiform inscriptions in three languages (old Persian, Elamite and Akkadian). The relief was of crucial importance in the decipherment of all three languages. Already familiar names and phrases in the same text in three different languages could be compared (in the same way, the Rosetta Stone led to the decipherment of Egyptian hieroglyphic).

This led to the translation of many lost works of Near Eastern literature (including the Epic of Gilgamesh).

In the inscriptions, Darius gives names of the rebel kings in three languages, and tells the story of how he secured the kingdom of Persia. It states that Cambyses killed his brother Bardiya, then that someone pretending to be Bardiya (Darius calls him Gaumata) rebelled after Darius had become king. Darius refers to himself conquering this uprising, which he refers to as 'the Lie' and restoring order in the Empire. Darius then describes his defeat of the other rebel kings who had taken advantage of the lack of a natural heir to Cambyses (Cyrus had no other sons, just Cambyses and Bardiya).

On the relief, the figure of the king surrounded by a winged disc hovers above the rebel kings. This is probably a representation of Ahuramazda, the god and protector of the Persian kings.

PRESCRIBED SOURCE

Rock relief at Bisitun

Date: 6th/5th century BC

Material: relief carved into a limestone cliff face

Location: Bisitun (also written as Behistun), Iran

Significance: commemorates the victory of Darius over Gaumata and the nine rebel kings

---

KEY INDIVIDUAL

Ahuramazda

Principal god of the Persian kings. Ahuramazda is probably represented by a winged disc that sometimes surrounds the figure of the king. However, some historians believe that the winged disc does not indicate Ahuramazda but instead that it shows the divine glory of the king. The god's name is sometimes written as Ahura Mazda.

Study question

Consider how the Persian kings used propaganda to help support their rule.

FIGURE 1.23
Rock relief at Bisitun.

As Darius was not the son of the previous king, and had instead succeeded after Cambyses had died suddenly, it was necessary for him to justify his right to rule. On a rock relief at Bisitun, Darius is shown in a dominant position over the men who had rebelled against him in the first months of his rule. The inscription that accompanies the image is translated into three languages. It tells the story of how Darius defeated the conspirators. The text also suggests that Darius, like Cyrus before him, was descended from Achaemenes but from a different branch of his family. Therefore, as an Achaemenid, he had a right to rule Persia. Most historians believe that Darius created Achaemenes as a fictional ancestor of both himself and Cyrus to legitimise his rule. Darius later married Atossa, the daughter of Cyrus and mother of Xerxes. On the same Bisitun relief, the winged disc that flies over Darius can probably be identified as the figure of the god Ahuramazda. Ahuramazda was the chief Persian god, and the kings were described as his worshippers. Darius is perhaps showing that Ahuramazda affirms his kingship.

All Xerxes' official inscriptions record that he is a descendant of Achaemenes (an Achaemenid) and that he rules with the favour of Ahuramazda.

THE ARTISTIC AND CULTURAL ACHIEVEMENTS OF THE ACHAEMENID DYNASTY

The cultural significance of Persepolis and the Palace of Darius at Susa

Cyrus had his capital city at Pasargadai in the Persian heartland. There are two palaces that feature an Apadana with covered porticoes. There were probably formal gardens laid out between these two palaces.

Darius expanded the royal palace at Susa and added an Apadana. The rooms of the palace were arranged around a large courtyard. The walls were decorated with polychrome friezes of glazed bricks depicting the Persian elite troops known as 'Immortals'. Susa was the administrative capital of the Persian Empire. The foundation inscription for the palace lists the nationalities that contributed their specialities to the building: Ionian and Lydian stonemasons, Median and Egyptian goldsmiths, and Lydian and Egyptian carpenters. He also gives an extensive list of the imported building materials, including Lebanese cedar wood and ivory from Ethiopia. Cyrus' list also cleverly suggests the breadth of the Empire that he has created.

The Tomb of Cyrus (shown in Figure 1.24), a large stone-built structure with a gabled roof, is at Pasargadai. Constructed from huge blocks, it is a dramatic and permanent memorial to the founder of the Persian Empire. The stone-working techniques show Egyptian and Lydian influences and some historians feel that there are also Ionian stylistic influences on the tomb.

The site of Persepolis (Figure 1.25) was a magnificent palace complex begun by Darius and later added to by Xerxes. It features fifteen major buildings including an Apadana, a hall of 100 columns and a treasury. The complex was built on a low artificial

FIGURE 1.24
The Tomb of Cyrus the Great, Pasargadai.

> **S**
> **&**
> **C**
> Alexander the Great's visit to the tomb of Cyrus is described by the Greek
> historian Arrian (6.29). Alexander is very upset when he arrives at Pasargadai
> and sees that the tomb has been looted. The achievements of Cyrus – the
> creation and management of an empire – were very influential on Alexander.
> Alexander also made use of the system of satrapies and he, like Cyrus, appre-
> ciated the power of his own image.

---

platform made of rock with a steep mountain behind it. Access to the plateau was through
the magnificent Gate of All Nations (Figure 1.26); visitors would walk between two huge
winged bulls with human heads, which were perhaps suggestive of the power and beauty
of the Persian king.

The Apadana was built on a platform accessed by staircases decorated with members
of the imperial court and twenty-three delegations from across the Persian Empire bearing
tribute. The Great King is also pictured, flanked by his attendants, waiting to accept the
offerings. Each group is distinguished by their offerings and by their dress. The differences between the various groups stress the breadth of the Empire. The Cappadocians,
wearing trousers, bring a horse to the king and the Parthians bring a camel. The Ionians
(Figure 1.27) bring bowls made from precious metals, wool and cloth.

The capitals of the columns throughout the complex have a variety of decorations:
adorned with pairs of bulls, with or without human heads, lions or griffins. On the door-
ways into the halls, there are friezes of heroic combat between a man and an animal, and
images of the king on his throne.

PRESCRIBED SOURCE

The Tomb of Cyrus the Great, Pasargadai

Date: 6th century BC

Material: stone, clay

Location: Pasargadai, Iran

Significance: tomb of the greatest of the Persian
kings

FIGURE 1.25
Aerial photograph of the palace complex at Persepolis (north is to the left).

PRESCRIBED SOURCES

Persepolis: the palace complex, the Gate of All Nations and the Apadana

Date: 6th/5th century BC

Material: stone

Location: Persepolis, Iran

Significance: large and impressive Achaemenid palace complex

FIGURE 1.26
The Gate of All Nations.

S & C Compare the Gate of All Nations with the Propylaia in Athens and the pylon of Ramesses II at the Temple of Luxor in Egypt – how does each serve its purpose of providing an entry to an important site?

FIGURE 1.27
Plaster cast taken from the Apadana staircase. It shows the Ionian delegation.

MODERN SCHOLARSHIP

The message of the Apadana reliefs seems rather one of solidarity or inclusiveness between the King – to whom the procession and the gifts are directed – and his subjects.

Waters, *Ancient Persia* (CUP, 2014), pp. 143–144

Would you agree with Waters' interpretation of the Apadana reliefs?

The relationship between Achaemenid and Greek art and the influence of each on the other

Due to the shared trading relationships with the Ionian Greeks, there would have been plenty of contact in peace time between the Persians and the mainland Greeks. Persian luxuries gained through trade and then, after the war, as spoils were a symbol of wealth in Athens. There are Persian influences evident in Athenian pottery of the fifth century. The shallow drinking bowl called a *phiale* has a shape that is copied from gold and silver Persian bowls.

The animal-headed drinking goblet called a rhyton commonly features amongst Greek pottery shapes. It was influenced by similar Persian vessels made from silver and gold. Figure 1.28 shows a beautiful silver rhyton, which ends in a horned, winged griffin (a mythical beast). The standard of the carving is very high. Gold detailing has been added to the face and wings of the griffin and to the floral decorations around the rim.

The Oxus Treasure is a large collection of beautiful gold and silver objects dating from the fifth and fourth centuries BC (including tableware, votive offerings and jewellery) found by the River Oxus in the Persian satrapy of Bactria.

Figure 1.29 shows a gold armlet with griffin heads at the ends. It is an excellent example of Persian metal-working skill. The Lydian delegation on the Apadana relief

Silver rhyton ending in a griffin

Date: 5th century BC

Material: gold, silver

Original location: Erzincan, Turkey

Current location: British Museum

Significance: beautiful example of Persian luxury tableware, showcasing metalwork skills; rhyton shape is also seen in Greek tableware

FIGURE 1.28
Silver rhyton ending in a griffin.

Gold armlets with griffins from the Oxus Treasure

Date: 5th–4th century BC

Material: gold (originally inlaid with coloured glass, faience and semi-precious stones)

Original location: River Oxus, Tajikistan

Current location: British Museum

Significance: beautiful example of Persian artistic skill

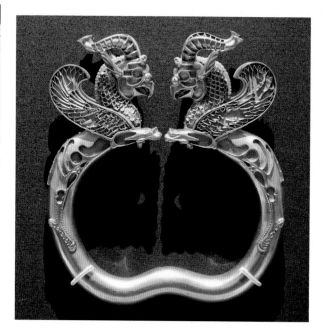

FIGURE 1.29
Gold armlets with griffins from the Oxus Treasure.

PRESCRIBED SOURCE

Statuette of a naked youth from the Oxus Treasure

Date: 5th–4th century BC

Material: gold, silver

Original location: River Oxus, Tajikistan

Current location: British Museum

Significance: small, possibly votive statuette showing the influence of Greek sculpture

FIGURE 1.30
Statuette of a naked youth from the Oxus Treasure.

bring similar armlets to the Persian king as gifts. Herodotus describes the Persian Immortals wearing golden accessories:

> Out of everybody, the Persians wore the most decoration, and they were the best-dressed. I have already described their clothing, as well as this they were distinguished from the rest by the enormous amount of gold which they wore.

Herodotus, *Histories*, 7.83

The nudity, facial features and pose of the small, silver statuette of a youth from the Oxus Treasure (Figure 1.30) suggest the influence of Greek sculpture, yet he is wearing a Persian headdress. Figure 1.31 shows a bronze statue of Apollo. Although the scale is very different (the Greek statue is life size), the similarities between the two poses are clear.

The Persians had no experience of building large-scale buildings from stone before the reign of Cyrus. Persian architecture, therefore, developed as a fusion of different styles and shows influences from across the Empire. They absorbed Lydian, Babylonian, Egyptian and Ionian architectural features as an imperial statement. Greek inscriptions were found in the quarries that provided stone for the palace complex at Persepolis. There is also evidence that the tools used on the Persian palaces were of the same design as the picks and chisels used on Greek buildings of the sixth century. Metal clamps were used to hold the stones together on both Persian and Greek buildings. There are also similarities in decoration: both Persian and Greek columns feature fluting (narrow, vertical grooves carved into the columns) and volutes (scroll-like decorations).

However, the message of the sculpted decoration in the palace of Persepolis is clear: the king is shown receiving tribute or sitting on a throne supported by subjugated

FIGURE 1.31
Greek bronze statue of Apollo, found in Piraeus, the harbour of Athens.

ACTIVITY

Look at other pieces from the Oxus Treasure either online or at the British Museum. Compare the themes and skills shown in Persian and Greek metal work.

FIGURE 1.32
Marble head found in
Athens *c.* 600 BC.

populations. Delegations march in ordered files bringing tributes or compliant animals.
The frieze on the Parthenon creates a different narrative: the horsemen build to a gallop
to hurry the viewer along, a lone heifer refuses to march along compliantly and a marshal
intervenes to control proceedings.

Two heads carved by Greek (Figure 1.32) and Persian (Figure 1.33) sculptors
both show the influence of earlier Egyptian art. The stylised eyebrows, almond-shaped
eyes and the tight curls of the hair are seen on Greek sculptures in the late seventh
and sixth centuries BC. The use of lapis lazuli also indicates the breadth of the
Persian Empire. The semi-precious stone, sought after for its deep blue colour, was
traded across the ancient world. Once Cyrus had conquered the Median kingdom in
550 BC, Arachosia, where the lapis lazuli mines were located, became a satrapy of the
Persian Empire.

PRESCRIBED SOURCE

**Head of a young Persian prince in lapis lazuli,
from the Apadana at Persepolis**

Date: 6th century BC

Material: lapis lazuli

Original location: Persepolis

Current location: National Museum of Iran

Significance: sculpture from a rare material showing
the influence of Greek sculptors

FIGURE 1.33
Head of a young Persian prince in lapis lazuli, from
the Apadana at Persepolis.

THE CONTRAST OF THE 'REALITY' OF PERSIAN CULTURE AND SOCIETY WITH THE GREEK VIEW

The extent to which Herodotus shows familiarity with the reality of Persia

Although Herodotus was born and lived within the Persian Empire, there are many aspects of Persian culture that are over-simplified or even incorrect in his *Histories*. It is likely that Herodotus used Persian as well as Greek and Egyptian sources. His catalogue of the Persian army and fleet in 7.61–98 is probably based on documentary evidence, as it seems so certain and detailed. Also the description Herodotus gives of the accession of Darius is very similar to the, almost certainly, fictitious story given on the Behistun relief, so there was probably a common original source for both. Herodotus was also probably misled by Egyptian sources about the cruelty of Cambyses. His sacrifice of the sacred Apis bull is not supported by other sources. The inscription on the tomb of the bull, which dates to this period, claims that Cambyses made generous offerings.

Herodotus does use Persian technical words – he explains that '*orosangae*' (8.85) is the word for 'benefactors of the Persian king' and explains that '*angareion*' (8.98) is the Persian message relay system. However, (at 1.139) he also claims that all Persian names end with an 's' (the Greek sigma), which shows a lack of understanding of the Persian language.

The explanation for the Persian invasions is over-simplified and made 'Greek-centred'. The conquest of Greece would be a natural move for the Persians to secure the western frontier of their Empire and control the entire Aegean basin. Herodotus, however, has Xerxes give the following explanation:

> I will punish Athens for what they did to the Persians and to my father.
> You saw that my father, Darius, was planning an expedition against these
> people. But he died and did not get the chance to punish them. For him, then,
> and for all the Persians, I will not rest until I have captured and burnt Athens
> in return for the wrongs which they instigated against me and my father.

Herodotus, Histories, 7.8

Earlier in this speech, Herodotus does have Xerxes explain that he feels pressure due to the successes of his predecessors; Cyrus, Cambyses and Darius had all made significant additions to the Persian Empire:

> Cyrus, Cambyses and my father Darius all conquered races and added their territories
> to our empire, no one needs to remind you of their accomplishments. Since I came to
> this throne, I have considered how best to match the accomplishments of my
> ancestors by increasing the power of the Persians by as much as they did.

Herodotus, Histories, 7.8

Matching the successes of those he claimed as his ancestors was probably a stronger motivation on Xerxes than revenge. The pride in conquest is shown in the following inscription on the tomb of Darius at Naqsh-I Rustam:

Study question

Is it possible to assess whether or not Herodotus deliberately misrepresents the Persians. If you feel that he does, what is his purpose?

EXPLORE FURTHER

On the Malice of Herodotus by Plutarch, and *Cyropaedia* and *Anabasis* by Xenophon are all useful ancient sources when considering the Greeks' representation of the Persians.

Look at the sculptures [of those] who bear the throne, then shall you know, then shall it become known to you: the spear of a Persian man has gone forth far; then shall it become known to you: a Persian man has delivered battle far indeed from Persia.

DNa

Herodotus does not explain the central importance of Ahuramazda in Persian religion, nor does he mention the prophet Zoroaster, whose teachings the Persian kings, at least, may have followed. The importance of Ahuramazda is clear from artistic representations on the Bisitun relief and elsewhere, and from the following passage (also from the tomb of Darius):

Darius the King says: This which has been done, all that by the will of Ahuramazda I did. Ahuramazda bore me aid, until I did the work. May Ahuramazda protect me from harm, and my royal house, and this land: this I pray of Ahuramazda, this may Ahuramazda give to me!

DNa

There are other oversights. Herodotus refers to Mitra as a version of the Greek goddess Aphrodite (1.131) when he is a male deity. He does not mention Persepolis, which was, at the time of Xerxes, the most important city in the Empire. Pasargadai, another important city, is only referred to as a tribal name.

TOPIC REVIEW

These questions should draw on your knowledge of the whole topic, so think carefully about the different things you have learned (check the Topic Overview on p. 71).

1. What were the contributions of each of the Persian kings to the Empire?
2. What can we tell about the Persians and their kings from the material culture?
3. How was the Persian Empire organised?
4. How does the Greek presentation of the Persian Empire correspond with reality?

Further Reading

Brosius, M. (ed.) (2000) *Lactor 16: The Persian Empire from Cyrus II to Artaxerxes I*. London: London Association of Classical Teachers

Curtis, J. (1989) *Ancient Persia*. London: British Museum Press

Curtis, J. (2013) *The Cyrus Cylinder and Ancient Persia*. London: British Museum Press

Curtis, J. and Tallis, N. (eds) (2005) *Forgotten Empire*. London: British Museum Press

Wiesehofer, J. (2001) *Ancient Persia*. London: I.B.Tauris

PRACTICE QUESTIONS

Source A: *The Cyrus Cylinder*

Source B: Aeschylus', *Persians*, 739–759

Darius: How swiftly came fulfilment of old prophecies! Zeus struck within one generation: on my son has fallen the issue of those oracles which I trusted the gods would still defer for many years. But heaven takes part, for good or ill, with man's own zeal. So now for my whole house a staunchless spring of griefs is opened; and my son, in youthful recklessness, not knowing the gods' ways, has been the cause of all. *He* hoped to stem that holy stream, the Bosporus, and bind the Hellespont with fetters like a slave; *he* would wrest Nature, turn sea into land, manacle a strait with iron, to make a highway for his troops. *He* in his mortal folly thought to overpower immortal gods, even Poseidon. Was not this some madness that possessed him? Now my hard-won wealth, I fear, will fall a prey to the first plunderer.

Atossa: Xerxes the rash learnt folly in fools' company. They told him you, his father, with your sword had won gold to enrich your children; while he, like a coward, gaining no increase, played the warrior at home. He planned his march to Hellas, this vast armament, swayed by the ceaseless slanders of such evil men.

Study **Sources A** and **B**.

1. What is the usual name for the artefact pictured in **Source A**?   [1]
2. How does Aeschylus suggest in **Source B** that Xerxes was responsible for the Persian defeat at Salamis?   [10]
3. 'The Greeks always represented barbarian women as intimidating.' Explain how far you agree with this statement and justify your response.   [30]

What to Expect in the A Level Exam for Invention of the Barbarian

This chapter aims to show you the types of questions you are likely to get in the written examination. It offers some advice on how to answer the questions and will help you avoid common errors.

THE EXAMINATION

This component of the A Level Classical Civilisation examination is designed to test your knowledge, understanding and evaluation of the Greek concept of the barbarian. The examination is worth 75 marks and lasts 1 hour and 45 minutes. This represents 30% of the total marks for the A Level.

There are two Assessment Objectives in your A Level, and questions will be designed to test these areas. These Assessment Objectives are outlined in the table below, together with the total number of marks available for each on the paper:

	Assessment Objective	Marks
AO1	Demonstrate knowledge and understanding of: • literature and visual/material culture • how sources and ideas reflect, and influence, their cultural contexts • possible interpretations of sources, perspectives and ideas by different audiences and individuals.	35
AO2	Critically analyse, interpret and evaluate literature and visual/material culture, using evidence to make substantiated judgements and produce coherent and reasoned arguments.	40

EXAM STRUCTURE AND QUESTION TYPES

The exam is divided into two sections, A and B.

There are four question types in this exam:

- a number of short-answer questions (5 marks in total)
- 10-mark stimulus questions
- 20-mark shorter essay
- 30-mark essay

Try to plan your time well. The shorter essay question and the long essay question together make up 50 of the 75 marks available, and so you should aim to spend the majority of your time on these two questions.

Section A has the following format:

There will be a prescribed visual/material source on the paper.

- One or more short-answer questions relating to the source (worth 2 or 3 marks in total). These questions will test AO1 only.
- You will then be asked a 10-mark stimulus question on this source.

There will also be a textual source, which will be a passage from one of your prescribed literary sources (in fact, the textual source could come before the visual/material source or after it). The questions follow the same format as above:

- One or more short-answer questions relating to the source (worth 2 or 3 marks in total, adding up to 5 marks when combined with the earlier short-answer questions). These questions will also test AO1 only.
- You will then be asked a 10-mark stimulus question on this source.

The final question in Section A will be the 20-mark shorter essay question.

- You may be asked to use one or both of these sources as a starting point for your answer, as well as your own knowledge.

Section B has the following format:

- You will be given a choice of two essays, of which you should **only do one**. This is worth 30 marks.

SECTION A

Short-answer questions and visual/material stimulus question

For example, you could be shown the following prescribed visual/material source.

Source A: *Section of the frieze from the Temple of Apollo at Bassae*

Short-answer question

An example of a short-answer question would be:

Question: This is a section of a frieze from the Temple of Apollo at Bassae. What does it show? [2]

Answer: An Amazon [1] fighting a Greek [1].

This question is AO1 since it requires you to show knowledge and understanding, but there is no analysis or evaluation required.

Stimulus question

After the short-answer questions, you will be asked a 10-mark stimulus question. Of the 10 marks available, 5 are for AO1 and 5 for AO2. AO1 marks are awarded for the selection of material from the source, AO2 marks for the interpretation, analysis or evaluation of this material. These questions are marked according to a marking grid which you can view on the OCR website.

For example, for the section of the frieze from the Temple of Apollo at Bassae, you might be asked a question such as this:

Question: Evaluate how useful this image is as a source of information about the Greek depiction of the barbarian. [10]

A key word here is 'evaluate'. You need to think about how far the image can give us accurate information about how the Greeks depicted barbarians. As the marking grid indicates, you should aim to make a range of points that give clear and thoughtful analysis and are backed up with good supporting evidence from the source. Here are examples of two points you could make (you do not need to separate them in your answers):

Point 1: The Amazon is in a position of dominance over the Greek warrior. Although this is a section of an expensive marble frieze, which would have been prominently displayed in a Greek temple, the sculptor is, nevertheless, willing to show a Greek being defeated. This is therefore a very important source as it proves that the Greeks were comfortable showing the barbarians as well-matched adversaries.

Point 2: The Amazon is wearing a distinctive Persian cap. The source is useful because it shows us not only how the Greeks portrayed the Amazons but also that they identified them with the Persians, who were their historical enemies.

Notice that in each case, evidence from the image leads to a point of analysis. Try to make your arguments as clear and distinct as possible, and always back them up with evidence from the source. In addition, notice that together the two points would then help you to evaluate the question further. The first point suggests that the Greeks saw themselves as vulnerable to barbarians, while the second point shows how the Greeks identified mythical barbarians with the Persians. This then starts to build towards a clear and well-reasoned evaluation of the Greek depiction of the barbarian.

Short-answer questions and textual-stimulus question

As an example of a literary source, look at the passage below from Euripides' *Medea*, lines 1323–1343.

Jason:	Hateful creature!
	O most detestable of women to the gods and me and all the human race!
	You could bring yourself to put to the sword the children of your womb.
	You have taken my sons and destroyed me.
	And can you still face the Sun and this Earth, guilty of the most unholy crime?
	Curses on you!
	Now I am sane.
	But I was mad to bring you from your home, from your savage land to a
	Greek family: a mighty trouble, already a traitor to your father and the
	country that had nurtured you.
	The avenging spirit meant for you the Gods have visited on me: you killed
	your brother at the family hearth and came on board the Argo, my
	fair-faced ship.
	That's how you began! You became my bride.
	You bore my children, and because of your feelings about our marriage
	bed, you killed them.
	No Greek woman could ever have brought herself to do that.
	Yet I rejected them, to marry you, a wife who brought me enmity and
	death, a lioness, not human, wilder than Tyrrhenian Scylla.

Short-answer question

An example of a short-answer question would be:

Question: Where was the mythical figure of Medea from? [1]

Answer: Colchis [1].

Once again, no analysis is required here, you simply need to show knowledge (AO1).

Stimulus question

As an example of a textual 10-mark stimulus question, you might be asked a question such as this based on the passage given from *Medea*:

Question: Explain how Euripides emphasises Jason's shock at Medea's behaviour in this passage. [10]

Notice that in this instance you are not being asked to evaluate but to explain. You should aim to make a range of points, using evidence from the passage. If possible, refer closely to the passage, either by referencing line numbers, or by quoting directly. One example of one point that you might make is as follows:

Answer: 'You've destroyed me! And yet, there you are, alive!': Jason is shocked and appalled at the injustice of his situation. He cannot understand how Medea has committed the heinous crime of murdering her own children and yet he is the one who is punished by grief. Euripides emphasises Jason's shock by juxtaposing the situations of Jason and Medea in this brief quote.

Once again, the point contains evidence from the source (in this case the passage), which enables a point of analysis to be made.

The shorter essay question

The final question in Section A will give you the opportunity to use one or both of the sources, as well as asking you to demonstrate your wider knowledge of the Invention of the Barbarian topic. There are 20 marks available, 10 for AO1 and 10 for AO2. This question has its own tailored marking grid, which you can view on the OCR website.

An example of such a question might be as follows:

Question: Explain why the Greeks found Penthesilea and Medea so disturbing. You may use Sources A and B as a starting point, and should justify your response.

When you **plan** your answer to this question, it might be a good idea to write down some key points of factual evidence which you are going to use for AO1. You could start by noting the evidence from the two sources on the paper. The Bassae frieze shows a barbarian woman defeating a Greek man in battle, although this is a scene from mythology and in other representations the Amazons are defeated. In the *Medea* passage, Jason blames Medea's status as a barbarian for her shocking behaviour, commenting that 'no Greek woman would dare do such a thing'. The power these transgressive barbarian women have over Greek men is clear. You might then list other examples and pieces of evidence from your wider studies.

Think about some of the key words and phrases in the question. The word 'disturbing' asks you to consider the contemporary Greek attitude to the barbarians. The phrase 'justify your response' gives you plenty of flexibility to choose which sources you wish to use in your argument. It will be important to explain the key differences between Penthesilea and Medea and Greek women. You really do have the opportunity to give exactly your own opinion on this question. There is no 'right' or 'wrong' answer to a question such as this – you simply need to back up your opinions with strong evidence from your studies.

SECTION B

The essay question

In Section B, you will be given a choice of two essays. **You should only do one essay.** The essay is out of 30 marks, with ten marks for AO1 and twenty marks for AO2 (this question also has its own tailored marking grid, which you can download from the OCR website). However, this does not mean that you should be aiming to give evidence and evaluation in exactly that ratio. A good essay is likely to have more evaluation than evidence in any case, and so you should just aim to write the best essay you can, where you back up your arguments with evidence from your studies. What you should avoid doing, however, is over-narrating: telling the examiner what happens in a literary source rather than analysing it according to the question.

The first thing you need to do is to decide which question to choose. Make sure that you read both questions carefully and think about what is being asked. It is a common mistake for candidates to read the question as they want it to be, rather than as it is. For example, consider the following question:

'The Greeks had as much in common with the Persians as they did with each other.' Explain how far you agree with this statement and justify your response. [30]

In this question, you should weigh up the differences and similarities between the Greeks and the Persians. However, notice that it would be possible to misread this question. A learner may previously have written a practice essay such as: 'How far did the Greeks use their common practices to distinguish themselves from the Persians?' If so, it would be very tempting to reproduce many of the arguments made in that essay. Be very careful not to do this. You must answer the question in front of you, which, in this case, is about whether or not the Greeks had more in common with each other than they did with the Persians. Therefore, when you make your choice about which essay to attempt, ensure that you have read each question carefully and are very sure about what each one is asking for. It may be that you think that you could answer both. This is a good problem to have! Make a clear decision one way or another and then stick with it.

Try to ensure that you give your essay a clear structure. Perhaps draw up a plan paragraph by paragraph or argument by argument. While it is a good idea to have a brief introduction and conclusion to the essay, try not to make these too long. Your introduction should briefly outline the key issues, and perhaps the line you are going to take, while the conclusion should be short and simply summarise the key points you have made to conclude your argument. To score good marks in AO1, make sure you choose a range of factual evidence. To score good marks on AO2, make sure you examine the issue and weigh up your arguments carefully. You will want to make a variety of points, and again you may find that there are arguments on both sides.

Modern scholarship

In this essay question, you are required to show knowledge of modern scholarship in your answer. This requirement of the exam is supported in the textbooks by 'Modern Scholarship' boxes. The OCR rubric says that 'Learners are expected to make use of scholarly views, academic approaches and sources to support their argument'. It is essential that you build in such material in order to do well on this question. How should you do this?

First of all, you of course need to read more widely about the topic. In this book, you have been given suggestions for articles and books to read on a variety of topics relating to the Greek Invention of the Barbarian. Try to follow up as many as possible, and take notes about some of the key arguments that scholars make. It is especially interesting when two authors disagree with each other on a topic, such as whether or not Aeschylus' *Persians* shows sympathy to the Persians. When referring to the view of a scholar, you need not quote them directly, although if you are able to remember a few words that they have written accurately, then that would be very impressive. However, it may be that you refer to a general argument that they put forward in a book, an article or a chapter.

Let us take an example relating to the question on p. 93. One of your books for recommended reading is *The Greeks* by Paul Cartledge (OUP 2002). On p. 3, he writes '"Greekness", that is to say, had at least enough purchase on reality to allow of a definition that was not purely wishful thinking'. This might well be a quotation or a view worth putting forward in your essay, particularly since it implies that, despite arguments to the contrary, it was possible to define 'Greekness'. Cartledge goes on to say, however, that this 'Greekness' had 'relatively little tangible impact in the sphere of practical politics', which is another opinion that you could compare with the speeches before the battle of Salamis in Book 8 of Herodotus' *Histories*. You do not necessarily need to quote the details of where you read the ideas, it will be enough to mention the scholar's name and explain what they say.

Above all, make your use of secondary sources relevant to the question you are answering. To use a secondary source well you should think carefully about why it is supporting your argument or showing a different argument, and make it clear why you are including it. You might want to agree or disagree with the scholarly view, in which case you will need to explain why you do so. You may not remember everything about the secondary source you have read, but if you ensure the examiner understands what you are using and why, this will strengthen your argument. Using secondary sources in this way gives you a skill that is crucial at university level in many different subjects because engaging with what other people have thought about a particular topic enriches your own understanding.

PART 2
GREEK ART

Introduction to Greek Art

This chapter introduces Greek Art (Component 24) in the OCR A-Level in Classical Civilisation. It begins by considering material sources and how to analyse them. It then discusses the advantages and disadvantages of using damaged and/or reconstructed pieces, as well as the usefulness and limitations of copies or reproductions.

The next section presents the sources for the free-standing sculpture element, beginning with the Archaic Period and moving through the various stages of the Classical period. An introduction to the block-carving and bronze-casting methods of production is included. This is followed by a section on architectural sculpture in the same format. This section also briefly covers the architectural orders and the functions of Greek temples. There is then a section introducing the sources for the vase-painting element, starting with black-figure scenes of the Archaic Period via the transitional period and the red-figure scenes of the classical period. This includes a consideration of the various vase-painting techniques and the movements of the mannerists and the pioneers.

The final section looks at the themes apparent in Greek art. It begins with mythology and everyday life as the main subjects for Greek art. It then considers the themes more specifically apparent in free-standing sculpture, architectural sculpture and vase-painting. Finally, there is an investigation of the pursuit of naturalism over time and the impact and influence of the Persian Wars on the production of ancient art.

General bibliography

Barringer, J.M. (2008) *Art, Myth, and Ritual in Classical Greece*. Cambridge: Cambridge University Press

Boardman, J. (1974) *Athenian Black Figure Vases*. London: Thames & Hudson

Boardman, J. (1975) *Athenian Red Figure Vases*. London: Thames & Hudson

Boardman, J. (1978) *Greek Sculpture: The Archaic Period*. London: Thames & Hudson

Boardman, J. (1987) *Greek Sculpture: The Classical Period*. London: Thames & Hudson

Jenkins, I. (2008) *Greek Architecture and Its Sculpture*. Cambridge, MA: Harvard University Press

Moignard, E. (2006) *Greek Vases: An Introduction (Classical World Series)*. London: Bloomsbury Academic

Osborne, R. (1998) *Archaic and Classical Greek Art*. Oxford: Oxford University Press

Spivey, N. (2013) *Greek Sculpture*. Cambridge: Cambridge University Press

Woodford, S. (2015) *An Introduction to Greek Art: Sculpture and Vase Painting in the Archaic and Classical Periods*, 2nd edn. London: Bloomsbury Academic

EXAM OVERVIEW: A LEVEL	H408/24

Your assessment is a written examination testing AO1 and AO2. It is:

30% of the A Level   1 hr 45 mins   75 marks

35 marks will test AO1: demonstrate knowledge and understanding of:

- literature, visual/material culture and classical thought
- how sources and ideas reflect, and influence, their cultural contexts
- possible interpretations of sources, perspectives and ideas by different audiences and individuals

40 marks will test AO2: critically analyse, interpret and evaluate literature, visual/material culture, and classical thought, using evidence to make substantiated judgements and produce coherent and reasoned arguments.

The examination will consist of two sections.

All questions in **Section A** are compulsory. There are three question types:

- short-answer questions
- 10-mark stimulus question using the prescribed sources
- 20-mark essay

Section B has one question type:

- 30-mark essay

There is a choice of one from two essays. In these essays learners will be expected to make use of secondary sources and academic views to support their argument.

TIMELINE

☆ Development of the Korai
☆ Development of the Kouroi

Free-standing Sculpture

590–580	New York Kouros	☆
580	Kleobis and Biton	☆
570–560	Berlin standing goddess	☆
530	Anavyssos Kouros	☆
530–525	Peplos Kore	☆
510–500	Aristodikos Kouros	☆
478–474	Delphi Charioteer	⎤ Transitional period
460–450	Artemision Zeus	
460–450	Myron's Diskobolos	⎦
440	Doryphoros	Polykleitos

420	Aphrodite of the Agora
375–371	Eirene and Ploutos
340	Hermes and Dionysus; Aphrodite of Knidos; Antikytheran Youth; Apoxyomenos

[handwritten: Female figures 5th century]

[handwritten: ⌉ 4th cent]

Architectural Sculpture

580	Pediment of Temple of Artemis at Corcyra
575–550	Metope at Temple C at Selinus
525	Ionic frieze on Siphnian Treasury at Delphi
510–500	West Pediment on Temple of Aphaia at Aegina
490–480	East Pediment on Temple of Aphaia at Aegina
460	Pediments and metopes on the Temple of Zeus at Olympia
447–442	Doric frieze on the Parthenon at Athens
442–437	Ionic frieze on the Parthenon at Athens
437–432	Pediments on the Parthenon at Athens
420–400	Ionic frieze on the Temple of Apollo at Bassae

Vases

580	Gorgons pursuing Perseus
580–570	The Wedding of Peleus and Thetis
550	The François Vase
540–535	Dionysus and the Maenads
540–530	Ajax and Achilles playing dice
540–530	Dionysus sailing on the ocean
530–510	Dionysus/Herakles Feasting in the Presence of Athena
515–510	Herakles and Antaios
510	Hector Arming/Three Men Carousing
510	Herakles and The Amazons
500–490	Dionysus and the Maenads
490–480	The Trojan War
490–460	Achilles and Hector/Memnon
480–460	Boreas pursuing Oreithyia
460	Perseus and Medusa

[handwritten: Attic black figure vases 6th century]

[handwritten: Transitional period]

[handwritten: Reference to the bilingual amphora]

[handwritten: ⌉ Attic red figure vases 5th century]

2.1 Sources

Materials

- Usefulness and limitations of damaged and/or reconstructed pieces
- Usefulness and limitations of copies of free-standing sculpture

The prescribed sources for the whole component are relevant here. Don't forget that you will be given credit in the exam if you study extra sources and make relevant use of them in your answers.

Due to the passing of time, and human actions through war, looting or vandalism, scholars often do not have access to original pieces of ancient art and are therefore limited to damaged, reconstructed, or copied pieces. This topic looks at the nature of our source material and highlights some of the general aspects to be considered when analysing the prescribed sources for this component.

ANALYSING MATERIAL SOURCES

The analysis of material sources is in many ways very similar to the analysis of literary sources with which we are often more familiar. In both cases, it is important to consider the context of the piece: what it is; why and when it was made; and by and for whom.

With vases and both architectural and free-standing sculpture there are two main elements to think about when analysing material sources: content and composition. Consider, for example, the metope depicting Herakles and the Kerkopes from Temple C at Selinus.

Content is more straightforward, and will probably seem more familiar to those new to studying material sources; it deals with what is depicted in any given scene or piece. In this metope we find the two Kerkopes, hanging upside-down from a pole across the shoulders of the figure of Herakles. This scene, in which Herakles tries to punish the Kerkopes for attempting to steal from him, is not particularly well-known today, but would have been easily recognisable to its ancient audience.

Analysis of the composition of the scene is more complex. It considers how a scene is put together, the positions of different figures or elements, and their relationship both to

FIGURE 2.1
Herakles and the Kerkopes, with lines added to show the vertical and diagonal lines.

each other and to the piece as a whole. In this case the arrangement of the figures side-by-side fills the space well. Avoiding any overlapping of the three characters in the scene results in a series of clear vertical lines. The diagonal lines created by Herakles' striding legs not only suggest movement but also add variety. The artist also relies heavily on mirroring and symmetry as the Kerkopes are reflections of each other, a particularly effective technique here given that they are twins. While the upper bodies of the Kerkopes are depicted in a frontal view, their lower bodies are shown in profile, with the resulting awkward twist at their waists covered by their folded arms. However, with Herakles, the artist has maintained the attempt at a profile view throughout the whole body, using only the frontal view for his face.

When analysing material sources of ancient art, give particular thought to the following series of questions, although not all will be relevant to every piece:

- Which elements of a story have been included and why? Are they integral to the scene? If not, why have they been included? Why has this moment of the story been chosen?
- What makes this scene and the characters intelligible/recognisable?
- How well does the scene fit with its location? Is the space well filled? Does the piece encourage viewing from a particular spot or angle?
- What makes the arrangement of different elements interesting? Repetition? Overlapping? Symmetry? Contrast? Variety?

USING DAMAGED/RECONSTRUCTED PIECES

Little art from the ancient world has survived in mint condition: vases and marbles are often chipped or cracked, if not made up of only fragments; bronzes are often missing accoutrements, such as weapons or eyes. Clearly such damage is a challenge for students of Greek art.

FIGURE 2.2
The François Vase.

Consider the Artemision Zeus (see p. 120). Found in a shipwreck off the coast of the island of Euboia in the late 1920s, this bronze conforms to the iconography of the older Olympian gods Zeus and Poseidon: the muscular, yet slightly older, physique combined with the bearded face. However, the statue is incomplete. Unfortunately, the projectile from the figure's right hand, which would probably have confirmed the god's true identity, is missing. Is the figure Zeus holding a thunderbolt or Poseidon holding a trident? The argument has recently swayed more towards Zeus on the grounds that the length of a trident held in that position would have meant obscuring the god's face. Although the identification of this bronze is problematic, the arguments in favour of studying it – including the quality of the casting, the innovation of the pose, the rarity of original bronzes – far outweigh the difficulties of using a damaged artwork.

The François Vase by Kleitias has also suffered damage, though more recent. In 1900 a museum worker threw a stool at the display case,

FIGURE 2.3
Slab North XLIII of the Ionic Frieze of the Parthenon.

smashing the vase into 638 pieces. It was painstakingly reconstructed in 1902, but one fragment had been stolen. In 1973, almost 70 years after the missing piece was located, another reconstruction was undertaken. Again, it would be a great oversight not to study vases such as this on account of their damaged state. Very many vases are discovered in fragments. Even when it is not possible to reconstruct whole pieces, the fragments offer their own insights.

Some of the more complete pieces often appear very differently today from how they would have done in antiquity. For instance, the sculptures of the Parthenon Frieze may appear fairly well preserved. However, on closer inspection we can see that the reins the riders held, originally made of metal, are now missing. Their hands are now grasping thin air. It is possible to make out the holes near the horses' mouths and ears where these attachments were added.

It is also very important to remember that sculpture would have been painted. Although most of this colour has not survived, we do occasionally see traces of it. As technology develops, it is becoming easier to gain a more complete picture of the original appearance of ancient art. For example, the use of UV light on the archer from the West Pediment of the Temple of Aphaia at Aegina reveals the original pattern painted on the figure's trousers. As in the case of the Peplos Kore, although it is not currently possible to determine the exact colouring, speculative reconstructions can be made based on the information available, such as those from the 2015 'Gods in Colour' exhibition at the Ashmolean Museum of Art and Archaeology (see p. 105).

USING REPRODUCTIONS

It is not possible for all students of Greek art to view original pieces. Although original vases survive in abundance, the story is quite different for sculpture, and bronzes in

EXPLORE FURTHER

Cast Collections

Two of the UK's largest collections of plaster copies of ancient sculpture, both architectural and free-standing, can be found at the Ashmolean Museum of Art and Archaeology in Oxford and the Museum of Classical Archaeology in Cambridge.

particular. Often the original pieces no longer exist as they were melted down when the material became more valuable than the object itself. However, the Romans were great lovers of Greek art and often copied pieces for their own collections. Due to changing tastes and the costs of materials, many of these Roman reproductions were carved in marble rather than being cast in bronze. Huge numbers of Greek bronze sculptures now survive only as Roman marble copies, including the Doryphorus of Polykleitos and the Apoxyomenos of Lysippos. While the general appearance of these sculptures is unchanged, in that the likeness of the original bronze is recognisable, a number of details in these reproductions are different. The poses achieved in bronze cannot always be replicated in marble, as the tensile strength of marble is much less than that of bronze. As a result, we often see the addition of supports, particularly tree-trunks, in marble copies, which were not present in the original pieces. Similarly, some of the intricacies of casting in bronze, such as the rendering of the skin, cannot always be replicated in marble with the same effect as in the original.

Reproductions also take many forms, from full-scale copies to miniatures, from depictions on coins to photographs and drawings. All of these have their uses. Viewing full-scale copies enables students of art to appreciate the size of sculptures or vases in a way that no photograph can. This is particularly useful when comparing one piece with another. For example, the Berlin Standing Goddess is much smaller than students often imagine, while the metopes of the Temple of Zeus at Olympia and the Berlin Painter's vase depicting Achilles and Memnon/Hector are larger than people tend to think having studied them in books.

In some cases, reproduction through photographs or drawings are all that remain of some pieces of ancient art. The metopes, frieze and pediments of the Parthenon are a prime example. Many of the central slabs of the friezes were destroyed during an explosion in 1687 and now remain only in the sketches made by Jacques Carrey when he had visited the Acropolis four years earlier. Similarly, when the victorious Venetian general Morosini took Athens a year later from the occupying Turks, he attempted to have the sculptures removed from the pediments. Unfortunately, the ropes supporting the heavy horses of the deities were not strong enough and they smashed to the ground on the Acropolis. Again, Carey's drawings are invaluable in reconstructing the scene as it would have originally appeared.

One of the problems to be aware of when using reproductions to study ancient art is that copies vary enormously in terms of their accuracy in replicating the original piece. For example, there are numerous copies of Myron's Diskobolos. While the figure is instantly recognisable, in some reproductions the athlete looks to the ground in front of his foot rather than back towards the discus, which is generally considered to be the correct direction.

There are both advantages and disadvantages to using reproductions in the study of ancient art. On the one hand, reproductions enable pieces to be studied by a wider audience than the original alone; on the other, no matter how accurate the reproduction, an original can never be replicated entirely. Students should therefore take care to familiarise themselves with the differences between originals and reproductions.

TOPIC REVIEW

These questions should draw on your knowledge of the whole topic, so think carefully about the different things you have learned (check the Topic Overview on p. 101).

Reconstructions of the Peplos Kore

1. What are the advantages and disadvantages of using/studying replicas?
2. To what extent should material sources be treated differently from literary sources?
3. Can material sources be studied in isolation? Give reasons for your answer.
4. Do you consider reconstructions or reproductions to be more authentic to the original piece? Give reasons for your answer.
5. Evaluate how useful the image above is for art historians.
6. How successfully do the pieces you have studied support the argument that studying reconstructions is a worthwhile exercise?

Further Reading

Boardman, J. (2008) *The History of Greek Vases: Potters, Painters and Pictures*. London: Thames & Hudson
Pedley, J.G. (2011) *Greek Art and Archaeology*. Cambridge: Pearson

2.2 Free-Standing Sculpture

TOPIC OVERVIEW

Functions

- Functions of free-standing sculpture including:
  - cult statue, votive, grave marker, memorial

Materials

- Effects of different types of materials, including:
  - marble and bronze in free-standing sculpture
- Advantages and limitations of different materials
- Usefulness and limitations of damaged and/or reconstructed pieces
- Usefulness and limitations of copies of free-standing sculpture

Techniques

- Block method of carving statues
- Lost-wax method of casting bronze statues

Stylistic features and development

- Stylistic features and development of the *kouros* and the *kore*, including:
  - pose, archaic smile, hair, adornment, geometric anatomy, elaborate drapery
- Stylistic features and development of the bronze statue, including:
  - action pose, chased detail; added detail in different metals

Composition

- Dominant verticals, horizontals and diagonals
- *Chiastic* composition
- Pose
- *Contrapposto*
- Portrayal of anatomy and physical form
- Portrayal of movement
- Portrayal of emotion

Subject matter

- Themes in free-standing sculpture, including:
  - mortals and gods
  - concepts in 4th-century BC sculpture

The following prescribed sources are covered in this topic:

- **Archaic Period**
  - New York Kouros
  - Kleobis and Biton
  - Berlin Standing Goddess
  - Anavysos Kouros
  - Peplos Kore
  - Aristodikos Kouros

- **Early Classical Period**
  - Delphi Charioteer
  - Artemision Zeus
  - Diskobolos by Myron

- **High Classical Period**
  - Doryphoros by Polykleitos

- **Late Classical Period**

  - Aphrodite of the Agora
  - Eirene and Ploutos by Kephisodotos
  - Hermes and Dionysus

Don't forget that you will be given credit in the exam if you study extra sources and make relevant use of them in your answers.

This part of the course examines **free-standing** sculptures from the sixth to the fourth century BC. It considers sculptures of both male and female figures, of mortals, heroes and gods. The majority of the sculptures are originals, although a number of originals have been lost since antiquity and remain to us only as later Roman copies.

Sculptures are vitally important for understanding ancient Greek society. They served a variety of functions, which will be discussed in relation to specific sculptures later on in this chapter. Free-standing sculpture could also function as **cult statues**. Since these were initially made out of wood and later frequently out of precious materials, such as gold and ivory, the majority of these have not survived.

Sculptures help us learn about how people viewed themselves and each other, as well as the gods. They allow us to draw conclusions about contemporary social values, how they commemorated victories and deaths and the role of mythology in people's lives.

> **free-standing** sculpture not used to decorate architecture. Sculpture that stands alone, without a background or supporting unit
>
> **cult statue** a statue that embodied and depicted a specific deity, and was situated within the main room of a temple

THE ARCHAIC PERIOD

Archaic free-standing sculpture usually had one of three purposes:

1. to depict a god, either independently from a temple or as a cult statue
2. to act as a votive offering to a god
3. to act as a grave marker or memorial.

It is difficult, and sometimes impossible, to understand the functions of all free-standing sculptures of the **Archaic Period**. Often it is only possible due to knowledge of the find-spot or an accompanying inscription.

> **Archaic Period** beginning around the start of the 6th century BC and ending between 490 and 480 BC, following the Persian invasions of Greece

The block method of carving statues

Sculptors used the 'block method' for carving statues. They drew a grid of lines on all four sides of a block of stone to determine the figure's proportions. They would then draw the front of the statue on the front of the block, the profile views on either side and finally the rear view on the back. Thereafter they would chip away at the block, getting rid of excess stone. Some stone would be left below the feet as a plinth to fit onto the statue base. Details on the figure, such as their musculature or facial features would have been rendered through incisions or modelled lines.

While this technique was effective in creating sculptures, we shall see that it has some limitations. Little to no attention is given to the diagonal viewpoint, such as the angle between the front and side views, and the sculptures appear flat. As sculpture developed and artists wanted to break free from rigidity and explore freer movement, modifications were made to this method.

FIGURE 2.4
The block method of carving statues.

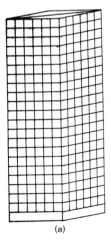 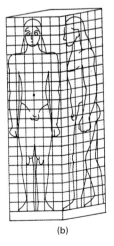  

(a)   (b)   (c)   (d)

Kouroi and korai

A **kouros** has the following key features:

- He is nearly always nude.
- He stands frontally.
- His left leg stands in front of the right in a 'walking pose', caught between walking and standing.
- His weight is evenly distributed between both legs.
- His arms are by their sides with fists clenched.
- He often has almond-shaped eyes.
- He often has wig-like hair that is schematically and symmetrically arranged.

A **kore** statue has the following key features:

- She is always draped.
- She stands frontally.
- Her feet are side by side.

kouros (pl. **kouroi**) literally, a male youth, and a type of sculpture from the Archaic Period

kore (pl. **korai**) literally, a maiden or unmarried girl, and a type of sculpture from the Archaic Period

FIGURE 2.5
Egyptian statues of Menkaura and queen, mid-third millennium BC.

The New York Kouros

The original purpose of the New York Kouros is unknown. The figure is not individual-ised but rather idealised. The life-size marble statue depicts a youthful nude male. His torso is marked with symmetrical and un-natural incisions that denote his chest muscles and pelvic arch. He has a very narrow torso and body, but broad shoulders. He follows the controlled and restricted pose of a kouros. He looks straight ahead and has the typical facial features of the Archaic kouros. His bead-like shoulder-length hair falls straight down his shoulders behind his neck and is tied with a fillet around the top of his head. This stylised hair reflects his aristocratic and idealised nature.

> **EXPLORE FURTHER**
>
> Archaic sculpture was influenced by Egyptian art. Draw a table comparing the kouroi and korai from this course with Egyptian sculpture, starting with Figures 2.5 and 2.6. Consider their poses, orientation, clothing and anatomy.

> **MODERN SCHOLARSHIP**
>
> Robin Osborne in his *Archaic and Classical Greek Art* argues that 'the Greek kouroi were certainly expensive and prestigious offerings but they do not embody power . . . They figure the male human body but not a particular body . . . Without attributes and without motion they give no grounds for telling a story . . . the plain features of the New York Kouros make no definitive statement about man at all.' Do you agree?

FIGURE 2.6
Mayor Nen-kheft-ka, mid-third millennium BC.

New York Kouros

Date: 590–580 BC

Material: marble

Height: 1.95m

Style: Archaic Kouros

Original location: Attica

Current location:
Metropolitan Museum
of Art, New York

Original or copy: original

Significance: depiction of
early Archaic Kouros

ACTIVITY

Draw the face and body
of the New York Kouros.
This will make you look
closely at the details of
the sculpture.

handwritten annotations:
almond eyes
expressionless
neat bead-like hair orishcrahc
broad shoulders but small waist unnatural
clenched fists by sides
unnatural musculature & pelvic arch
walking pose but weight distributed evenly
not convincing

FIGURE 2.7
New York Kouros, front and rear views.

PS

Kleobis and Biton

Kleobis and Biton are twin kouroi, identical sculptures dating to the early Archaic Period.
Sculpted by the Argive sculptor [Poly]medes, they were discovered at the oracular sanctuary of Apollo at Delphi, making them likely votive offerings. The presence of sculptures
from Argos in the Peloponnese at Delphi, which is in mainland Greece, demonstrates the
Panhellenic nature of the sanctuary.

Over life-size, the sculptures stand in the typical kouros pose. The figures appear
more robust and fleshier than the New York Kouros, a development in Greek sculpture's
naturalistic depiction of the male figure. The twin kouroi have been identified as the
famous twins Kleobis and Biton, based on a passage from Herodotos (1.31), which tells
the tale of twin brothers in Argos who showed exceptional devotion to their mother.

The sculptures have also been identified as the Dioskouri, Castor and Pollux. They
were sons of Zeus, and half-brothers to Helen of Troy and Clytemnestra. Their cult was

Panhellenic literally
means 'all' (pan) 'Greeks'
(Hellenes). Panhellenic
sanctuaries refer to those
that were open to all
Greeks

EXPLORE FURTHER

Without animals to pull the wagon so their mother could go to the sanctuary of Hera, the sons pulled the cart 45 stades. Upon arrival, their mother prayed to Hera to reward her sons for their piety with whatever is best for a man to receive. After performing sacrifices in honour of the goddess, the boys fell asleep and did not rise again. The Argives considered them to be the best of men, passing away after their greatest achievement.

widespread in the Peloponnese as patrons of travellers and sailors. They were also popular with athletes as they were often associated with horses. The absence of their traditional helmet, however, as well as a lack of horses suggests this is a false identification.

EXPLORE FURTHER

Twin kouroi were discovered in May 2010 in Corinth. Compare these with Kleobis and Biton. Do you think they represent the same figures? Is there sufficient evidence to identify these kouroi?

same pose & hair & facial features

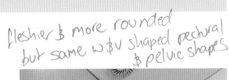
fleshier & more rounded but same w & v shaped pectoral & pelvic shapes

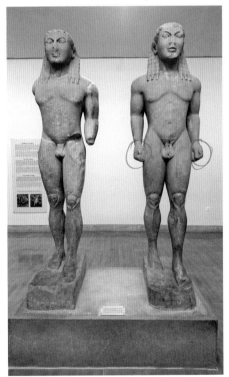

FIGURE 2.8
Kleobis and Biton, front view.

FIGURE 2.9
Kleobis and Biton, side view.

PRESCRIBED SOURCE

Kleobis and Biton

Date: *c.* 580 BC

Material: marble

Height: 2.18 m

Style: Archaic Kouros

Protagonists: probably Kleobis and Biton

Original location: Delphi

Current location: Delphi Archaeological Museum

Original or copy: original

Significance: example where kouroi perhaps represent real or mythical individuals

---

FIGURE 2.10
The Berlin Standing Goddess.

chiton a rectangular piece of linen clothing, worn by both men and women, sown at the shoulders or tied with buttons and frequently tied at the waist with a belt; in sculpture it is frequently worn by women, often as the thinner under layer to either a **himation** or a **peplos**

himation a mantle, or cloak; a thicker piece of clothing, that was often worn on top of the chiton or peplos

peplos a rectangular piece of woollen clothing, without sleeves, that was belted and tied or sewed at the shoulder

Berlin Standing Goddess

The Berlin Standing Goddess stands in a typical kore stance and displays Archaic facial features.

The Berlin Standing Goddess wears a red **chiton** with a **himation** on top. Her body is entirely covered, as befits a modest, respectable woman. Her clothing is so thick that nothing beyond her female hips and posterior denotes her anatomy. Her drapery and jewellery is used instead to denote beauty and status. She wears earrings, a necklace and a bracelet to show her wealth, as well as elaborate sandals on her feet. On her head she wears a painted headdress, a *polos*, which was commonly worn by goddesses. Her wig-like hair frames her face with stylised segments and is neatly arranged behind her back. The back view of the sculpture is made attractive by the contrast between the curved lines of her himation, the vertical plait of hair and folds of her chiton.

The kore's arms are active. Her left arm is bent at the elbow and crosses over her chest, holding the right side of her shawl in place, preserving her modesty. Her right arm is also bent at the elbow and holding a pomegranate. This fruit was commonly associated with death, as it was eaten by Persephone when she was abducted and taken to the Underworld by its god, Hades. It has therefore become a symbol of death and might suggest that this sculpture is a grave marker. The *polos* might even indicate that this is Persephone herself, in her role as the wife of Hades.

PRESCRIBED SOURCE

Berlin Standing Goddess

Date: 570–560 BC

Material: marble

Height: 1.93 m with plinth; plinth 0.10 m

Style: Archaic kore

Original location: Attica

Current location: Antikenmuseen in Berlin

Original or copy: original

Significance: depiction of early Archaic Kore

Study questions

1 Who do you think the Berlin Standing Goddess represents? A grave marker or Persephone herself?
2 The New York Kouros and the Berlin Standing Goddess were sculpted within a few decades of one another; how similar are they? What do their differences suggest about attitudes to sculpting male and female forms?

[handwritten margin notes: jewellery & headdress; stylised braid pattern; curved lines; feminine hips; vertical lines; shift pose]

Anavyssos Kouros

The Anavyssos Kouros and the New York Kouros may be compared to highlight the development of the male nude throughout the Archaic Period. The Anavyssos Kouros is much more rounded and fleshier than the New York Kouros. The figure seems far more three-dimensional, instead of flat. This is best seen in his thighs, arms and cheeks. Greek sculptors were making headway towards creating naturalistic, lifelike images that reflected the human figure. The musculature is likewise developed. The modelled lines on the torso are less straight and harsh, but rounded and gentler, denoting more than simple anatomy.

The mouth of the Anavyssos Kouros is also different from that of the New York Kouros. Instead of having straight lips, he is smiling what is known as the Archaic Smile. This is not an attempt at showing expression, but rather to make the sculpture appear more lifelike.

We know the context of the Anavyssos Kouros from an inscription found nearby:

Stay and mourn at the tomb of dead Kroisos
Whom raging Ares destroyed one day, fighting in the foremost ranks.

IG I³ 1240

It evidently marked the grave of a man who died while fighting. Nothing in the sculpture reflects this, however; the viewer had to read the words in order to understand. The

PRESCRIBED SOURCE

Anavyssos Kouros

Date: *c.* 530 BC

Material: marble

Height: 1.94 m

Style: Archaic kouros

Function: funerary

Original location: Anavyssos, southern Attica

Current location: National Museum in Athens

Original or copy: original

Significance: The development of the musculature and anatomy of kouroi in the Archaic Period.

ACTIVITY

Create a table charting the similarities and differences between the New York Kouros and the Anavyssos Kouros.

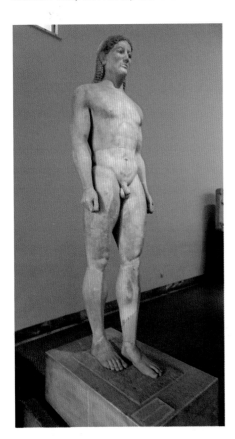

FIGURE 2.11
Anavyssos Kouros, front and side views.

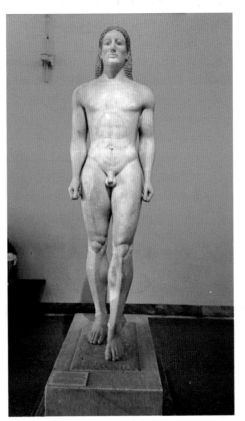

FIGURE 2.12
Anavyssos Kouros, face.

Study question

Cover up the next section. Draw a table comparing the New York Kouros and the Anavyssos Kouros. Consider their poses, orientation, viewpoints, anatomy, musculature and facial features.

S & C

Consider the following grave markers from the ancient world:

- The Dexileos Grave Stele
- The Ilissos Grave Stele
- The Hegeso Grave Stele
- The Alexander Sarcophagus
- The Nereid Monument
- The 'Mourning Women' Sarcophagus from the royal necropolis at Sidon

How do these compare with the Anavyssos Kouros? Which do you think is the most successful grave marker and why?

EXAM TIP

Decide which of these features are similar and which different. Group the features together. Each feature should be its own paragraph and try to link them together to show fluidity in your argument.

ACTIVITY

Read Robert Browning's, 'The Bishop orders his tomb at St Praxed's Church'.

Consider any cemeteries and tombs you may have visited yourself. Design a tomb, inspired by Browning's poem.

Compare these tombs with the Anavyssos Kouros and evaluate how successful it is at commemorating the deceased.

sculpture may therefore have represented the deceased or acted as a symbol for the life lost. Stewart, in his *Greek Art*, suggests that 'as grave markers, they could be regarded as *agalmata* to delight the dead, reminding everyone of the pinnacle of life on earth, and perpetuating it for all to see' (*agalmata* are statues designed as offerings).

Peplos Kore

The Peplos Kore was found on the Athenian Acropolis, making her a likely votive offering to the goddess Athena. Like the Berlin Standing Goddess, she stands frontally, feet next to each other. Her left arm, although missing below the elbow, would have extended out in front of her, holding an offering. She wears a peplos, a popular garment in sixth-century Greece and typically associated with Athena, over a thin chiton. The clothing provides a straight outline, offset only by a belt around her waist. Although this clothing covers her entire body, it does reveal her anatomy. This suggests an increasing awareness and ability at depicting the female figure.

Although her peplos appears simple in comparison with the chiton and himation that the Berlin goddess wore, it would have been painted with bright colours and elaborate patterns, which would have further enhanced the aesthetic of the sculpture. Bronze earrings and a wreath would have been attached separately.

The Peplos Kore appears more delicate and feminine than the Berlin Standing Goddess. Although both faces betray the typical kore features, the face of the Peplos Kore is no longer exaggerated and almost masklike, but was carved with gentleness, making each feature appear more naturalistic. Likewise, her hair is now carved with individual strands that define her neck and shoulders, and emphasise her breasts.

As a votive offering on the Athenian Acropolis, the Peplos Kore's purpose would have been to delight the goddess Athena, as well as to demonstrate the dedicator's own virtues. This is achieved through embodying and reflecting the female ideals of the time, namely beauty, modesty and respectability.

Although at first glance the statue looks somewhat plain, there are very subtle asymmetries that bring it to life. Her left leg is just in front of the right, her left shoulder is fractionally above the right and her head is slightly turned. This development of the kore figure corresponds to the contemporary development of kouroi, as discussed with the Anavyssos Kouros.

FIGURE 2.13
The Peplos Kore with suggested reconstructions of her original colours.

PRESCRIBED SOURCE

Peplos Kore

Date: *c.* 530–525 BC

Material: marble

Height: 1.18 m

Style: Archaic kore

Function: votive offering

Original location: Acropolis in Athens, west of the Erechtheum

Current location: Acropolis Museum in Athens

Original or copy: original

Significance: the development and variety of the kore in the Archaic Period

MODERN SCHOLARSHIP

In his *Understanding Greek Sculpture,* Nigel Spivey argues that korai were sexy; the visibility of their breasts through the drapery, as well as the careful arrangement of her hair to accentuate breasts make them a somewhat erotic sculpture. On one hand, the Peplos Kore is covered and respectable and, on the other, she is attractive and alluring.

Study question
Considering the kouroi were entirely nude, why do you think so much debate surrounds the erotic nature of the draped korai? Do you think the kouroi might also have been considered erotic?

Aristodikos Kouros

The sculpture of Aristodikos is identified because his name is engraved on the statue base, suggesting that it was a grave marker. The statue marks the transition from the Archaic to the Early Classical Periods.

Although Aristodikos' pose and orientation are the same as other kouroi, there are various features that mark development. Firstly, he no longer has long, wig-like hair;

PRESCRIBED SOURCE

Aristodikos Kouros

Date: *c.* 510–500 BC

Material: marble

Height: 1.95 m

Style: Archaic kouros

Function: funerary

Original location: Attica

Current location: National Museum in Athens

Original or copy: original

Significance: the stylistic development of the Kouros in the late Archaic Period

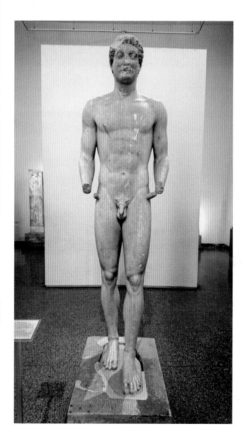
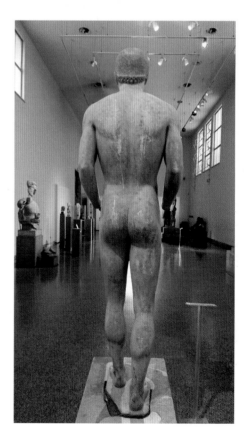

FIGURE 2.14
Aristodikos Kouros, front and rear views.

Study question

Stewart in his *Greek Sculpture* states that 'it was perhaps the very lack of specificity of the kouros and kore that made them so popular. For not only could they fulfil . . . two quite different functions (votive and funerary), but were also easily adaptable to represent the gods. There were secular satisfactions to be had from them too . . . as symbols of a united, ageless and all-enduring aristocracy of individually brilliant men and women, these statues both made concrete and perpetuated its values from generation to generation.'

Why do you think the Kouroi and Korai were so popular?

ACTIVITY

Draw a timeline for sculpture in the Archaic Period. Include images of the sculptures and annotate each one with its key features. In a separate colour, write out how the sculptures have developed from the ones before.

Afterwards, answer the question: to what extent was there any development, as opposed to variety, in sculpture during the Archaic Period?

although still arranged in rows of spiral curls across the brow and back of neck, his hair is now short. Traces of red were found on the top of his hair, suggesting a hair colour.

The arms are another key difference. These are now bent at the elbow and would have required struts to support their distance from the body, as marble is too weak to stand without it. Although this development in movement marks a significant breakthrough in the depiction of male free-standing sculpture, sculptors now faced difficulties with the material they were used to using, as the struts disrupt the aesthetic and illusion of extended arms.

Finally, there is further realism to the way the shin, knee, bone and sinew are depicted. The knee is no longer marked with stylised and symmetrical patterns. The slender body appears with more natural musculature, a further development from the Anavyssos Kouros. The collar bone is likewise more pronounced but natural.

This development in movement and musculature, which seems to have happened very quickly, is remarkable and crucial for the progress of Western sculpture and art. There are, however, still stylised features, particularly with his pubic hair, which has been arranged into a star-like shape, reminding us that development was a gradual process.

EARLY CLASSICAL PERIOD

Lost-wax method of casting bronze statues

Bronze was a far more effective material than marble due to three key features:

1. Since bronze statues are sculpted in sections, a mistake or damage does not mean that the whole piece has to be re-made.
2. The strength of bronze means that it does not require supports for extended limbs, and sculptors can therefore create movement in their pieces with greater freedom.
3. Additional materials, such as gold, silver, ivory or copper, can be used to make the statue more lifelike.

Like marble, bronze was originally painted. However, bronze was a much more expensive material.

The introduction of the hollow-bronze technique was extremely significant in the development of bronze statues and of sculpture in general. The sculptor began by creating a clay model of the statue, distinguishing the various sections that it could be sculpted

ACTIVITY

Create a poster advertising the process of the hollow-cast bronze and its benefits.

in. Each section of the clay model would then be covered in wax. A clay covering was put on top of the wax and attached to the core with metal rods. This was then put into an oven in its entirety so that the clay hardened and the wax melted away. Molten bronze was then poured in the gap between the clay core and the clay mould. When the bronze cooled and solidified, the clay mould was taken off and the sculptor could fix any minor problems and smooth the sculpture.

Delphic Charioteer

S & C Read Pindar's *Pythian Odes*, which celebrate the athletic victories at Delphi. Some of these were written in honour of Sicilian tyrants like Polyzalus.

The Delphic Charioteer is a life-size bronze sculpture, which would originally have been part of a far bigger monument. According to the epigram on the base found alongside it, it was dedicated by Polyzalus, a tyrant from Sicily, who reigned between 478 and 467 BC. He likely won a four-horse chariot race at the Pythian Games, the athletic contests that took place every four years at Delphi. The sanctuary's records state that Polyzalus' brother Hieron won the event in 470 BC so this dedication likely marks a victory in 478 or 474 BC. The original monument would have included the four-horse chariot; parts of the legs and tail of a horse have been found. An extended left arm was also discovered, suggesting that a slave boy may have stood in front of the horses, attending to them. Instead of sculpting the charioteer in the midst of his event, the sculptor has chosen to commemorate him after his victory, the calmness after the chaos and fervour of the race.

The charioteer was a slave, not Polyzalus himself. He stands still, but has a number of subtle movements that enliven him. His arms are outstretched before him, holding the reins,

FIGURE 2.15
Drawing and surviving sections of the monument featuring the Delphic Charioteer.

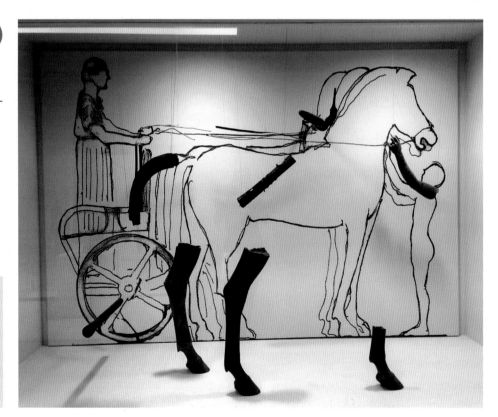

Study question
The victor Polyzalos is not depicted in this sculpture and is only mentioned in the inscription. Why do you think he chose this?

and his feet are at an angle from one another. His head is turned slightly to the right and is tilted downwards. This suggests modesty, a highly valued trait in ancient Greece, where arrogance was believed to be punished by the gods. His attentive gaze indicates his concentration on his horses, a focus that doubtless contributed to his victory. The artist's choice to sculpt the athlete after his victory, instead of during the action that led to the victory, is significant. It allows the figure to act as a model for other athletes: calm and modest, gracious to the gods for his success. Perhaps the choice of narrative was also easier for the sculptor; casting an action scene involving moving horses would have been much more complex.

The sculpture was created using the lost-wax technique. It was made in three sections: the head and torso, lower torso from waist to feet, and right arm. Only the left arm is missing. As was customary for charioteers, he is depicted wearing a chiton. This garment was tied at his waist by a belt, which creates a break in the folds. The chiton has numerous uneven folds around his shoulders and chest, particularly around the straps that cross his back. The folds clearly respond to these straps, creating greater realism in the sculpture. The bottom half, however, has a more columnar pattern, probably because this would not have been visible behind the chariot and horses that would have stood before him. The straight lines of the drapery further add to the stillness of the figure.

His head is particularly noteworthy. He wears a ribbon around his forehead, indicative of his victory, and his hair curls around his temples and the side of his face. The top of his hair is marked in shallow relief, likely because it was not visible from ground level. Since the charioteer was a slave, the figure is not his portrait but is rather idealised and unspecified. He has additional materials that make him lifelike: bronze eyelashes and headband, and glass and stone eyes. These additions would also have demonstrated Polyzalos' wealth. The ambition to sculpt idealised figures becomes a greater priority throughout the fifth century, culminating in the works of the High Classical Period, with the Doryphoros or the sculpture on the Parthenon.

FIGURE 2.16
Delphic Charioteer.

FIGURE 2.17
Delphic Charioteer, rear view.

FIGURE 2.18
Delphic Charioteer's face.

PRESCRIBED SOURCE

Delphic Charioteer

Date: 478–474 BC

Material: bronze with copper (lips), silver (headband), glass and stone (eyes)

Height: 1.80 m

Function: victory monument

Technique: hollow-bronze technique

Original location: Delphi

Current location: Archaeological Museum in Delphi

Original or copy: original

Significance: a commemorative monument made of bronze

Artemision Zeus

The Zeus of Artemision is a life-size bronze sculpture, discovered off the coast of Artemision in Greece. It was probably being shipped to Rome when the ship capsized.

Zeus stands in a very bold pose, a significant development from previous statues, made possible only because of the lost-wax technique. Although frontal, he faces his left where he is about to throw a thunderbolt, now missing from his right arm. His left arm is extended to mark where he is about to throw his weapon. His right arm is drawn behind him, anticipating the key event. His right leg is turned frontally, resting on the ball of his foot, which makes it rather an unrealistic pose, but stresses the anticipated movement. His elongated arms and legs, as well as the open stance, mean that he occupies a large space, making him appear grand and authorial. The narrative movement of the figure reflects and reveals the characterisation of the deity. His neatly arranged beard portrays him as a mature figure.

His pose – he is about to throw a thunderbolt – demonstrates his power. His torso shows his physical strength, as his musculature is exaggerated, something that the bronze further emphasises as it glistens in the sunlight. Zeus' face is expressionless but his focus is clearly on the victim of his attack.

Diskobolos of Myron

Only Roman marble copies survive of this original bronze piece. Myron sculpted the athlete just before he throws his discus, a highly active and innovative pose which,

FIGURE 2.19
Artemision Zeus, frontal view.

FIGURE 2.20
Artemision Zeus, rear side view.

KEY INDIVIDUAL   Myron

Dates: first half of 5th century BC

Attic sculptor

Myron was famous in antiquity for sculpting a wide range of subjects, from divinities and heroes to animals, from athletes to sea-monsters. The Roman author Pliny writes the following about him:

> He seems to have been the first to extend the representation of natural truth, being more rhythmical in his art than Polykleitos and more careful over proportion; yet though he was very attentive to the bodies of his figures he does not seem to have expressed the feelings of the mind.
>
> Pliny, *Natural Histories*, 34.57–58

S & C Why do you think Myron's Discobolos statue was very popular among the Romans? Why do you think the Romans sculpted this statue in marble, rather than in bronze? What effect does the different material have on the sculpture?

PRESCRIBED SOURCE

Diskobolos

Date: 460–450 BC

Sculptor: Myron

Material: bronze (original)

Scale: lifesize

Technique: hollow-bronze technique

Function: victory monument?

Original or copy: copy (original lost)

Significance: free-standing sculpture of a discus thrower

FIGURE 2.21 PS
Roman marble copy of the Diskobolos from the Palazzo Massimo in Rome, front and rear views.

however, is entirely artificial and does not correspond to any known position. The focus instead is on potential movement and energy and on the contrast between the curved right side of the statue with the zig-zag created on the left. The mathematical ideal is the priority in this sculpture, a potential explanation for other aspects, such as naturalism being compromised. This becomes an increasing priority for sculptors of the fifth century BC, as we shall soon see with Polykleitos' Doryphoros.

The figure is most successfully viewed from the front where his muscular torso is also visible. Neither the side views nor the back view demonstrate the power and skill that Myron intends, though they do demonstrate a new interest in the height of the figure. Unlike previous sculptures, which stood upright and sought to demonstrate a sense of power and presence, the athlete is crouched down, focused on his sport, through which he hopes to gain victory and honour.

FIGURE 2.22
Roman marble copy of the Diskobolos from the Palazzo Massimo in Rome, side view.

PS

ACTIVITY

Do you think the Diskobolos would have looked better in bronze than it does in marble? Explain the effect of the material on the sculpture.

Study questions

1 What characteristics does this figure suggest about Zeus?
2 Imagine you are an ancient Greek who worships Zeus regularly; how do you feel when seeing this statue?
3 To what extent do you think that sculptors of the early fifth century were only concerned with developing the poses of their figures? In your answer refer to the musculature and facial features, as well as the poses.

HIGH CLASSICAL PERIOD

Doryphoros of Polykleitos

Doryphoros means 'spear-bearer' in Greek. This name merely identifies and describes the statue, rather than giving insight into its aims or character. The original was in bronze but only Roman marble copies survive. This standing male nude retains the suggestion of movement through the left leg, which rests on the ball of the foot, placed slightly behind his right leg. The figure is caught between standing and walking. It creates a tension between movement, or potential movement, and stillness.

KEY INDIVIDUAL   Polykleitos

Dates: *c.* 480 to end of 5th century BC

Sculptor

Polykleitos mostly worked in Argos in the Peloponnese, a rich city that held a significantly high status. Polykleitos is one of the most famous ancient Greek sculptors of the Classical Period. Pliny the Elder, a later Roman author who wrote about art and sculpture, stated that Polykleitos' lost sculpture of the 'Boys Playing Knucklebones' was 'generally considered to be the most perfect work of art in existence'.

Polykleitos' sculptures became famous because of the deep interest he had in portraying human anatomy. He prioritised this over the depiction of drapery, which is better achieved in marble. He developed a theory of mathematical proportions, the so-called Canon, whose aim was not to explain the statue, but to depict the *kalos* (the *beautiful*) or the *eu* (the *good* or the *perfect*). He believed that this was achieved through *symmetria*, a proportionality of all parts of the body. This is best seen in his Doryphoros, the spear-bearer.

The statue is enlivened by a series of contrasts, a balance of opposites in the pose, which is known as **contrapposto**. The figure stands with most of its weight on one foot so that its shoulders and arms drop slightly. A contrast and balance is hereby created between one tense leg and a tense arm, with the relaxed leg and arm on the opposite side. In the case of the Doryphoros, the lowered right shoulder contrasts with the heightened left, while the straight right leg balances the bent, relaxed left leg. Likewise, the lowered and straight right arm contrasts with the bent left arm that would have held a spear.

The Doryphoros marks a significant development in the depiction of standing male nudes. There are four key developments:

1. Unlike the previous sculptures, the relaxed leg is now moved back slightly so that it looks like the figure is between walking and standing.
2. The upper body is less severe and tense, causing the shoulders to incline.
3. There is greater correspondence between the torso and the limbs, creating the series of contrasts mentioned above. This mathematical balance of opposites developed a notion of harmony within the figure, an idea we already considered with Myron's Diskobolos. Due to the interest in proportions, however, the body almost appears to have been formed in sections, dividing the head from the torso and the torso from the legs.
4. The side views are realistic and animated in their individual ways, granting attention and interest beyond the front and back view. This is a significant development in the creation of sculptures intended to be viewed from all angles.

A key limitation of the sculpture is that the figure's head appears to be more youthful than its body. The face is so idealised that it is devoid of any expression or even life. This suggests that Polykleitos' focus was on the body.

It is unclear who the Doryphoros is meant to represent, if anyone at all. He has been identified as Achilles and Patroclus, both heroes from the Trojan War.

> **contrapposto** literally, counter-pose: the figure's shoulders and hips are angled in different directions because its weight is on one foot

PRESCRIBED SOURCE

Doryphoros of Polykleitos

Date: *c.* 440 BC

Material: bronze (original)

Scale: lifesize

Technique: hollow-bronze technique

Function: victory monument?

Original or copy: copy

Significance: free-standing sculpture of the spear-bearer, which shows the first example of contrapposto and Polykleitos' canon

ACTIVITY

Print out a picture of the Doryphoros and draw on it all the contrasts described. Then, in a different colour, annotate it with all the developments it has made from previous standing male figures.

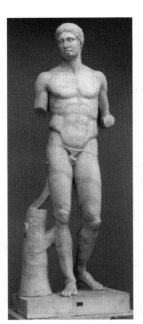
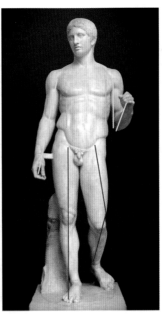

FIGURE 2.23
Roman marble copy of the Doryphoros.

FIGURE 2.24
The Doryphoros, with lines showing the contrapposto.

ACTIVITY

Try standing like the Doryphoros; is it a comfortable stance? Why do you think Polykleitos has chosen it?

MODERN SCHOLARSHIP

In his *Archaic and Classical Greek Art,* Robin Osborne argues that 'we no longer look on a "real man": we cannot square the over-developed architectural musculature with the clear skin of the face; we know we look at a construct . . . The personal is no longer on the sculptural agenda.' Do you agree?

wet drapery technique used from the mid-fifth century BC onwards for female figures only, particularly Aphrodite, minor goddesses or nymphs. The drapery is so thin that it clings tightly to the figure's body, as though wet, emphasising attractiveness and sexuality, or denoting movement or flight, as the wind forces the garment to cling to the body

LATE CLASSICAL PERIOD

Aphrodite of the Agora

This over life-size marble sculpture has been identified as Aphrodite, the goddess of love and beauty, by her alluring pose and revealing dress; other goddesses were portrayed in more modest manners. This marks a significant contrast and development from the korai, whose purpose was to denote female modesty and respectability. The statue may be one of the two Aphrodites in the sanctuary of Ares described by Pausanias, a travel-writer from the second century AD (1.8.4). Ares, the god of war, and Aphrodite had a long love-affair, so her presence by his sanctuary would not be unusual.

Aphrodite wears a chiton of extremely fine cloth and a himation is wound around her hips and thighs. The thin chiton clings to her body, revealing the shape of her breasts and body. The sculptor has evidently employed the **wet drapery technique** to emphasise Aphrodite's sexuality and enticing nature. The contrast between the thin chiton and the thick folds of the himation make the sculpture even more interesting and appealing.

PRESCRIBED SOURCE

Aphrodite of the Agora

Date: *c.* 420 BC

Material: marble

Height: 1.83 m

Function: female deity

Original location: Agora in Athens

Current location: Agora Museum in Athens

Original or copy: original

Significance: free-standing sculpture of the goddess Aphrodite, showing the wet-drapery technique

FIGURE 2.25
Aphrodite of the Agora, front and side views.

The himation's position around her waist draws extra attention to this area, emphasising her hips. This is further denoted by the pose, which pushes the right hip outwards. This stance, which has clear contrapposto, is further reminiscent of the Doryphoros' pose as the left leg is similarly slightly behind the right, again capturing an otherwise uncomfortable moment between movement and stillness.

Eirene and Ploutos by Kephisodotos

The original bronze Eirene and Ploutos by Kephisodotus has not survived, but it is well known through literary references and Roman marble copies. Pausanias (1.8.2) recorded that the sculpture stood in the Athenian agora, the market place where social, political and economic activities took place. The statue was also depicted on Attic coins from the Roman imperial period, indicative of how famous and significant it was in the Ancient world. Copies of the statue measure 2.07 metres high.

The statue is an allegory. Eirene, a personification of Peace, is shown as a matronly figure who cradles the baby Ploutos, a personification of Wealth. The message behind the sculpture is that wealth is reliant on peace and that peace breeds and nurtures wealth. This political and economic message was likely created to coincide with the foundation of a cult of Eirene in 374 BC, when peace was made between Athens and Sparta after a series of wars, or in 371 BC when peace was signed between all Greeks. Since an image of the statue appears on a Panathenaic amphora of 360/359 BC, a prize for athletes in the quadrennial Athenian games, it must have been erected by then.

The sculpture depicts a standing woman holding an infant in her left arm and likely a now-missing staff in her right. In certain Roman copies she is also holding an oinochoe, a wine jug, in her left hand, which Ploutos is also touching with his left hand. She wears a peplos with a himation draped over her shoulders, both marking her as respectable and modest. While the shapes of her breasts and right leg are visible through the drapery, the loose fit suggests that her sexuality is not the focus of the sculpture. The simple, heavy enveloping drapery reflects the dignity of the figure. There is a realistic contrast between the curved horizontal folds across her torso and the vertical folds that cover her legs. She stands with weight on her left leg and there is a distinction between her raised right arm and her lowered left. Her hair is arranged around her forehead, kept in place by a fillet, and falls naturally in deep curls around her shoulders. She would also have worn earrings.

MODERN SCHOLARSHIP

Read the article 'Hellenistic Free-standing Sculpture from the Agora, Part I: Aphrodite' by Andrew Stewart in *Hesperia*, 81, 2012, pp. 267–342. Stewart argues for a later date.

KEY INDIVIDUAL

Kephisodotos

Dates: unknown, active *c.* 400–360 BC

Greek sculptor

Father or uncle of the famous sculptor Praxiteles.

FIGURE 2.26
Roman marble copy of Eirene and Ploutos in the Glyptothek, Munich.

Study questions

1 Why do you think the original sculpture was in bronze? Would the original material change your perception of the statue, and if so, how?

2 What kind of a relationship has Kephisodotos created between these two figures and how was it achieved? Consider their positions, eye contact, clothing, size and identities.

The infant Ploutos is depicted in a three-quarter view, sitting on his mother's left arm, reaching towards her face with an outstretched right hand. According to the illustration on the Panathenaic amphora, Ploutos was holding a *keras*, a horn of plenty, in his left hand, a typical attribute for Wealth.

The figures and poses are very accessible and relatable, inviting the viewer to engage more deeply with the sculpture of these gods, than they could with sculptures of gods up until this point.

Hermes and Dionysus

Praxiteles' Hermes and Dionysus is a marble group statue, showing a youthful Hermes cradling baby Dionysus in his arms. Pausanias records seeing this sculpture in the Temple of Hera at Olympia (5.17.3–4). The sculpture is now at Olympia, though some scholars argue this is a copy of the original work, which is lost.

The composition of Praxiteles' group is clearly inspired by his father's Eirene and Ploutos. Instead of a maternal scene, however, Praxiteles has created a jovial image of the trickster, god of thieves who was given charge of Dionysus while still a baby. Here, Hermes holds Dionysus in his left arm, while in his right he likely dangled grapes above Dionysus' head, teasing him. Although this right arm is missing, scholars have re-constructed the statue to show the close relationship between the two figures. Not only does holding grapes show how well Hermes knew the god of wine, but also shows his mocking nature as he holds it tantalisingly out of Dionysus' reach. What's more, Hermes looks down at the baby who is reaching out to the grapes and looking directly at them, to see how his teasing is affecting Dionysus. This very relaxed scene therefore shows the gods not as the all-powerful, unapproachable figures that we see elsewhere, but much more humanised and accessible, caught in a private moment that we might relate to ourselves.

Hermes and Dionysus

Date: c. 340 BC

Sculptor: Praxiteles

Material: marble

Height: 2.11 m

Function: two male deities

Original location: Temple of Hera, Olympia

Current location: Archaeological Museum at Olympia

Original or copy: original

Significance: group sculpture of Dionysus and Hermes, showing the Praxitelean S-curve

FIGURE 2.28
Hermes and Dionysus

Since the sculpture was made of marble, the extended left arm of Hermes that holds Dionysus requires extra support. Praxiteles has hidden this by using drapery. This allusion to clothing accentuates Hermes' nudity, highlighting his divine form, and creates a setting for the scene. Praxiteles has hereby exploited the weakness of marble for his own narrative benefit. The use of marble further enables this scene between two gods to appear relatable and approachable for a mortal viewer. This marks a significant development from images such as Poseidon of Artemisium, where the gods appear distant, powerful and threatening.

Aphrodite of Knidos by Praxiteles

Aphrodite of Knidos is another lost Praxitelean sculpture that only survives through Roman copies. The original marble sculpture was commissioned by the people of Kos, an island in the Aegean Sea, but they found her nudity to be too shocking and inappropriate and requested another statue to be made; the people of Knidos, a city on western Asia-Minor, modern Turkey, took it instead.

The heights differ but the tallest is 2.04 metres. Aphrodite stands nude, her hair tied in a bun, either before or after bathing. Her cult-title at Knidos was *Euploia*, fair voyage. This likely refers to a passage from the Homeric Hymn to Aphrodite (lines 60–66), where her bathing and anointing by the three Graces is described before she goes to Troy. The position of her head, downwards and slightly tilted to the left, suggests that she has been spotted by an onlooker and she is quickly attempting to cover herself up, her right arm concealing her crotch, which she also tries to hide with her inwardly bent right leg, while

EXPLORE FURTHER

Read Pliny's description of the Knidian Aphrodite and its contemporary reception in *Natural Histories*, 36.20–21.

FIGURE 2.29
Aphrodite of Knidos.

PRESCRIBED SOURCE

Aphrodite of Knidos

Date: *c.* 340 BC

Sculptor: Praxiteles

Material: marble

Scale: over life-size

Function: female deity

Original location: Knidos

Original or copy: copy

Significance: first free-
standing image of
a nude female and
an example of
contrapposto used for
a female figure

---

her left hand grabs a garment that was resting on top of a *hydria*, a water-carrying vessel. Her quick movements contrast with the still life of the drapery. Although her intention is to protect her modesty as her privacy has been intruded, Praxiteles is also playing on her role as goddess of beauty and sex, as her right hand draws attention to her pubic area, while her extended left hand leaves her breasts exposed.

Praxiteles appears to be mocking the goddess as he is adapting a familiar type of myth. Most famously the myth of Artemis and Actaeon shows what happens when a mortal intrudes on a goddess bathing: Actaeon was punished by having his own hunting-dogs attack and kill him. In this case, however, Praxiteles has reversed the roles; instead of the intruding mortal being punished, the goddess herself suffers a bad fate as she is forever cast in marble, unable to prevent others from seeing her body. Moreover, the viewer has been involved in this narrative, forcing us to participate in this uneasy relationship with the goddess.

The choice of marble was entirely appropriate for this sculpture because it accentuates her softness and vulnerability as she is caught naked. Gilding was probably used for her hair, jewellery and for the hydria, and her cloak was probably painted. These colours would enliven the statue further and also contrast with her pure skin. Aphrodite's anatomy is not entirely accurate. Her hips are rather broad compared to her shoulders, her breasts seem rather small for her height and the head is relatively small. Her pose, however, is reflective of Praxiteles' innovative style as he took the contrapposto even further and created an S-curve through his figures.

Although it is uncertain whether this applied to the original sculpture, we know that in the Hellenistic period, a circular structure was set up around the sculpture so that it could be admired from all angles. It was set outside, in a garden, further enhancing its beauty.

> **Study question**
> Do you think Praxiteles was insulting Aphrodite by this statue? Was he claiming that she is powerless or was the implied mythology behind it enough to reinforce her authority over mortals?

S & C Ancient sources praised the Knidian Aphrodite. Pliny writes about a man who was overcome with love for the statue (*Natural Histories*, 36.21). Pseudo-Lucian records that 'she is a most beautiful statue . . . smiling just a little haughty smile . . . So great was the power of the craftsman's art that the hard unyielding marble has done justice to every limb' (*Amores*, 13–14).

Do you agree with these responses to the statue? If not, explain your thoughts and try to consider why the ancient Greeks did respond in this way to them.

Read Aphrodite's opening speech in Euripides' *Hippolytus* (lines 1–57), where she explains how she will punish a mortal who insults and rejects her.

Do you think Praxiteles' statue captures the powerful and threatening nature of the goddess? Do you think that was his intention?

Antikytheran Youth

The Antikytheran Youth was uncovered along with a number of other bronze artefacts off the coast of Antikythera, an island in the Aegean. It was likely being transported from Greece to Rome in the first century BC when the shipwreck occurred. This reflects the contemporary Roman favour for Greek sculptures.

The Youth stands, resting his weight on his right leg, holding out his right arm, which held a now-missing object. This extended arm invites the viewer to engage with the statue and share in the figure's look. His tilted head and eyes, which still remain, focus on the object, giving it further significance. His face shows a development from the idealised into the individualised. His thoughtful gaze, full lips and tousled hair show features that become common in the Hellenistic Period, particularly with the statues of Lysippos and the images of Alexander the Great.

There are two interpretations for whom this youth might depict: Perseus, the Gorgon-slayer, and Paris, the Trojan Prince who had to judge who was the most beautiful between Hera, Aphrodite and Athena. If it is Perseus, then his right hand would have held the head of the Gorgon Medusa, whom he had slain with the help of Athena. Legend had it that whoever looked on her head, which was famously hideous and had snakes instead of hair, would turn into stone. It is therefore a wonder that Perseus is looking at the head, though perhaps because it was severed, it no longer held that power. Perseus is an attractive identification as the statue's emphatically muscular physique suits the hero who was

PRESCRIBED SOURCE

Antikytheran Youth

Date: *c.* 340 BC

Material: bronze

Height: 1.94 m

Protagonist: either Perseus or Paris

Original location: off Antikythera

Current Location: National Museum at Athens

Original or copy: original

Significance: free-standing bronze sculpture depicting either Perseus or Paris

---

FIGURE 2.30
Antikytheran youth, front and side views.

renowned for heroic feats. The stocky body, with its muscular torso and exaggerated abdominal muscles, complements the image of a strong hero.

The second interpretation is Paris, about to give the now-missing golden apple to Aphrodite, the goddess of beauty. This identification better suits the shape of his right hand, whose fingers are positioned as if curved around a small circular object. His thoughtful and solemn gaze upon the apple might signify the severity of his decision and foreshadow the future suffering that would arise as a result of it. On the other hand, Paris was often characterised as a relative weakling, lacking the strength and bravery of a front-line soldier, but rather relying on his arrows. This would contrast with the muscular physique of the Antikytheran Youth.

Regardless of identity, the youth is a remarkable bronze figure. Not only has the body survived extremely well, but even his eyes are still intact. They demonstrate how lifelike bronze sculptures were.

Apoxyomenos by Lysippos

Lysippos' Apoxyomenos (the man scraping himself) is renowned for three main reasons:

1. The choice to sculpt an everyday moment.
2. Breaking the frontal plane by extending the right arm straight in front of him.
3. Using an innovative approach to depicting the male figure and face.

The figure in the statue is shown scraping the oil off his body. Athletes would cover themselves in oil before partaking in events such as wrestling to make it difficult for their opponents to grab onto them. After exercise, they used a *strigil*, a metal tool to scrape oil, sweat and dust off their bodies. This was not a glamorous or heroic part of an athlete's life and contrasts with previous sculptures, which depict an athlete, either in the midst of his event, or afterwards, when they have been crowned the victor. Lysippos is therefore innovative in his choice of narrative, opting for an everyday action that many viewers would be able to relate to.

Lysippos' decision to extend the figure's right arm directly in front of his body breaks the frontal plane. The viewer is required to walk all the way around the sculpture in order to understand it, as there is no single viewpoint where something is not hidden. While previous sculptures had encouraged the viewer to walk around, so that the sculpture could be admired from multiple angles, it was never because a part of the statue was obscured. With Lysippos' sculpture, the viewer cannot see the whole statue from a single viewpoint. This innovation forces the viewer to engage with the sculpture.

Finally, the proportions and facial features of the figure mark a third innovation. Unlike Polykleitos' canon, which stresses balance in the figure, Lysippos' youth has slightly elongated legs and a slenderer physique. This probably suits his role as an athlete quite well. The face is also far more personalised, with tousled hair and frown lines on the forehead.

FIGURE 2.31
Roman marble copy of the Apoxyomenos, front and side views.

PRESCRIBED SOURCE

Apoxyomenos ('man scraping himself')

Date: *c.* 330 BC

Sculptor: Lysippos

Material: bronze (original)

Scale: over life-size

Function: victory monument?

Original or copy: copy

Significance: an example of a free-standing sculpture portraying an everyday action. It is innovative for breaking the frontal plane

---

TOPIC REVIEW

These questions should draw on your knowledge of the whole topic, so think carefully about the different things you have learned (check the Topic Overview on pp. 106–107).

1. What were the uses of free-standing sculptures?
2. How successfully did sculptors tell a narrative through their free-standing sculptures?
3. How effectively was bronze and marble used in free-standing sculptures?
4. To what extent did sculptures of the male nude develop more as a result of the development of sculptor's techniques, than of differing narrative contexts?
5. To what extent is marble a more effective material than bronze for sculpting statues? Answer with reference to both male and female figures.
6. How much can we learn about ancient Greek society from studying these sculptures? Consider their attitudes to the gods, men and women, the role of athletic competitions, and the significance of sculptors and sculpture in society.

Further Reading

Osborne, R. (1998) *Archaic and Classical Greek Art.* Oxford: Oxford University Press

Spivey, N. 1996) *Understanding Greek Sculpture.* London: Thames and Hudson Ltd

Spivey, N. (2013) *Greek Sculpture.* Cambridge: Cambridge University Press

Stewart, A. (1993) *Greek Sculpture: Exploration.* New Haven: Yale University Press

Woodford, S. (1997) *An Introduction to Greek Art.* London: Gerald Duckworth and Co Ltd, pp. 38–56, 75–90, 128–133, 153–155, 164–169

PRACTICE QUESTIONS

Source A

1. Identify this sculpture. [1]

2. Do you think that bronze was used effectively in this sculpture? Explain your answer. [10]

2.3 Architectural Sculpture

Function

- Purpose and positioning of different types of architectural sculpture including:
  - metopes, Ionic friezes and pediments

Materials

- Effects of different types of materials, including:
  - limestone and marble in architectural sculpture.
- Advantages and limitations of different materials
- Usefulness and limitations of damaged and/or reconstructed pieces

Stylistic features and development

- Unity of theme and scale in architectural sculpture

Composition

- Dominant verticals, horizontals and diagonals
- Pose
- Portrayal of anatomy and physical form
- Portrayal of movement
- Portrayal of emotion

Subject matter

- Mythology, including reflection of everyday life in mythological scenes
- Themes in architectural sculpture, including
  - Medusa, Centauromachy, Trojan War

The following prescribed sources are covered in this topic:

- **Archaic Period**
  - Pediment of the Temple of Artemis, Corcyra
  - Metopes of Temple C, Selinus
  - Ionic Frieze of the Siphnian Treasury, Delphi
  - West Pediment of the Temple of Aphaia, Aegina

- **Early Classical Period**
  - o East Pediment of the Temple of Aphaia, Aegina
  - o Temple of Zeus, Olympia (pediments; metopes (Augean Stables, Cretan Bull, Garden of the Hesperides))

- **High Classical Period**
  - o The Parthenon, Athens: pediments, Ionic frieze, metopes (XXVI, XXVII, XXVIII)

- **Late Classical Period**
  - o Ionic Frieze of the Temple of Apollo, Bassae

Don't forget that you will be given credit in the exam if you study extra sources and make relevant use of them in your answers.

Some of the most beautiful and famous Greek statues were originally part of a bigger architectural masterpiece. This topic examines a series of such architectural sculptures, from 600 to 300 BC and from buildings of both the Doric and Ionic orders. They come from all over the Greek mainland and give us a strong understanding of how cherished and significant the decoration of architecture was in the ancient Greek world.

THE CONTEXT FOR ARCHITECTURAL SCULPTURE

Ancient Greek architecture spanned a variety of different buildings: from temples to fountains, from houses to palaces, or from shops to political buildings. Unlike several

FIGURE 2.32
Doric and Ionic architecture.

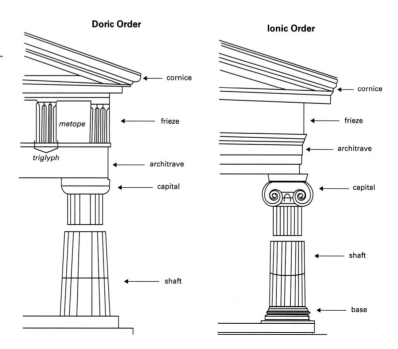

modern religions, rituals such as sacrifices and prayers took place around an altar, often located outside a temple, dedicated to a specific deity. Temples, therefore, were not traditionally the location for religious practices, but rather housed sacred cult statues of the deity to whom the temple was dedicated. They also frequently housed votive offerings, dedications made to the god. Since worship took place outdoors, temples were predominantly decorated on their exterior, as that was visible to the public. Two main areas were decorated: the **pediment** and the **frieze**.

As we shall see, architectural sculpture differed between buildings. Architects and sculptors had the freedom to decorate their temples in a variety of ways. Nevertheless, there are some common themes: myths associated with the deity to whom the temple is dedicated, or the land where the temple is located; and myths symbolising the victory of civilisation over barbarity, such as the Trojan War, the Gigantomachy, the Centauromachy and the Amazonomachy. In the fifth century BC, when these myths were frequently depicted in sculptures and on vases, they came to symbolise the Greek victory against the invading Persians. These myths are often shown with a presiding deity, implying that the gods are securing human society.

The vast majority of temples were adorned with myths, illustrating stories about gods and/or heroes. Only one temple, the Parthenon, breaks this convention and shows an event in which contemporaries took part: the Panathenaic Festival in honour of Athena.

> **pediment** (pl. **pediments**) the triangular-shaped gable end of the roof at the front and back of a Greek temple, usually facing east and west
>
> **frieze** (pl. **friezes**) a rectangular band that wraps around all four sides of the temple

KEY EVENTS

Trojan War

This war is most famously described in Homer's *Iliad*. It was between the Achaeans, or Greeks, and the Trojans, who lived in north-west Asia Minor, modern-day Turkey. The Greeks were victorious and destroyed King Priam's city of Troy.

Gigantomachy

This battle was between the Olympian gods and the Giants, for authority and power over the world. The gods won.

Centauromachy

This was fought between the Centaurs, mythical creatures that are part-man, part-horse, and the Lapiths, humans from Thessaly, in the North-East of Greece. The king of the Lapiths was hosting a wedding party for his daughter and the Centaurs, who in some versions were invited and in others were not, drank too much and attempted to rape the bride and other female guests. A battle ensued and the Athenian hero Theseus played a crucial role in the Lapiths' victory.

Amazonomachy

This was fought between the Greeks and the Amazons, a tribe of warrior women.

in the round sculptures that are not attached to anything else, but are free-standing

relief sculptures attached to a background surface; if in low relief, they project only slightly from this background surface, but if in high relief, they project at least half or more of their natural circumference from the background

It is easy to forget that architectural sculptures would have appeared very lifelike to a contemporary audience. Firstly, they would have been painted. Traces of bright colours, in particular blues and reds, have been found on the sculptures and this would have enlivened them significantly. Moreover, they were either sculpted **in the round**, or in **relief**, both of which gave them a three-dimensional effect that would have made the sculptures seem lifelike.

Additional materials, such as bronze and gold, were added to make the sculptures more engaging. They would have glistened in the sunshine and would have further attracted the eyes of onlookers.

THE ARCHAIC PERIOD

Pediment of the Temple of Artemis, Corcyra

The Temple of Artemis, goddess of hunting and unmarried maidens, was built around 580 BC on the Greek island of Corfu, in a city called Corcyra. This Archaic-Period Doric temple is believed to have been the first of its order built entirely of stone (earlier temples were constructed from wood or a mixture of the two).

The centre of the pediment is occupied by Medusa, almost three metres tall. Medusa was a gorgon, a mythical female monster, with wings and snakes in her hair.

PRESCRIBED SOURCE

Pediment of the Temple of Artemis, Corcyra

Date: *c.* 580 BC

Material: limestone

Central narrative: Medusa

Current location: Archaeological Museum of Corfu

Significance: early archaic architectural sculpture depicting a variety of myths on one pediment

> **EXPLORE FURTHER**   **Perseus and Medusa**
>
> Medusa features in a popular myth with Perseus, who was tasked with going to slay her. The challenge for the hero was that anyone who looked at Medusa's face turned into stone. With the help of Athena, the hero used the reflection of his shield to see where Medusa was and cut off her head without looking directly at it.
>
> You can read the full myth in the Roman poet Ovid's *Metamorphoses* (4.770).

FIGURE 2.33
Pediment of the Temple of Artemis, Corcyra.

FIGURE 2.34 PS
Medusa figure at the centre of the Pediment of the Temple of Artemis at Corcyra.

Medusa is depicted facing ahead. She is probably running away from Perseus, though he is not featured on the pediment. She wears a belt made of two intertwined snakes, whose heads face one another. There are two further snakes on either side of her torso, and two more coming out either side of her hair. Although literature describes Medusa with snakes instead of hair, artistic depictions portray her with both hair and snakes. Snakes represent rebirth, but also reflect Medusa's monstrous and demonic side, and suggest danger and threat.

ACTIVITY

Compare the sculpture of Medusa to the Archaic free-standing sculptures we have studied on pp. 109–117. List the Archaic features you can spot.

The choice of Medusa in such a prominent position was not unusual. Her purpose was to act as an apotropaic spirit, to ward off evil and, in doing so, protect the temple. The six snakes that adorn her, likewise function to prevent malice entering the temple.

Medusa is likely to have been depicted alongside her children, Pegasus and Khrysaor. The sculpture of Pegasus has not survived beyond one of his forelegs that rests affectionately on his mother's arm, but the head, torso and hips of Khrysaor do remain. Although both children were born from her blood after Perseus decapitated her, the artist chose to depict them all together, hereby playing with chronology and showing consecutive scenes at once. Thus, the artist can depict both the middle part of the myth, when Medusa is being chased, as well as the end, when she has been killed and her children are born from her neck. Khrysaor is shown in a significantly smaller scale to his mother, perhaps to maintain focus on her as the central, apotropaic figure. It might also be a result of the awkward shape of the pediment.

On either side of Pegasus and Khrysaor, are sculpted two panthers. Like Medusa and the snakes, these exotic and dangerous animals act as guardians of the temple. The panthers are decorated with a number of concentric circles, representing their impressive spots. Although their bodies face inwards towards Medusa, their faces look out towards onlookers. In arranging the panthers in a crouching position, the sculptures both occupy the whole available space effectively, and symmetrically frame the central figure.

FIGURE 2.35
Close-up of seated figure on the left side of the pediment of the Temple of Artemis at Corcyra.

FIGURE 2.36
Close-up of the fighting figures on the right side of the pediment of the Temple of Artemis at Corcyra.

On the left side of the pediment, behind the panther, are two figures. The figure furthest to the left appears to be that of a fallen, wounded warrior. The second is seated in profile, facing the centre of the pediment. He has been interpreted as King Priam of Troy. If this is the case, the fallen figure in the corner may represent a fallen Trojan warrior. The seated figure may, however, represent either Rhea, a Titan daughter of the Earth Goddess Ge, or Cronus, the father of Zeus, in which case the scene might represent part of the Gigantomachy, the battle between the gods and giants. Throughout the sculptures, we can see the change in size and scale of the figures to accommodate the triangular shape.

On the right side of the pediment two figures are shown fighting. The figure nearest to the panther is likely to be Zeus, as he wields a thunderbolt against his opponent. The other figure tries to hold off his attacker with both hands. This could also therefore depict a scene from the Gigantomachy, the battle between the gods and the giants. Symmetry was a common feature of Archaic architectural decoration. Given this, it is likely that there was another fallen warrior on the right corner of the pediment also. The pediment might therefore depict three individual myths, all united in narrative of civilisation overcoming barbarity.

Metopes of Temple C, Selinus

Selinus was an Ancient Greek colony in Sicily, modern-day Trapani. Temple C was an Archaic Doric temple made and sculpted from local limestone, built between 575 and 550 BC. The temple, which has been partially rebuilt, was decorated with a number of architectural sculptures on both the pediments and on the **metopes**. The central space of the pediment was occupied by an enormous gorgon head, similar to that of Medusa on the Temple of Artemis at Corcyra. The metopes depict snapshots of individual myths, all of which represent the victory of civilisation over barbarity. We are studying one of the three fully surviving metopes; there were originally ten fully sculpted metopes on the façade of the temple.

metope (pl. **metopes**) a square-shaped panel decorated with relief sculpture (where the sculpture remains attached to the background). These panels would decorate the space between the bottom of the roof and the tops of the columns of a Greek temple

triglyph (pl. **triglyphs**) a series of three vertical grooves separating metopes

PRESCRIBED SOURCE

Metopes of Temple C, Selinus

Date: 575–550 BC

Material: Limestone

Height: 1.47 m **PS**

Narratives: Herakles and the Kerkopes

Current location: Archaeological Museum of Palermo

Significance: metope depicting Herakles and the Kerkopes

FIGURE 2.37
Temple C at Selinus.

Herakles (Hercules) and the Kerkopes

This metope represents a lesser–known myth associated with Herakles and is not one of his twelve labours. It is not, however, unique to this temple but is seen on a metope from the Archaic Heraion at Foce del Sele in Poseidonia, dating to 570–560 BC.

The metope on Temple C shows the central moment of the myth, when Herakles has tied the Kerkopes up to a pole and is walking along with it resting on his shoulders. The bonds are visible around their ankles and on the arms of the right Kerkopes; this is a nice detail that the sculptor has chosen to include to accurately narrate the story.

EXPLORE FURTHER   Diodorus Siculus, *Library of History*, 4.31.7

Herakles and the Kerkopes
Herakles once fell asleep and two mischievous, forest creatures, known as Kerkopes, stole his weapons. When Herakles woke up and realised what had happened, he caught them and, to punish them, tied them upside down to a pole and carried this pole on his shoulders. The Kerkopes, who could see Herakles' hairy bottom from this vantage point, started to laugh. When Herakles asked them why they were laughing, they explained and Herakles himself joined in the laughter. He then untied them and let them go.

FIGURE 2.38
Herakles and the Kerkopes.

There are numerous features of the style and composition that reflect the Archaic Period. Herakles' face and torso are frontal, and his body is twisted at the waist somewhat unnaturally so that his hips and legs are in side view. This twist is similar to that of Medusa in the centre of the Pediment on the Temple of Artemis at Corcyra, as the sculptors have not yet mastered the subtle transitions of rotating sideways.

The symmetrical composition of the metope is also reflective of the Archaic Period. The Kerkopes' mirror arrangement frames the central figure of Herakles, in the same way the panthers framed Medusa on the pediment at Corcyra. Rather than it being merely a compositional preference, however, the nature of the Kerkopes as twins makes this arrangement appropriate. The metope is dominated by vertical lines, created through the hanging bodies of the Kerkopes and Herakles' torso. The triangular shape created by Herakles' walking legs provides some diversity. By hanging the Kerkopes upside down, as the myth dictates, and by having Herakles striding forth, his legs apart, the sculptor has maximised the space available on the rectangular metope.

Within the stylistic and compositional trends of the Archaic period, the sculptor has successfully managed to narrate the myth. The choices about depiction and arrangement both fully complement the narrative and present the onlooker with an identifiable moment in a specific myth.

Ionic Frieze of the Siphnian Treasury, Delphi

The Siphnian Treasury at Delphi was built around 525 BC. Located along the Sacred Way to the Temple of Apollo at Delphi, this Archaic building would have been seen and doubtless admired by all pilgrims who came to this oracular site. The treasury was the first religious structure made entirely of marble, and served to house dedications made by the island of Siphnos. Although it no longer remains, the treasury would have been particularly eye-catching because it had two **Caryatids** acting as columns along the front.

The Ionic frieze wrapped around all four sides of the treasury. Each side depicted a different myth: the Judgement of Paris (west); an abduction, perhaps Helen or Persephone (south); Greeks fighting Trojans, with the Gods in council (east); and the Gigantomachy (north). On all four sides, the sculptors have maximised the use of the continuous frieze in two main ways; firstly, they have exploited the ability to show more than one aspect or

Caryatid clothed female figures used in architecture in place of columns

Ionic Frieze of the Siphnian Treasury, Delphi

Date: *c.* 525 BC

Material: marble

Narratives: Gigantomachy (north), Trojan War (east), Abduction Scene (south), Judgement of Paris (west)

Current location: Delphi Archaeological Museum

Significance: Ionic frieze depicting four different myths on each of the sides of the treasury

FIGURE 2.39
Reconstruction of the Siphnian Treasury at Delphi.

Study question
Bearing in mind that these architectural sculptures were set up high on a building and that the small size of the frieze would have made its visibility even more difficult, why do you think sculptors put such effort and details into their work?

EXPLORE FURTHER

Herodotus III.57 describes the Siphnians:

. . . the Siphnians were at this time very prosperous and the richest of the islanders, because of the gold and silver mines on the island. They were so wealthy that the treasure dedicated by them at Delphi, which is as rich as any there, was made from a tenth of their income; and they divided among themselves each year's income.

Now when they were putting together the treasure they inquired of the oracle if their present prosperity was likely to last long; whereupon the priestess gave them this answer:

"When the prytaneum on Siphnus becomes white
And white-browed the market, then indeed a shrewd man is wanted
Beware a wooden force and a red herald."

At this time the market–place and town–hall of Siphnus were adorned with Parian marble.

part of a myth. Secondly, they have sculpted numerous figures, overlapping one another, to reflect the action of the narratives.

East: the Trojan War

The Trojan War was depicted on the east side of the Treasury. The mortal scene portrayed here shows groups of soldiers, dueling over the dead body of a warrior. The Trojans are on the left and the Achaeans are on the right. On both sides, the warriors are in mid-action, striding forwards. The back foot of each rests only on the ball, suggesting movement, and

FIGURE 2.40
East frieze of the
Siphnian Treasury,
depicting the Trojan War.

their torsos lean forwards, ready to attack. The scene is given depth by the figures overlapping one another. The figures are all armed with breastplates, helmets and shields, and wear short skirts that show their muscular thighs. There are holes for where bronze attachments would have been fitted, glistening in the sunshine to enliven the scene.

The left side of the frieze depicts the gods holding an assembly. As Homer's *Iliad* describes, the gods played a key role throughout the war. Trojan supporters, such as Ares, Aphrodite and Apollo are all depicted together, making dramatic gestures with their hands and interacting with one another. They are evidently highly engaged with the mortal events. Their divine status is cleverly distinguished through their size: the gods are shown as larger than the mortals because, despite being seated, they occupy the full height of the frieze. The mortals, on the other hand, occupy the space by standing. This subtle way of differentiating between the two was later used on the Parthenon Frieze for exactly the same purpose.

ACTIVITY

Has the sculptor created individual figures in this scene or do you think they are merely repetitions of one another? Refer to specific figures from the frieze to support your argument.

FIGURE 2.41
East frieze of the
Siphnian Treasury,
depicting seated gods.

143

North: the Gigantomachy

This side was visible to pilgrims walking up the Sacred Way to the oracle. It is perhaps not coincidental that as they walked to consult their god Apollo, they were faced with the story that explains why these gods were being worshipped, instead of the Titans.

The war between the gods and the giants was another myth typically chosen to adorn architecture, as it too symbolised the victory of civilisation and order over barbarity, chaos and anarchy. On one side of the frieze, the gods are shown attacking from the left with spears, swords and arrows. Individual gods are identifiable, such as Hephaistos, Demeter, Herakles, Artemis, Apollo and Athena. On the other side, the giants are shown heavily armed with helmets, breastplates, shields and greaves.

FIGURE 2.42
North frieze of the Siphnian Treasury, depicting the Gigantomachy.

West: the Judgement of Paris

While this frieze has not survived beyond a few relief figures, it seems as though it showed the Judgement of Paris.

FIGURE 2.43
West frieze of the Siphnian Treasury, depicting a goddess stepping down from a chariot.

FIGURE 2.44
West frieze of the
Siphnian Treasury,
depicting Hermes leading
a chariot.

EXPLORE FURTHER

The Judgement of Paris
You can read about this
myth in Ovid's *Heroides*,
16.51ff, and in Pausanias
5.19.5.

This choice of myth functions as a nice counterpart to the decoration of the east side of the treasury, which shows the Trojan War. This relationship between the two friezes indicates that the sculptors considered the overall effect of the sculptural decoration.

The first figure is Athena, shown on a winged chariot, with Hermes acting as her charioteer. Aphrodite is also shown stepping off her chariot, perhaps anticipating her receipt of the golden apple. It is likely that Hera was also shown on a chariot, although this has not survived.

Study question
Compare all four sides
of the frieze. Bearing
in mind the differing
amounts of surviving
sculpture, why do you
think some scenes are
more action-packed than
others? What do you
think the overall effect
of the frieze is on the
decoration of the
building?

South: an abduction scene

As with the west frieze, the majority of this scene is missing. The surviving fragments depict lively horses. This may suggest it shows the abduction of Persephone by Hades into the Underworld, or the abduction of Helen by Theseus.

FIGURE 2.45
South frieze of the
Siphnian Treasury,
depicting an abduction
scene.

Pediments of the Temple of Aphaia, Aegina

PRESCRIBED SOURCE

West pediment of the Temple of Aphaia, Aegina

Date: 510–500 BC

Material: limestone

Narrative: second sack of Troy with Paris and Ajax

Current location: Glyptothek, Munich

Significance: late Archaic depiction of the second sack of Troy

Aegina is an island close to Athens. In the late Archaic and early Classical times, Aegina was one of the most important, prosperous and powerful city-states in the Greek world, in part thanks to its navy. In this period, there was great competition between different city-states, and chiefly between Aegina and Athens, as they were neighbouring, naval cities. Aphaia is a local goddess, worshipped seemingly exclusively on Aegina. The Athenians later identified her both as Artemis and Athena.

The first Temple of Aphaia in Aegina was built in *c.* 570 BC, during the early Archaic Period, and it was succeeded by a second temple in the late Archaic Period. The sculptures from the west pediment were used in the first temple and are dated to the Archaic Period, whereas the sculptures from the east date to the Early Classical Period when sculptors made new decoration for their temple.

The west pediment on the Temple of Aphaia

Both pediments show the two sackings of Troy. The west pediment shows the war described in Homer's *Iliad*, with characters such as Paris and Ajax. The east pediment shows an earlier sacking of Troy by Herakles. The temple is therefore united by a common narrative. This was not an unusual choice of myth, as we saw it also on the Siphnian Treasury at Delphi and we shall see it again on the Parthenon in Athens. It was, however, also chosen to make a specific political statement. The first sack of Troy involved the hero Telamon, while the second included his son Ajax. Aegina claimed

FIGURE 2.46
Reconstruction drawing of the west pediment of the Temple of Aphaia on Aegina.

West

FIGURE 2.47
Reconstruction of the west pediment in the Glypothek Museum in Munich.

Study question
Compare the reconstructions in Figures 2.46 and 2.47. Scholars have suggested different arrangements for these figures. Which do you think is the more successful arrangement and why?

Telamon and Ajax, father and son, to be their local heroes, descended from Aiakos, the son of Zeus and the nymph Aegina, after whom the island was named. At the time these sculptures were made, however, Athens had also claimed Ajax and Telamon as their own. Both city-states, Aegina and Athens, who had been long-time rivals, were therefore competing over the heroes. The sculptor's choice to give Ajax and Telamon such prominent positions, not only in the central, tallest part of the pediment, but also directly next to the goddess Athena, was a deliberate political statement of ownership of the heroes.

The west pediment shows the second Trojan War, the one described in Homer's *Iliad*. The central apex of the pediment is occupied by Athena.

Athena stands frontally, though her legs are sideways. She wears a thick peplos and her **aegis**, and is armed with a helmet, spear and shield.

A bronze gorgon was likely attached onto her aegis, making Athena even more imposing and powerful, as it would have glistened in the sunshine. She is clearly identifiable as the warrior goddess. She stands vertically, making no gestures towards the chaotic fighting unfolding around her. She presides over the action but does not engage with it at all.

The fighting is arranged outwards around Athena. In designing the layout of the sculptures, the sculptors have utilised the potentially awkward triangular shape of the pediment to showcase a variety of poses. In doing so, a series of mini-conflicts and engagements

Study question
Why do you think the sculptor has chosen to fill the central space with a goddess? Consider the space available and the issue of scale. What does it reveal about Greek attitudes to the gods?

aegis this was often carried or worn by both Athena and Zeus, though its precise nature is unclear: it sometimes appears as a garment, worn around Athena's chest, or as a shield, and often has the head of a gorgon on it

EXPLORE FURTHER

Athena's aegis is referred to in Homer's *Iliad*:

It produced a sound as from a myriad roaring dragons and was borne by Athena in battle . . . and among them went bright-eyed Athene, holding the precious aegis which is ageless and immortal: a hundred tassels of pure gold hang fluttering from it, tight-woven each of them, and each the worth of a hundred oxen.

Homer, Iliad, 4.17

Study questions

1 Athena's pose may be interpreted in numerous ways. Perhaps it suggests that she is not on the same plain as the other warriors around her, or maybe that her presence is invisible to them. Her attendance may provide comfort for onlookers, as her support for the Greeks brought about their ultimate victory, but it may also cause concern, as she is not involving herself with their struggle. How do you respond to her pose and how do you think an ancient Greek might have responded?

2 Compare Athena's drapery with that of the Berlin Standing Goddess and Peplos Kore; how varied was the use of drapery and depiction of female figures and how can we explain it?

S & C Compare this scene with passages from Homer's *Iliad*, e.g. 5.1–8 (helps Diomedes); 17.543–574 (urges on the Achaians) and 21.391–433 (injures Ares and Aphrodite). Do you think the image of Athena here matches that of Homer? Do you think the differences are due to various interpretations of the goddess or the different possibilities of literature and art?

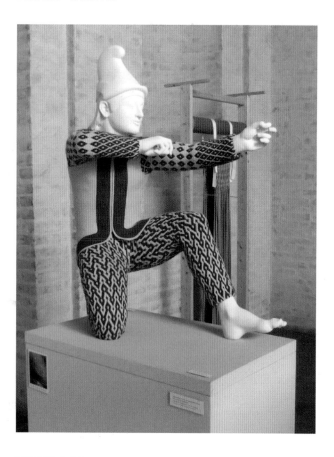

FIGURE 2.48
Painted cast of the archer

(PS)

FIGURE 2.49
Another painted reconstruction of the archer from
the west pediment of the Temple of Aphaia on Aegina.

(PS)

Study question
Study the warriors on the pediment. Do you think the scene shows the Greeks as the clear victors? Why do you think the artist has chosen to depict the battle in this way? Support your answer with specific figures.

are shown, without any repetition. The soldiers next to Athena have their backs towards her, separating her further from their engagement.

Two individual sculptures deserve greater attention as they will be compared with their counterparts on the east pediment: the archer identified as Paris, and the fallen warrior in the corner. The archer is featured on the left side of the pediment, in a mid-action pose, about to shoot his arrow. He is bent down on his right knee, filling the space that the triangular pediment requires. He looks ahead at his target and rests delicately on the heel of his left foot and the knee of his right. Much thought and detail has gone into this sculpture and the pose is very daring for its time. He has been identified as Paris because of his role as an archer and because of his eastern clothing. Unlike the other warriors who are shown heroically nude, he wears long-sleeved and long-legged clothes with a leather cuirass, and an easterner's hat. This clothing would have been painted with bright colours and decorated with patterns. It is very important to remember that these figures were originally painted in eye-catching, bright colours as that would have doubtless impacted the viewer's experience of them. It characterises Paris as slightly effeminate, a common contemporary attitude to easterners, as we can see on depictions of Persians on vases. His skill as an archer is, however, possibly praised, as the fallen warriors on the left side of

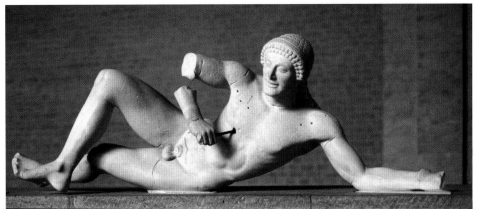

FIGURE 2.50
Fallen warrior from west pediment of the Temple of Aphaia.

Study question
Why do you think that on the same pediment there is both Paris, in a daring pose, and a fallen warrior who embodies typical Archaic features?

ACTIVITY
Compare the Athena from the east and west pediments. How do you respond to each? Do you think it is problematic to have the same figure behaving differently on two sides of the same building? How can we explain this?

the pediment could be his victims. The surviving figure immediately to the left of Paris appears to have just been hit as he still holds himself up by his right hand and bent knee, while the furthermost figure is dying.

The fallen warrior in the right corner of the pediment is very reflective of the Archaic style. He is lying down, resting his weight on his extended left arm, while with his right arm he tries to pull a weapon out of his chest. The arrangement of his legs and facial expression, however, are highly unusual and unnatural. His right leg is bent at the knee, folded over his lying left leg. This appears almost casual, and yet greatly at odds with the idea of his dying. His face moreover betrays all the typical features of the Archaic style, complete with an Archaic smile that again contrasts with the narrative.

The east pediment on the Temple of Aphaia

The east pediment depicts an earlier destruction of Troy by Herakles and Telamon. At first glance, the composition and figures appear very similar to the west pediment; however, there are numerous differences that show its later date and a deliberate sculptural choice for variety.

Athena still occupies the central part of the pediment. Here, however, she is far more engaged with the ongoing battle around her.

The east pediment has not survived as well as the west pediment, but the surviving sculptures and fragments suggest that the action faces inwards. The duals and conflicts between the individual warriors face towards the centre of the pediment, further emphasising Athena's relevance, importance and dominance.

The archer on the East pediment is Herakles, identified by his lion-skin head-dress. He is crouching down, taking aim before firing his arrow. He seems similar to Paris, but there are differences that reflect his superiority and victory. Most obviously, his pose is subtly different. He is twisted slightly outwards and appears at an angle from the viewer.

PRESCRIBED SOURCE

East pediment of the Temple of Aphaia, Aegina

Date: 490–480 BC

Material: limestone

Narratives: first sack of Troy with Herakles and Telamon

Current location: Glyptothek, Munich

Significance: early classical depiction of the first sack of Troy

FIGURE 2.51
Reconstructed drawing of the east pediment of the Temple of Aphaia.

East

FIGURE 2.52

Herakles from the
east pediment of the
Temple of Aphaia.

Study question
The figures of Herakles
and Paris both depict
archers; how similar are
the two and how can this
be explained?

ACTIVITY

Compare the depiction
of Herakles on this
pediment with that on
the metope of Temple C
at Selinus. Was there a
consistent iconographic
depiction of this hero or
are sculptors free to
portray him in any way
they like, that suits their
specific narrative?

His extended left arm is entirely straight, level with his shoulder, fully focused on his target.

The fallen warrior on the left corner of the east pediment is similarly comparable with that of the west pediment. Here, the warrior's pose fully demonstrates his pain and suffering as he dies. He lies on his side, one leg extended, the other bent, his left arm still in the strap of his shield. He faces downwards, looking towards the ground and his death.

FIGURE 2.53
Fallen warrior from
the east pediment of the
Temple of Aphaia.

PS

EXPLORE FURTHER

Horace's line 'dulce et decorum est pro patria mori' (meaning 'it is sweet and right to die for one's country') has been used ironically as the title and last line in Wilfred Owen's poem about the First World War. Do you think the sentiment applies to the depictions seen on the pediments at Aphaia?

These details fill the onlooker with pathos and we feel great sympathy for this victim. While other sculptures in the pediments boast the glory one can win in battle, this figure demonstrates the cost and suffering. War is hereby considered from a number of angles.

THE EARLY CLASSICAL PERIOD

The Temple of Zeus at Olympia

The Early Classical Temple of Zeus at Olympia was the centerpiece of the sanctuary. Its construction was funded by the spoils of a local war between Elis and Pisa, whose defeat and destruction occurred in about 470 BC. The temple was apparently completed by 457 BC, when a golden tripod was dedicated by the Spartans on the peak of the gable after their defeat of Athens in the battle of Tanagra in the same year. The architect was a local man named Libon, and he designed the structure in the pure Doric style. The temple was decorated with sculptures in both pediments, on the metopes above the east and west porches, and inside with the chryselephantine statue of Zeus, made by the famous artist **Pheidias**.

KEY INDIVIDUAL
Pheidias

Dates: *c.* 480–430 BC
Athenian sculptor, artist and architect
Pheidias is most famous for his chryselephantine sculptures of Zeus at Olympia and of Athena in the Parthenon at Athens.

East pediment of the Temple of Zeus at Olympia

The east pediment depicts the chariot race between Oinomaos and Pelops. It shows an intense scene, but one wholly without action. The composition of the pediment is arranged almost as a mirror-image, balanced but not symmetrical, apart from Zeus who seems to rest above the whole scene. Each half of the composition features a chariot team with various servants and grooms, a seer, and a reclining figure representing one of the local rivers, the Kladeos or the Alpheios. In the very centre, Zeus oversees the events, and on either side of him stand the protagonists of the myth: Pelops and Oinomaos, and their respective wives – Hippodameia, who will marry Pelops after the race, and Sterope, Oinomaos' wife.

EXPLORE FURTHER

Read Pausanias' description of the sculptures on the Temple of Zeus: 5.10.6–9.

FIGURE 2.54
Drawn reconstruction of the east pediment of the Temple of Zeus at Olympia.

PRESCRIBED SOURCE

East pediment of the Temple of Zeus, Olympia

Date: *c.* 460 BC

Material: marble

Narrative: contest between Pelops and Oinamaos

Current location: Archaeological Museum of Olympia

Significance: pediment sculpture showing myth of Pelops and Oinomaos

EXPLORE FURTHER Pindar, *Olympian Ode*, 1.66ff; *Pseudo-Apollodorus, Bibliotheca*, E2. 2–10

Pelops and Oinomaos

Pelops fell in love with Hippodameia, daughter of Oinomaos. Pelops had been taught to ride chariots by Poseidon. Oinomaos did not want his daughter to get married (because he had received a prophecy that told him that his son-in-law would kill him), so he challenged every suitor to a chariot race. Each time, Oinomaos won and he stuck the suitors' heads on a stick and displayed them outside the palace walls. Pelops decided to compete and asked Poseidon for help. Poseidon supplied him with a chariot and winged horses. To ensure that he would win the race, Pelops convinced the king's charioteer Myrtilus (a son of Hermes) to help him, promising him half of the kingdom. To make sure he would win, he replaced the bronze linchpins attaching the wheels to the chariot axle with fake ones made of beeswax the night before the race. The race started, and went on for a long time, but just as Oinomaos was catching up to Pelops and readying to kill him, the wheels flew off and the chariot broke apart. Myrtilus survived, but Oinomaos was dragged to death by his horses. Pelops then killed Myrtilus after the latter attempted to rape Hippodameia. Pelops became king and is said to have founded the Olympic Games.

FIGURE 2.55
From left to right, horse and servant, Sterope, Oinomaos, Zeus (central), Pelops, Hippodameia, slave and horse

Zeus is depicted in the centre of the pediment, just as Athena had been in the pediments at Aphaia. Only his body survives, but it shows that he was turned towards his right, likely towards Oinomaos. His physical strength, revealed by his bare upper torso, would have been highly impressive considering also that the figure was over three metres tall.

Oinomaos is shown standing to the right of Zeus. He has a beard, which indicates his older age and his shoulders are covered with a small cloak. His hand is confidently placed on his right hip. His open mouth suggests that he is perhaps speaking, possibly explaining the conditions of the race. This makes him the only active member of the otherwise still tableaux.

Oinomaos' competitor Pelops stands on the other side of Zeus. The two contrast as Pelops is depicted as a young nude, wearing only a helmet, to show off his physical strength. His head is bowed, reflecting his modest character, and contrasts with the arrogant stance of Oinomaos, perhaps indicative of their fates; the haughty is overcome by the modest.

Sterope, Oinomaos' wife, is depicted in a gesture well known from grave reliefs: she holds her head in her hand and her other arm is crossed in front of her breast. This gesture clearly indicates grief. She is grieving about the forthcoming death of her husband. The sculptor has hereby chosen to suggest the outcome of the events through his characters' gestures. Her pose is very inward and closed, reflecting her sorrow.

Hippodameia, Oinomaos' daughter and Pelops' future wife, is shown in the typical bridal gesture, adjusting her veil. Her open body language hints towards her future marriage with Pelops.

The principal figures are flanked by two chariots, horses' heads turned toward the centre. The horses create a context for the myth depicted; it helps identify the figures as those anticipating a chariot race. Servants in attendance sit or kneel in front of or behind the horses. Unlike the main characters who are consumed with the events about to take place, the servants are indifferent; a servant-boy plays with his toes as he waits for the race to begin. This furthers the narrative and creates a realistic contrast between the figures who are involved and whose lives will be immediately affected by the race, and those who are merely bystanders. Moreover, their crouched and lying figures suit the problem of the awkward triangular shape well.

On the right side of the pediment, sits an old man, identified as a seer. He is particularly noteworthy in Greek art as great detail and thought has gone into depicting him as an old man. Unlike other contemporary, and even later Greek sculpture, where age was denoted merely by a beard, the seer has a belly, a sagging chest, is balding and has frown lines on his forehead. His lips are slightly parted, giving life to the sculpture as if he breathes. His right fist is closed and rests on his cheek; he too is therefore in the grieving pose, like Sterope. Seeing the future, he mourns for the forthcoming death of Oinomaos.

On either side of the pediment, the sculptors have chosen to fill the awkward space with personifications of the two local rivers of Olympia: the Alpheios and the Kladeios. Both figures are lying on their sides, their waists covered by thin drapery whose folds mimic ripples in the river. They are highly muscular, youthful bodies, perhaps suggesting

Study question
Compare this portrayal of Zeus with Zeus of Artemision; to what extent is this same deity depicted in the same way throughout Early Classical sculpture? Give reasons for your answer.

Study question
Compare the portrayals of Hippodameia and Sterope. How has the sculptor distinguished between these two female figures? Consider their poses, drapery, anatomy and orientation. Do you think he has done so effectively?

FIGURE 2.56
Seer from the east
pediment of the Temple
of Zeus at Olympia.

PS

MODERN SCHOLARSHIP

Read and evaluate these interpretations of the seer:

Pollitt has the following to say about the seer:

. . . one of the great, original, conceptions of Early Classical Sculpture. Not only is the extreme adaptation of the figure's physical characteristics – his sagging body and bald head – to his dramatic role something new, but new is also the clear state of consciousness which he projects, setting him apart from all the other characters in the group . . . As he contemplates the implications of his knowledge he shrinks back in dismay.

Pollitt, *Art and Experience in Classical Greece* (CUP, 1972), pp. 14ff

Osborne writes:

The moment at which he is caught is not just a moment in the course of a physical action . . . but a moment of new mental clarity. Although the face is moulded with very simple forms, the attention devoted to eyes and the slightly open mouth, along with the gesture of the right arm, afford to this one actor a single moment of vision that transforms the rather static tableau at the centre of the pediment by illuminating their past action, present intentions and future fates.

Osborne, *Archaic and Classical Greek Art* (OUP, 1998), pp. 171ff

FIGURE 2.57 PS
Kladeos personified
in the east pediment
of the Temple of Zeus.

the abundance and strength of the Olympian landscape. Their presence locates the events of the myth in Olympia, which is entirely appropriate since this chariot race was the reason why chariot races were held as part of the Olympic Games.

The narrative on the east pediment is thoughtful and unique. The figures stand vertically and very still; they anticipate the action. It shows the calm before the storm. The horses on either side of the main characters foretell the chariot race but the race has not begun. Nevertheless, the poses of the figures foreshadow the end of the story. Oinomaos' confident stance indicates his arrogance, which will be punished. Pelops' modesty shows his nobility and his youthful musculature implies his heroism. Sterope's grieving pose implies the death of her husband Oinomaos. Hippodamia's bridal gesture demonstrates how open she is to her future marriage with Pelops.

There are numerous stylistic advances that can be seen in the sculptures of the east pediment. The anatomy, movement and facial features have developed since the Archaic Period. The muscles on figures such as Oinomaos and Pelops is rendered by gentle modelled lines. Although still schematic, the lines have not been carved so strongly and definitively, paving the way for a more naturalistic depiction of musculature.

This is, however, not true for all of the sculptures; the personified rivers, for example, have highly exaggerated musculature and their rib cages are also very schematic. The rotation of the rivers' bodies is likewise still unnatural, but it is a clear progression from the fallen warriors on the west and the east pediments at Aphaia. It is clear that sculptors were seeking to depict this movement more naturally, and that it was an on-going development.

EXPLORE FURTHER

Compare this depiction of the myth with that from a mid-fourth-century Apulian red-figure clay vase in the St. Petersburg State Hermitage Museum. How have the artists chosen to depict the events and the characters involved? Which do you think is a more successful treatment of the myth?

FIGURE 2.58
Side view of Kladeos personified.

Severe Style the transitionary period between the Archaic and Classical Periods, dating to roughly between 490 and 450 BC; the style is characterised by thick eyelids, heavy and simple drapery, and an increase in individual characterisation

---

PRESCRIBED SOURCE

West pediment of the Temple of Zeus, Olympia

Date: *c.* 460 BC

Material: marble

Narrative: Centauromachy

Current location: Archaeological Museum of Olympia

Significance: pediment sculpture depicting the Centauromachy with Apollo in the middle

There are further advances from the Archaic depiction of the face. The Archaic smile has now gone and instead figures have their mouths slightly parted, as though they are breathing. The almond-shaped eyes are also no longer there, but now thick eyelids indicate the **Severe Style**. This is best seen on the seer, whose face has survived very well.

West pediment of the Temple of Zeus at Olympia

The west pediment depicts the Centauromachy, the battle between the mythical part-man, part-horse Centaurs and the Lapiths, people from Thessaly.

In the centre of the pediment, Apollo presides over the events. The god of order and justice stands entirely frontally, except for his extended right arm and his head, which face his right. The extended arm forms a ninety-degree angle with his body and means his figure occupies greater space on the pediment. This neat, simple and static pose reflects the calmness and order Apollo will provide. This contrasts significantly with the chaotic scenes around him, where Lapiths and Centaurs are brutally fighting one another.

Unlike the east pediment, the west is filled with action. Figures overlap and interact with one another and fill the space entirely. Here the movement is horizontal. Women, Lapiths and Centaurs are viciously fighting for their lives. The Centaurs are characterised as disorderly and uncivilised not only through their attacks on the women, but also through their wild hair and mask-like, bestial faces. The narrative is expressed not only through their physical contact and the range of ways in which the figures are attacking and defending, but also in the anguish shown in some of their faces. While we need to be cautious of using the term 'emotion', and numerous figures still have vacant expressions,

FIGURE 2.59
Drawing reconstruction of the west pediment of the Temple of Zeus at Olympia.

FIGURE 2.60
Apollo.

FIGURE 2.61
Centaur bites a
Lapith's arm.

ACTIVITY

Draw a table comparing
the depiction of narrative
on the east and west
pediments at Olympia.
Consider the following
features:

- Moment of narrative
  depicted.
- Arrangement of
  figures.
- Characterization of
  figures.
- Movement of figures.

FIGURE 2.62
A Lapith woman tries to fight off an attacking Centaur.

some begin to show pain in their faces, as well as in their body language. This is particularly seen on the Centaur's face where his open mouth might suggest him screaming in anguish as the woman grabs his head and punches his chin (Figure 2.63).

FIGURE 2.63
Centaur being attacked by Lapith women.

Metopes on the Temple of Zeus at Olympia

The metopes above the east and west porches of the Temple of Zeus were adorned with scenes depicting the twelve labours of Herakles. Six sculpted metopes decorated the east side, and six the west. We shall consider three. Herakles' labours were not an unsurprising choice for this temple; Herakles was the son of Zeus and the great-grandson of Pelops. He was also the founder of the Olympic Games and the archetypal hero, to whom athletes would aspire. He exemplified the ideal athlete with his determination, courage and self-discipline. His labours are also symbolic of the victory of civilisation over chaos and barbarity, as he rid the world of monsters.

Herakles and the stables of Augeas

One of Herakles' labours was to clean out the ever-filthy Augean Stables.

The metope depicts Herakles mid-cleaning out the dung, with Athena behind him, guiding and supporting him. Since it was a victory of intelligence, it is no surprise that the goddess of wisdom is shown beside him. Athena stands frontally but her head and right arm focus on Herakles and his task. Besides her helmet, which enables us to identify her, she wears no armour. Instead, her gesture and her everyday clothing – the peplos – present her as a supportive, approachable deity, who helps Herakles. She is not

PRESCRIBED SOURCE

Metopes of the Temple of Zeus, Olympia

Date: *c.* 460 BC

Material: marble

Narrative: Labours of Herakles (Cretan Bull, Garden of the Hesperides, Stables of Augeas)

Current location: Archaeological Museum of Olympia

Significance: metopes depicting the individual labours of Herakles

EXPLORE FURTHER

Herakles' labours were carried out as punishment for killing his wife and children. He went to the oracle of Apollo at Delphi, where he was told that he had to serve King Eurystheus for twelve years, performing twelve difficult tasks, or labours. Each labour was a significant trial, many taking place in the Peloponnese, but some further afield.

Pausanias lists the labours in 5.10.9.

FIGURE 2.64
Herakles and the stables of Augeas

EXPLORE FURTHER

Cleaning the Augean stables was not as seemingly heroic or impressive as the other labours were, but it was purposefully impossible. Over a thousand immortal cattle lived in these stables and they had not been cleaned out in over thirty years, hence the amount of dung was immense. Herakles overcame this difficulty, however, by routing the river Alpheios through the stables to wash out the dung. His ingenuity is hereby celebrated, over his physical strength.

the same military goddess that we saw on the pediments at Aphaia, but her power is still evident through her calm stance and presence. Her vertical lines contrast with Herakles' diagonal action; while he struggles with his whole body to carry out a task, she stands serenely, in control of the situation. This recalls the contrasting poses and action we saw on the west pediment.

Herakles' body has not survived entirely; however, from the outline of his head and limbs, we can see he is concentrating on his activity. He appears bearded, showing his mature age.

Herakles and the Cretan Bull

Another of Herakles' labours was to capture the Cretan Bull. He sailed to Crete where King Minos allowed him to remove the bull because it had caused a series of problems for Crete, destroying the agriculture. In capturing the bull, Herakles was bringing civilisation by ridding the area of a monster.

The composition of this metope consists of two diagonal lines as Herakles and the bull cross one another. Herakles leans to the left, by resting his weight on his bent right leg and seemingly lunging to the side. He has pulled the bull's head round so that beast and man confront each other. Their eyes bring the focus into the centre of the metope. The dramatic turn of his head behind him shows he is in full control of the animal, as he

FIGURE 2.65
Herakles and the Cretan Bull.

tames it. The bull, however, probably rested on its back feet with the front two in the air; this mid-action pose makes the scene more dramatic and active, and reflects how the bull is in a weaker position than its new master. The X-shape formed by the two bodies creates a powerful composition as the contestants strain away from one another. This dynamic design reflects the difficulty of the task, as well as the strain Herakles experienced when taming this wild beast. The sculptor has tried to fill the whole available space of the metope, using the bull's tail to occupy the top-left corner.

Herakles is depicted as a mature figure, with a beard. His developed musculature does not show youth, but rather his mature physical strength. The sculptor has tried to make his torso respond to the twist in his body while still showing off his exaggerated strength, but it is not yet a naturalistic depiction of the human form.

Herakles and the Garden of the Hesperides

One of Herakles' final labours was to go to the Garden of the Hesperides and get some golden apples. Herakles asked Atlas to get the apples from the garden, while he carried

FIGURE 2.66
Herakles and the Garden of the Hesperides.

> **Study question**
> Compare the support Athena gives Herakles here with that given to Perseus on Temple C at Selinus. Which sculpture do you think best emphasises her help to these heroes? Explain your answer.

Study question

Compare the scene of
Herakles and the apples
of the Hesperides with
the metope of Herakles
and the Augean Stables.
Is the depiction of Athena
similar in both scenes?
What responses might it
invoke from the viewer?

ACTIVITY

Debate whether
metopes are more
effective for telling a
story than pediments.

MODERN SCHOLARSHIP

Read 'The Temple of Zeus
at Olympia: Heroes and
Athletes' by Judith
Barringer in *Hesperia*, 74
(2005), pp. 211–241.

the world. This is the scene shown in the metope: Herakles, in the centre of the metope, carries the world on his shoulders, while Atlas presents the apples to him. Athena stands behind Herakles, supporting the hero in his task.

The composition of this metope is vertical as the three figures stand upright. The main horizontal lines are Atlas' outstretched hands, which would have held the golden apples. Athena stands fully frontal, with only her head and left arm turned to the side. Herakles is in profile but Atlas' body is in a three-quarter view. Each figure is hereby depicted in a subtly different way, avoiding repetition.

Athena's role in this metope is to help Herakles. Her left hand is raised above her head and gently assists Herakles as he holds the world on his shoulders. Her power and divinity are emphasised, as she is not straining to do this in any way.

Herakles occupies the central part of the metope. Unlike the previous two metopes, his action here is not one of dynamic movement and strength, but instead shows great concentration and focus. He stands with his arms above his head, holding the world. In contrast to how we have seen him before, he appears restricted and still. Sculptors evidently focused on the individual narratives, and wanted variety in the metopes.

Atlas is depicted on the far right and, with his outstretched arms, he occupies the most space on the metope. The apples would have been added with a different material, most likely bronze. This glistening material would have really stood out against the painted marble, reflecting the divine nature of the objects.

Study questions

1 Compare the depiction of Herakles in these three metopes; how similar is his depiction? To what extent do you think the differences make the sculptures more effective and interesting? Explain your answer.
2 Contrast the depictions of Athena here with those on the pediments at Aphaia; how differently has the goddess been characterised? Do you think this is a result of the different chronology or narrative, or because the former are on metopes and the latter on pediments? Explain your answer.
3 How do you think an ancient Greek would have responded to the depiction of the gods on the Temple of Zeus at Olympia? Explain your reasoning.

THE HIGH CLASSICAL PERIOD

The Parthenon

The Parthenon was dedicated to Athena Parthenos, Athena the virgin or maiden, and was set up on the Acropolis in Athens. The Acropolis was the religious heart of Athens and already had a number of religious buildings on it before the Parthenon was built.

FIGURE 2.67
The Parthenon from the west.

EXPLORE FURTHER

When the Persians sacked Athens in 480/479 BC, they destroyed everything on the Acropolis, including the Pre-Parthenon. Read Herodotus' *Histories*, 8.52–53, for a full description. In the aftermath of this, the Athenians decided to leave the site in ruins, as an eternal reminder of Persian impiety, but later, as their wealth and political stability increased, they chose to re-build the Acropolis and to construct a new Parthenon.

By the mid-fifth century BC, Athens was flourishing. They had set up the Delian League, which was an alliance with a number of Greek city-states, mainly in the Aegean, to protect one another against potential Persian attacks. City-states would contribute ships or money to the League, in return for defence. The money was stored on the island of Delos, in the centre of the Aegean. As foreign attacks did not materialize, however, and as Athens grew increasingly strong and wealthy through the League, so did its nature change into one of an Empire. Athens moved the treasury from Delos to the Parthenon.

The Parthenon was the largest temple on the Greek mainland at the time, and was the first one built entirely from marble. It also housed more architectural sculpture than any other temple: both pediments were sculpted; all four sides of the temple were decorated with sculpted metopes; and an Ionic frieze ran along all four sides of the cella wall. It was also the first time that the Doric and Ionic orders were mixed quite so much: the temple had both a Doric and an Ionic frieze.

EXPLORE FURTHER

Read Pausanias' brief description of the sculpture of the Parthenon: 1.24.5.

PRESCRIBED SOURCE

East pediment of the Parthenon, Athens

Date: 437–432 BC

Material: marble

Narrative: the birth of Athena

Current location: British Museum, London; the Acropolis Museum, Athens

Significance: pediment sculpture showing the birth of Athena

Study question
Compare the depiction and use of drapery in these three reclining goddesses with that of Aphrodite of the Agora; how similar are they and what might that suggest about the purpose of drapery and its stylistic development in the High Classical Period?

FIGURE 2.68
Reclining goddesses from the east pediment on the Parthenon.

East pediment: the birth of Athena

The east pediment shows the birth of Athena, the patron goddess of Athens, to whom the temple was dedicated. According to the myth, Athena was born fully grown and fully armed from the head of her father Zeus. Zeus probably sat in the middle of the pediment and Athena, in full armour, was likely next to him. The news of her birth was carried from the centre to the sides, decreasing in intensity as it approaches the corners. In the two corners are horses – on the left is Helios' chariot (god of the sun), symbolising dawn; on the right is Selene-Nyx's chariot (god of the evening), symbolising dusk. This gives a temporal element as the narrative progresses from morning to evening.

Unfortunately, the vast majority of the pediment is lost, in particular the central part. Reclining figures from the outside of the pediment survive, however, which depict the gods in a different manner from that we have seen before. The reclining male nude on the left side appears relaxed, perhaps holding a drinking vessel. The three goddesses on the right are likewise shown to be at ease, one resting on the lap of another, showing a great intimacy and familiarity. These mirrored reclining figures contrast both in their use of drapery and in their interaction with other figures. The figures are not looking at the events at the centre of the pediment, however, perhaps suggesting that the news of Athena's birth has not yet reached them. Alternatively, it may indicate that the sculptors did not really know how to fill the awkward triangular shape and have not brought the narrative together. The drapery on these figures, however, is noteworthy, as it reflects the High Classical style. The goddesses wear thin drapery that clings to their bodies; in particular, their breasts and thighs are very visible despite their clothing. This delicate material is then contrasted with a thicker cloak, the deep folds of which would have created shadows on the sculptures. The downward folds of the drapery, moreover, emphasise the calmness of the figures as they recline, rather than engage in movement.

West pediment: the contest between Athena and Poseidon

This shows the contest between Athena and Poseidon over who should name the city.

The majority of the sculptures from this pediment are lost. The two central figures, which are only fragmentary, were probably striding away from each other but turning to look back. Poseidon's torso survives, however, and it gives a very good indication of how he was portrayed. This massive piece of marble already indicates the level of musculature that was shown. Poseidon's physical strength was clearly a focus, and the back view of his extensive muscles is noteworthy. The attention paid to the back of the sculptures suggests that they were probably put on public display before being attached to the pediments, and that when sculpting figures dedicated to the gods, every angle and viewpoint was significant, even if mortals would not have been able to see it. This explains why such detail and attention has gone into the sculptures when they would have been placed so high up; the gods could still see them. This would have contrasted with the clothed Athena, whose power is shown in a very different way. This opposition would have made for an interesting visual dynamic.

The Ilissos River is personified in the left corner of the pediment. As with the east pediment on the Temple of Zeus at Olympia, this locates the events of the myth. If we

PRESCRIBED SOURCE

West pediment of the Parthenon, Athens

Date: 437–432 BC

Material: marble

Narrative: the contest for the patronage of Athens

Current location: British Museum, London; the Acropolis Museum, Athens

Significance: pediment sculpture showing the contest between Athena and Poseidon for the patronage of Athens

FIGURE 2.69
Fragment of Poseidon's torso from the front and back.

PS

EXPLORE FURTHER

The contest for Athens
Athena offered the citizens the olive tree, while Poseidon offered salt water. The people chose the former and the city was thereafter named after the goddess: Athens. It is no surprise that this myth is chosen for the temple; the Parthenon's sculpture celebrated the city as much as the goddess. It was thanks to their patron goddess that they thrived. This choice of myth forms a nice pairing with the birth myth shown on the east pediment. These are the two central myths about the goddess for the Athenians: how she was born and why she is so important to them.

FIGURE 2.70
Personification of the
River Ilissos.

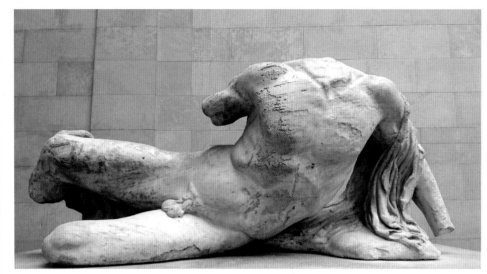

contrast the two rivers, we can see a significant development in the treatment of the body. The sculptor here has managed to depict a successful twist of the body. The figure's anatomy is likewise more realistic as its ribs are not as protruding and exaggerated. The flesh seems softer.

Ionic frieze: the Panathenaic Procession

When studying the frieze, it is worth bearing in mind how inaccessible it was. The location of the frieze was behind the metopes and colonnade that surrounded the temple. If a viewer stood within the peristyle, the colonnade that surrounded the temple, they would have had to strain their necks to see it. Outside the peristyle, however, only the columns would have interrupted their view of the continuous frieze. It is very different from the current layout and visibility in the British Museum.

The Ionic frieze was 160 metres long and just over a metre tall. It contains about 378 human and divine figures and at least 220 animals, though substantial parts of the frieze are lost. It is entirely unique in its choice of narrative because it shows a human event: the Great Panathenaic Procession, an event that took place every four years in honour of Athena. During the procession, Athenian men and women showed their devotion to their patron goddess through sacrifice and offerings. The climax was the presentation of a peplos to the statue of Athena outside the Erechtheion. The frieze was planned by Pheidias, who also sculpted the chryselephantine statue of Athena inside the temple.

The procession gathers and starts from the west side and walks along the north and south sides to the presentation of the peplos, probably shown on the east side. This route was not coincidental; visitors to the Acropolis would have seen the west side of the Parthenon first, and they too would have walked along the north or south sides to reach its entrance, which was on the east. The figures of the sculptures hereby accurately mimic the real-life worshippers.

FIGURE 2.71
North side procession
of cavalry.

Individuals on the west side are shown gathering by their horses. Some are standing, waiting; others are already on horseback, signalling more to join. Each figure is shown as an individual, different to the others around them. The sculptors have accurately portrayed their youthful bodies, and their poses are realistic depictions of movement. The horses too are distinct; some are galloping, others stand calmly, others are neighing. They have been made smaller in proportion to the men so as to leave as little empty space in the composition as possible.

Women are also shown taking part in the procession. They are shown fully clothed, indicating their respectable and modest nature, but their drapery and poses are all different. While they wear a chiton covered in a himation, the clothing falls differently over their bodies, and the folds are neither repetitive, nor symmetrical.

They each carry their own offerings or contributions to the festival; one carries an incense burner, another a jug, another a libation bowl. Just as the men are depicted distinctly, so are the women.

FIGURE 2.72
Women on the north
side of the frieze.

MODERN SCHOLARSHIP

Read Ian Jenkins' *The Parthenon Frieze*, pp. 25–26, on the various interpretations of the frieze.
  Explore an alternative interpretation of the Parthenon in Joan Connelly's *The Parthenon Enigma*.

EXPLORE FURTHER

Explore the festival of the Panathenaia further in Erika Simon's *Festivals of Attica*, pp. 55–74.

The east side of the frieze shows the climax of the festival. In the central part, the presentation of the peplos is shown. Framing this are the gods, who sit, watching the procession around them. They have their backs turned to the central dedication, which makes us question to what extent they really care about this moment, but they are facing the parading worshippers.

Here, Hermes, Dionysus, Demeter and Ares sit together. As with the mortals, there is no repetition in the depictions or poses of the gods. Each one is identified by certain attributes: Hermes has his traveller's hat and winged sandals; Dionysus leans on his now missing thyrsus; Demeter has her torch and Ares would have had a bronze spear resting on his right shoulder.

Hera and Zeus sit next to each other, reflecting their status as a married couple. Hera is making the bridal gesture we saw Hippodameia make on the Temple of Zeus at Olympia, as she plays with her veil. Her thin chiton falls naturally around her body, emphasising her breasts. Zeus sits facing his wife, relaxed, leaning casually on the back of his seat with his left arm. They appear to be deep in conversation, paying no attention to the dedication of the peplos, which occurs to the right of Zeus. It is not likely, however, that the Greeks thought their gods did not care about their offerings, but rather it might indicate their different planes: the mortals on Earth, the gods on Olympus.

FIGURE 2.73
Hera and Zeus.

Study question
Compare the scene of the gods from the Parthenon with that on the Siphnian Treasury from Delphi. To what extent is there development in the following areas:

● drapery and anatomy
● composition and poses
● characterisation
● interaction between the figures
● relevance and role in the wider narrative?

Doric frieze: metopes XXVI, XXVII and XXVIII

The metopes were sculpted between 447 and 438 BC. All four sides of the Doric frieze were decorated with sculpture. Each side represented a different myth, each symbolising the victory of civilisation over barbarity:

- East: Gigantomachy
- South: Centauromachy
- West: Amazonomachy
- North: Trojan War.

The best surviving side is the south. Unlike the pediment on the Temple of Zeus at Olympia, these metopes show only a snapshot of the Centauromachy. We will only be studying three metopes. The differing quality and style of each metope reflects the involvement of different artists.

Metope XXVI

This metope shows a Lapith and a Centaur mid-struggle. The Lapith has raised his left leg to kick the Centaur before him, and with his left arm he is about to hit the Centaur's head with a stone. His weight rests on the ball of his right foot, indicating a spring in his attack. His body is turned outwards so that we can see his muscular torso. Behind him, his cloak drapes onto the ground, hanging from his neck. His pose is highly unrealistic and overly dramatised. The sculptor was more concerned with showing off physical strength, depicting a range of poses and of occupying the whole space of the metope, than with naturalism.

PRESCRIBED SOURCE

Metopes of the Parthenon, Athens

Date: 447–442 BC

Material: marble

Height: 1.20 m

Narrative: Centauromachy

Current location: British Museum, London

Significance: metopes showing different myths on each of the four sides of the Parthenon

FIGURE 2.74
Metope XXVI.

Likewise, the Centaur has numerous problematic features. He stands on his hind legs and his body rises up diagonally, his front legs lifted and his arms, now missing, probably raised upwards. His body similarly shows off his musculature, which is even more exaggerated than that of the Lapith. It appears as though the sculptor did not get the measurements right because the Centaur has no neck. His face is characterised with the same bestiality that we saw on the Centaurs at Olympia: a big beard and moustache, wild hair and exaggerated features.

Although the metope is filled with action, and despite the figures' physical strengths, there does not appear to be much strain or trial in their fight. They seem almost placed next to each other, rather than really engaging or responding to one another.

Metope XXVII

This metope is very different from the previous one. The Lapith and the Centaur open out away from one another for very different reasons. The Centaur stretches out because his head is being pulled back by the Lapith, whereas the Lapith's open body language reflects his strength and power. The sculptures occupy the whole space of the metope effectively and the cloak behind the Lapith provides a background, as it increases his size. The

FIGURE 2.75
Metope XXVII.

realistic folds in the drapery provide a curved line that contrasts with the largely vertical Lapith, who in turn is different from the horizontal and curved Centaur. Although the heads of the figures are missing, it seems as though the Lapith turned to face his victim, adding focus and determination to his action.

Metope XXVIII

This third metope depicts a very different scene from the previous two; instead of showing the Centaur and Lapith mid-fight, it shows the victory of a Centaur, who rises above his victim. The Lapith lies contorted on the floor, seemingly writhing in pain.

His legs are bent at the knee, his torso is flung upwards but his head falls to the ground, clearly devoid of any further energy. The Centaur, in contrast, dominates the scene; he puts his weight on his hind legs and rises diagonally upwards, his tail swinging in the air and holding out a panther-skin with his extended left arm. The panther-skin represents the savage bestiality of the Centaurs, reflective of their monstrous and exotic nature.

> **EXPLORE FURTHER**
>
> Some scholars have identified the Lapith in Metope XXVII as Theseus, the Athenian hero who fought in the battle. Read Plutarch's *Life of Theseus*, 39–40, for his account of Theseus' involvement. Do you think there is enough evidence to make this link?

FIGURE 2.76
Metope XXVIII.

> **Study question**
>
> Compare the depiction of the Centauromachy in the Parthenon metopes with the west pediment at Olympia. How similar are their portrayals of the battle?

MODERN SCHOLARSHIP

Read *Architecture and Meaning on the Athenian Acropolis* by Robin Rhodes, especially Chapter 4, entitled 'The Integrated Parthenon', where the sculpture on the Parthenon is compared with the Olympian sculpture. How unified do you think the sculptural decoration on the Parthenon is?

For a history of the Parthenon, read Mary Beard's *The Parthenon*.

PRESCRIBED SOURCE

Ionic frieze of the Temple of Apollo, Bassae

Date: 420–400 BC

Material: marble

Height: 0.63 m

Narrative: Amazonomachy and Centauromachy

Current location: British Museum

Significance: internal architectural frieze showing the Amazonomachy and the Centauramachy

THE LATE CLASSICAL PERIOD

Ionic frieze of the Temple of Apollo at Bassae

The Temple of Apollo at Bassae is located in the middle of the Peloponnese and was built between 450 and 425 BC. The temple was probably dedicated to Apollo, god of healing, following a plague. The temple is found in a very remote, mountainous location and, unfortunately, little-to-nothing is known about who set up the temple and how they paid for it.

The temple is renowned for its architectural oddities. Most relevant to its sculpture is the fact that it combines the three architectural orders: it has a Doric exterior, complete with sculpted pediments and metopes, an Ionic frieze around the interior of the cella, and the earliest known Corinthian capital. The presence and location of the Ionic frieze are particularly noteworthy as never before has sculptural decoration focused on the inside of a temple.

The frieze is 31 metres in length and 0.63 metres in height. It would have stood about 7 metres above ground, and therefore is carved in very high relief so that onlookers from

FIGURE 2.77
Amazon dragging away a wounded companion.

Study question
Compare this dying Amazon with the dying warriors from Aegina; which do you think creates a deeper sense of pathos? Explain your views.

below could see it. It consisted of 23 marble slabs, showing the Centauromachy and the Amazonomachy. We have seen both these myths depicted alongside one another on the Parthenon, but we should not be surprised at this similarity considering that the architect of the Parthenon, Iktinos, was also the architect of the temple at Bassae.

Figure 2.77 shows three Amazon women, each at a different stage of the battle. The one on the left is fighting off a man, just off the image, while the central figure is lifting and supporting a dying Amazon, who lies in her arms. The close relationship between these figures, as well as the limp body of the figure on the right, draw pathos for these women, who represent the uncivilised.

Between the figures, their drapery is seen billowing in the wind, filling the space and providing a dramatic backdrop. Nevertheless, while it makes sense that the attacking Amazon's cloak is in the air, giving force and speed to her attack, the billowing cloak of the central figure seems more to be filling in the space than reflecting a narrative. There is a nice contrast also between the thick folds of their cloaks and the thin chiton that clings to their waists, particularly seen with the dying Amazon.

Figure 2.78 shows a different side of the battle and indicates the range of poses and scenes depicted on the frieze. On the left, a man and Amazon woman prepare to fight. Their diagonal and crossed composition recalls that of Herakles and the Cretan Bull from Olympia and is probably how Athena and Poseidon stood on the west pediment of the Parthenon. The proportions of the figures are, however, inaccurate; on the male figure, for example, his legs are too long and his torso seems contracted to fit in the space. To the right of the slab, an Amazon woman lies over a collapsing horse. This scene shows great variety and attempts at the depiction of daring movements by the sculptor, as the horizontal figures contrast with the largely vertical remainder of the frieze. Behind the Amazon stands a man, holding her by the feet, wearing a cloak around his shoulders. Although the woman is dying, she appears to have grabbed his right arm in a last attempt to protect herself.

The other myth shown on the frieze was the Centauromachy. Figure 2.79 shows a Centaur, which has galloped over a dead Centaur's body and is biting the neck of an attacking Lapith. The sculptor has varied between vertical, diagonal and horizontal lines,

FIGURE 2.78
Herakles fighting.

FIGURE 2.79
Centaur attacking a
Lapith.

making the composition visually interesting. Moreover, the tension between the Centaur about to bite the Lapith and the Lapith who is stabbing the Centaur shows the even level of this duel. This scene is reminiscent of the west pediment on the Temple of Zeus at Olympia, where a Centaur to the right of Apollo is biting the Lapith's arm. Despite these achievements, this slab also reveals the limited talent of the sculptors at Bassae. Firstly, it would be impossible for the profile galloping Centaur to be biting the Lapith's neck at that angle. The sculptor has instead used the body of the Lapith to hide this problem. Likewise, the Centaur on the floor is very difficult to interpret as there appears to be a face on its shoulder; the legs are also too short and the arm too long. These flaws are not surprising, however, as Bassae was such a remote area and would not have attracted the best sculptors.

Figure 2.80 emphasises the bestiality of the Centaurs, a feature we have seen both at Olympia and on the Parthenon metope XXVI. Their faces are wild and savage, reflective

FIGURE 2.80
Attacking Centaur.

FIGURE 2.81
Close-up of the
Centaur's face.

of dramatic masks. Like the latter sculpture, the Centaur appears without a neck, but with highly exaggerated musculature on its torso to reflect its strength and, therefore, threat. In this scene, the Centaur is extended, grabbing a Lapith woman with his right arm and punching a Lapith soldier with his left. The diagonal arrangement of the Centaur and kneeling Lapith suggests the Centaur's dominance; however, the Lapith may still bring his shield before him to attack. This mid-action scene exploits the multiple relationships between figures that a frieze composition can enable.

Figure 2.81 again shows different scenes and dynamics. On the left, a Lapith is kneeling on a Centaur's back, holding the Centaur's arms back with his knee and his head with his right hand. His cloak hangs behind him, magnifying his size and presence, and his muscular torso and right arm show his strength. Meanwhile the Centaur, although in the weaker position, does not show any anguish in his face or his body; this lack of tension again reflects poor craftsmanship. On the right, a Centaur is pulling away a Lapith woman, who is trying to run away, while carrying her child. This emotive scene, draws its tension from the crossed, diagonal composition that we have seen numerous times before.

TOPIC REVIEW

These questions should draw on your knowledge of the whole topic, so think carefully about the different things you have learned (check the Topic Overview on pp. 133–134).

1. How effectively did Greek sculptors tell narratives on architectural sculpture?
2. To what extent did the development of architectural sculpture reflect the contemporary development of free-standing sculpture?
3. How varied are the choices of scenes depicted on architecture?

Further Reading

Barringer, J. (2005) 'The Temple of Zeus at Olympia, Heroes and Athletes', in *Hesperia*, 74: 211–241

Beard, M. (2010) *The Parthenon*. London: Profile Books, Chapter 2

Jenkins, I (2002) *The Parthenon Frieze*. London: British Museum Press

Mayor, A. (2016) *The Amazons: Lives and Legends of Warrior Women across the Ancient World*. Princeton, NJ: Princeton University Press

Pollitt, J. (1972) *Art and Experience in Classical Greece*. Cambridge: Cambridge University Press, Chapters 2 and 3

Rhodes, R. (2005) *Architecture and Meaning on the Athenian Acropolis*. Cambridge: Cambridge University Press, Chapter 6

Simon, E. (2002) *Festivals of Attica*. Madison, WI: University of Wisconsin Press, pp. 55–74

Spivey, N. (2013) *Greek Sculpture*. Cambridge: Cambridge University Press, Chapter 6

Woodford, S. (1997) *An Introduction to Greek Art*. London: Gerald Duckworth and Co., pp. 27–37, 91–103, 110–127

PRACTICE QUESTIONS

Source A

1. Which part of the temple does this drawing show? [1]
2. Where was this temple located? [1]
3. Which had a greater narrative impact, scenes which were calm and still or action-packed? You may refer to **Source A** as a starting point. [20]

2.4 Vase-Painting

Function

- Shapes and uses of pots, including:
  - storage vessels, mixing pots, water pots, jugs and drinking cups, cosmetic and sporting equipment

Materials

- Effects of different types of materials, including:
  - clay, added colour and slip
- Advantages and limitations of different materials and shapes

Techniques

- Black-figure technique in vase-painting, the use of added colour and incision
- Red-figure technique in vase-painting, the use of different sized brushes and diluted slip to create effects

Subject matter

- Themes in vase-painting, including:
  - Achilles, Athena, Dionysus, Herakles, Trojan War

The following prescribed sources are covered in this topic:

- Archaic Period
  - Gorgons pursuing Perseus, dinos and stand by the Gorgon Painter
  - François Vase, volute krater by Kleitias
  - Wedding of Peleus and Thetis, dinos and stand by Sophilos
  - Dionysus and the Maenads, neck amphora by the Amasis Painter
  - Achilles and Ajax Playing Dice, belly amphora
  - Dionysus sailing on the ocean, kylix by Exekias

- Transitional Period
  - Dionysus/Herakles feasting in the presence of Athena, bi-lingual belly amphora by the Lysippides Painter and the Andokides Painter
  - Trojan War, hydria and Dionysus and the Maenads, pointed amphora by the Kleophrades Painter

- Classical Period
  - Achilles and Hector/Memnon, volute krater by the Berlin Painter
  - Herakles and Antaios, calyx krater by Euphronios
  - Herakles and the Amazons, volute krater by Euphronios
  - Hector arming/Three men carousing, belly amphora by Euthymides
  - Perseus and Medusa, hydria and Boreas pursuing Oreithyia, oinochoe by the Pan Painter

Don't forget that you will be given credit in the exam if you study extra sources and make relevant use of them in your answers.

Although the vast majority of ancient pottery was not decorated, painted vases survive in large quantities. First, let us look at how they were produced.

PRODUCTION

Vases were produced on a wheel. The image was painted in a more refined clay, which would turn black on firing. There is evidence to suggest that in some cases the image was sketched on the surface of the vase prior to painting. Other colours, including red and white, were occasionally added. Sometimes more colours, such as green or blue, might be added after the firing process.

Once the painted scene had been prepared, vases were fired in a kiln. Here they were heated to around 800°C and **oxidation** was allowed to take place. This gain in oxygen caused the whole vase and decoration to turn red. Then, by closing the air vents and burning green wood, the amount of oxygen inside the kiln was reduced. At this point the vase and its decoration all turned black. During this phase the temperature rose to around 950°C before cooling again to around 900°C. Finally, the air vents were opened again as the kiln was allowed to cool completely. While the body of the vase returned to a red colour, the areas painted with the slip would remain black and glossy.

> **oxidation** the process whereby oxygen interacts with other materials; on vases, the iron in the paint turned red

DEVELOPMENT

During the Geometric Period, vases were decorated with geometric patterns, such as zig-zag lines, triangles, diamonds or circles, which could be drawn with a compass. At this point, artists had a fear of empty spaces and so decorated the whole of the vase. Artists began to experiment with depicting the human body in a highly stylised manner, representing the various parts with different geometric shapes.

During the eighth century BC, the Greeks made more contact with the East, particularly with places such as Assyria, Egypt and Phoenicia. Over the next century this gradually led to the adoption of Eastern designs and motifs, such as panthers, sphinxes,

> **KEY EVENT**
>
> **The Geometric Period**
>
> The period from around 1100 BC to 700 BC when vases were predominantly decorated using lines and geometric patterns.

FIGURE 2.82
Monumental Attic grave amphora, 760–750 BC. Athens, National Archaeological Museum, 804.

palmettes and lions, being used by Greek artists on Greek vases. Due to these Eastern, or Oriental, influences, Greek vase-painting in the seventh century BC is decribed as belonging to the **Orientalising Period**.

The final phase before the introduction of Attic black-figure vases is the Corinthian style. In the seventh and early sixth centuries BC, Corinth was the most important Greek city-state politically and commercially. Its location on the Isthmus between the Peloponnese and northern Greece made for easy access to the main trade routes, both within Greece and overseas. The Corinthian style of vase-painting is exemplified by a smoothing of the angular forms of the Geometric Period into curvier decoration. Animals were also particularly prevalent. Over the course of the sixth and fifth centuries BC, Athens adopted and improved on the Corinthian style with higher quality of both potting and painting, before becoming the dominant manufacturing centre for painted vases.

KEY EVENT

The Orientalising Period

The period from the late eighth century BC to the early sixth century BC, during which vase decoration was heavily influenced by the East. Designs such as panthers, lotus blossoms and sphinxes became commonplace in Greek vase-painting.

FUNCTION

Most vases were designed for use around the home. As such, and in order to keep the costs low, they were undecorated. The less common, more expensive painted vases tended to be used for a few specific functions: ceremonial vases were used as prizes, such as the amphorae of olive oil awarded to victors of the Panathenaic Games, or for more ritual purposes, such as the loutrophoros, which held the water for the bride's bath at a wedding; there were also a series of painted vases designed for use at symposia, or drinking parties.

FIGURE 2.83
Vase shapes.

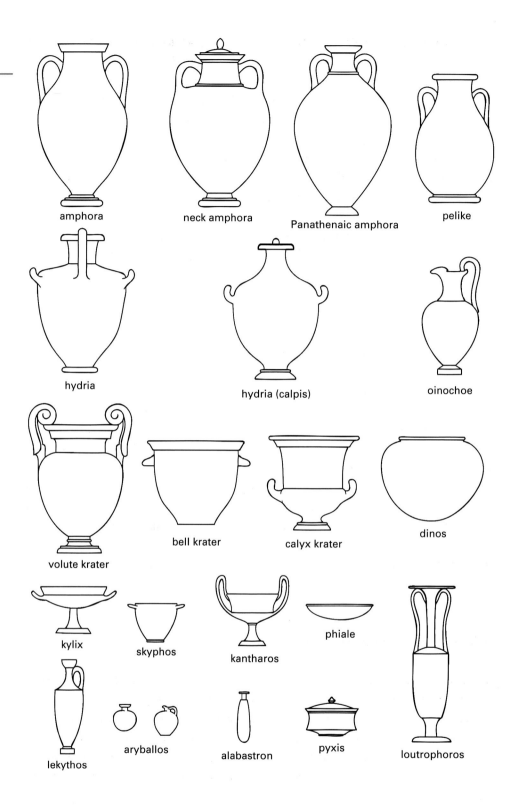

Let us look briefly at some of the more common vase shapes. A lekythos (pl. lekythoi) was a tall, thin vessel. They ranged in size with the largest being around 2 metres in height. They contained olive oil, which was used for lighting, cooking and washing. These were used both in the household and on graves. The latter were an offering to the dead and were painted white. Such pots were known as **white-ground**. A lekythos had a good pouring lip, so that the precious olive oil would not drip and be wasted.

The oinochoe was not dissimilar to the lekythos and is the shape that most closely resembles the modern-day jug, both in terms of form and function. Sometimes the lip of the jug might be modified to appear more ornate into a variation known as a trefoil oinochoe, where the lip is formed into three parts.

A krater was a large bowl used for mixing wine and water, as the Greeks liked to dilute their wine, typically with three parts of water to every one part of wine. Its function meant that a krater would have a wide mouth to allow the liquids to be mixed more easily.

The amphora (pl. amphorae) again, could differ dramatically in size. There were several variations on the basic amphora shape including the belly amphora, where the main bulge in the vase was in the belly area, and the neck amphora where the bulge was much closer to the top of the vessel. Amphorae usually held wine, particularly during a symposium. On some occasions they also held olive oil. Panathenaic amphorae were slightly narrower at the neck and foot than standard amphorae and used their own decorative scheme: Athena would be shown on one side and the relevant sport on the other.

The hydria (pl. hydriae) was another large vessel used to store water. Its function as a liquid container can be seen through its wider shoulders and narrow neck. Hydriae had three handles, two on the sides for lifting and one at the back for pouring. During the Classical Period the sharp angles between the lip, neck and shoulders evolved into a continuous curve.

A kylix was a very shallow bowl with small handles on either side and a narrow stem with a foot. The attendees at a symposium would drink their wine from kylixes. Again, these would vary from the size of a small saucer to bigger than a large dinner plate. Sometimes the handles of these cups would be flush with the lip so that they could be hung on the wall. A deeper drinking cup was the kantharos, which was easily recognisable by its large looping handles.

> **Study question**
> To what extent do you think the shape of a vase had an impact on the scene an artist would paint on it? Give reasons for your answer.

VASE-PAINTING TECHNIQUES

Three main techniques were used in Attic vase-painting: **black-figure**, **red-figure** and **white-ground**. Black-figure vase-painting, as the name suggests, sees the figures depicted in black against the unpainted, and therefore red background. The figures were painted as silhouettes and details were then incised so that the red of the clay showed through once the pot had been fired. Occasionally, other colours were also used for details, such as white paint for the skin of female figures or reddish-purple for hair and beards.

In the red-figure technique, figures were painted in outline and the background was painted around them. Although incision was sometimes used for effect in red-figure painting, the majority of details were added using paint instead. By using brushes of different sizes and varying the thickness of the slip used, red-figure artists were able

> **black-figure** figures are depicted in black against the unpainted, and therefore red background
>
> **red-figure** figures are outlined in paint then the background is filled in around them.
>
> **white-ground** figures are painted as on red-figure vases, but the slip is white

kaolinite a clay that is free from iron-oxide and appears white. It was used to produce the background colour of white-ground vases

FIGURE 2.84
White-ground funerary lekythos, British Museum GR1873.8–20.303.

motif either a recurring idea, scene or situation in artistic works (such as duelling warriors or the Master of the Animals), or a repeated pattern

to achieve a greater degree of differentiation in the modelling of figures than their black-figure counterparts.

White-ground vases achieve quite a different effect to those of the black- or red-figure techniques. Before the figures were painted, the whole vase was covered with a slip made from **kaolinite**, which appears white, rather than red. Once this slip was dry, the figured decoration was added in much the same way as with red-figure painting. The white-ground technique also allowed for a greater range of additional colours to be used for detailing, so we often find pinks, greens and blues being used. As the kaolinite slip is more fragile than the black- and red-figure vases, the white ground technique tended to be reserved for use on funerary or ritual vases, such as the grave offering shown in Figure 2.84.

THE ARCHAIC PERIOD

Gorgons pursuing Perseus

The earliest Attic vase to be decorated entirely with figurative, rather than geometric, ornamentation is a black-figure dinos dating from around 580 BC, depicting the Gorgons pursuing Perseus. The painter is unknown but the decoration on the vase is used to identify him as the Gorgon Painter.

On one side of the main frieze, the hero Perseus flees the Gorgons having killed their sister Medusa, who is shown collapsing following her decapitation. Two gods, Hermes, identified by his caduceus and travelling hat, and a female figure, usually thought to be Athena because of her association with this particular myth, are pursuing the Gorgons in an attempt to protect Perseus.

In terms of composition, the monotonous repetition of the Gorgon figures is broken by the falling Medusa; the diagonal lines comprising her figure stand in sharp contrast to the strong verticals of the accompanying deities.

The reverse side shows two warriors, Herakles and Kyknos, fighting in the centre; a **motif** that gains further popularity in later periods. The two figures are flanked on either side by their chariots, each attended by a charioteer who turns back, enthralled by the action. These figures are generally considered to be Herakles' companion Iolaos and Kyknos' half-brother Phobos. However, a lack of distinguishing features amongst the four figures in this scene makes it difficult to identify either.

In these entirely narrative scenes, devoid of any purely decorative elements, the Gorgon Painter heralds the rise of Attic pottery, which progressively shook off the Corinthian influence during the second quarter of the sixth century BC. Nevertheless, much of the decoration still very much demonstrates the Eastern influence on Greek art. The majority of the bowl and stand is decorated with bands of orientalised creatures, including deer, sphinxes and panthers. Some bands also include the 'Master of the Animals' motif.

The dinos itself is supported by a stand decorated in the same banded style, as is the interior. The elaborate shape of the stand is explained by the fact that the dinos was originally a bronze vessel, which has here been reproduced in clay.

FIGURE 2.85
Gorgons pursuing Perseus, dinos by the Gorgon Painter.

PRESCRIBED SOURCE

Gorgons pursuing Perseus

Date: *c.* 580 BC

Artist: Gorgon Painter

Vase type: dinos

Height: 93 cm

Provenance: Etruria

Current location: Musée du Louvre, Collection Campana, 1861, E874

Significance: earliest Attic vase featuring figurative rather than geometric decoration.

EXPLORE FURTHER
Perseus and Medusa

The tyrant Polydectes wished to marry Perseus' mother, Danae. In order to prevent the marriage, Perseus needed to acquire the head of the Gorgon, Medusa, whose gaze could turn any living thing to stone. Aided by Athena and Hermes, Perseus used his shield as a mirror to avoid looking directly at Medusa as he cut off her head. On his return, he showed the head to Polydectes and his court, turning them all to stone.

EXPLORE FURTHER

Compare the Gorgons from this vase with the Medusa of the Temple of Artemis at Corcyra; how different was the depiction of this mythical monster in vases and in sculpture?

The François Vase

The François Vase moves further from the Orientalising Period as this volute krater replaces the bands of repetitive Eastern animals with even more narrative scenes. Named after Alessandro François, who found the krater in 1844, this vase has been reconstructed, twice, after it was broken into 638 pieces when a disgruntled museum custodian threw a stool at its display case. The six bands of decoration feature over 200 figures. As is often the case in early black-figure works, many of these are identified by their accompanying inscriptions.

FIGURE 2.86
The Caledonian Boar
Hunt on the François
Vase.

The François Vase

Date: *c.* 550 BC

Artist: Ergotimos as potter
and Kleitias as painter

Vase type: volute krater

Height: 66 cm

Diameter of rim: 57 cm

Provenance: Necropolis
of Fonte Rotelia, near
Chiusi

Current location: Museo
Archeologico di
Firenze, Florence,
4209

Significance: banded
black-figure krater

The uppermost frieze, on the neck of the krater, depicts the Calydonian Boar Hunt on side A. The boar itself, as the main focus of the hunt, occupies the centre of the scene, brought down by four arrows. The hunters approach from either side, drawing the viewer's attention towards the boar, their raised feet help to instill a sense of speed and motion. Peleus and Meleager, the former clean-shaven and the latter with a beard, stand to the left of the boar while Antaios, the fallen hunter, lies below the boar. Peleus is followed by Melanaion and Atalanta, her white flesh helping to further highlight her as the only female participant in the famous hunt.

Side B shows Athenian youths and maidens dancing the Crane Dance, having escaped from the Labyrinth on Crete. They are led by Theseus who wears a long chiton and carries a lyre. Facing Theseus is Ariadne, ball of thread in hand. To the left of the scene is the ship with jubilant crew returning to carry the young men and women back home to Athens.

The second band shows the chariot race with five competitors from Patroclus' funeral games on side A. Achilles stands in front of a bronze tripod, which would have been one of the prizes, while the participants include Diomedes and Odysseus. Side B depicts the Centauromachy, including the demise of the Lapith Caeneus, as he is pounded into the ground due to his invulnerability.

The third frieze depicts the wedding of Peleus and Thetis. Thetis sits inside the house while Peleus stands at the altar, greeting his teacher, the Centaur Chiron, who leads the procession with the goddess Iris. The procession of deities extends around both sides of the vase. The overlapping figures in the procession increase the sense of depth in this two-dimensional scene.

FIGURE 2.87
Theseus and the
Athenians on the
François Vase.

The fourth frieze is once again divided into different scenes on each side of the vase. Side A depicts Achilles' ambush of Troilus, shown on horseback, outside the gates of Troy. Achilles is followed by Athena, Hermes and Thetis, all adding to the sense of Troilus' inevitable downfall. Apollo enters from the far left, suggesting the outrage at the imminent descration of his altar. The reverse shows the return of Hephaistos to Olympus. The god is portrayed riding a mule and led by Dionysos.

The fifth frieze is the most reflective of the Oriental origins of vase-painting. It shows sphinxes and griffins flanking lotus blossoms and palmettes, and panthers and lions attacking bulls, boar and a deer. The foot shows the battle between the Pygmies and the Cranes. The handles feature the Lady of the Animals above Ajax carrying the body of Achilles. The inner sides of the handles each show a Gorgon.

Every inch of this vase is covered with elaborate figured scenes. Each band of decoration would hold its own as the main scene, yet here so many are combined into this swarm of characters and stories that has been described as a 'wealth of elegant miniture-painting' (Williams, D. (1999) *Greek Vases*, 2nd edn. London: British Museum Press, p. 59).

The Wedding of Peleus and Thetis

This black-figure dinos, depicting the Wedding of Peleus and Thetis, is the earliest Attic vase by a known painter. Between the columns of Peleus house is the inscription 'Sophilos megrapsen', meaning 'Sophilos painted me'. Like the Gorgon Painter's name-vase, the figured scene that occupies the highest register contrasts with the animal friezes below to show the move away from contemporary Corinthian vase-painting.

PRESCRIBED SOURCE

The Wedding of Peleus and Thetis

Date: *c.* 580–570 BC

Artist: Sophilos

Vase type: dinos (with stand)

Height: 71 cm

Current location: British Museum, GR 1971, 1101.1

Significance: earlist Attic vase by a known painter

The gods, goddesses, nymphs and other mythical figures are shown processing to the house of the hero Peleus to celebrate his marriage to the sea-nymph Thetis. The names of the figures are written neatly alongside them. Although the dinos is painted using the black-figure technique, Sophilos uses red and white slip as well as using the background clay itself to such great effect that one almost forgets that there are only three painted colours in use on this vase.

Peleus stands in front of his house, holding a kantharos and ready to greet his guests, who arrive either on foot or by chariot. Leading the procession, in her red-winged boots, is the messenger goddess Iris. Behind her are four goddesses, Hestia, Demeter, Chariklo and Leto, wrapped in red cloaks. Dionysus follows the goddesses, occupying the central position in the scene, carrying a vine branch laden with grapes symbolising the wine that will be drunk at the wedding. He is followed in turn by Hebe and the Centaur Cheiron, who looks back to Themis, holding a sceptre, and three nymphs behind him.

FIGURE 2.88
Procession of deities on the dinos by Sophilos.

FIGURE 2.89
Procession of deities on the dinos by Sophilos.

The other section of the procession features deities in chariots alongside those arriving on foot. The first of these features Zeus and Hera. The goddess is shown holding her veil near her face in a gesture that is often used to represent brides or married women. Unfortunately, the label accompanying the three goddesses walking behind Zeus' horses has been lost, but they are usually identified as the Horai, the goddesses of the seasons. Poseidon and Amphitrite ride in the next chariot with three Charites, or Graces, walking alongside. These are followed in turn by Aphrodite and Ares in the next chariot with five of the Muses, and then Hermes, identifiable, as usual, by his hat and winged boots, with Apollo, whose mouth is open, presumably singing as he plays the cithara. The three figures with them are more of the Muses. Athena drives the final chariot with Artemis by her side, holding a bow. They are escorted by the three Morai, or Fates.

Behind the chariots we find the figure of Oceanus, bull-horned and with the body of a fish. With him are his wife Teithys, and Eileithyia, the goddess of childbirth. Bringing up the rear of the procession is Hephaistos, riding side-saddle on a mule.

The animals and monsters of the lower friezes are depicted conventionally rather than carelessly; the artist is more concerned with the mythological scene above. This style became the norm for a number of artists following on from the work of Sophilos. Found almost exclusively in Etruscan cemeteries in Italy, these vases, mainly amphorae, filled the gap after Attic ceramic ware took over the market from the Corinthian style.

Dionysus and the Maenads

This black-figure amphora, painted by the Amasis Painter, shows the god Dionysus and the Maenads. The painter is named after the potter, Amasis, with whom he regularly worked. Some scholars go so far as to suggest the potter and painter may be the same man. This vase bears the inscription 'Amasis mepoiesen', meaning 'Amasis made me'. Although some of his features and his name may seem slightly foreign to the mainstream style and suggest Egyptian origins, the Amasis Painter completed his apprenticeship in Athens.

Dionysus is bearded and holds a kantharos in one of his hands. He raises his left hand to greet two maenads approaching from the right. They are intertwined and clad in dark, intricately detailed garments. One of the maenads holds a hare, while the other is carrying a deer. Each of the female figures is also grasping a sprig of stylised ivy. Rather than picking out the flesh of the maenads in white, the Amasis Painter instead chooses to retain their pale skin by using the background colour, which results in a more subtle and sophisticated effect.

Repetition is used in the two female figures. Their front feet are raised together and their back feet are also in line. Their arms are almost mirror images of each other. Lines

FIGURE 2.92
Dionysus and the Maenads on the amphora by the Amasis Painter.

are incised on their garments to suggest repeated patterns. The intricate detailing of their drapery makes it easier to distinguish between the two figures. The overlapping of the maenads creates a greater sense of depth and texture than would be offered by a straight-forward mirroring of Dionysus by a single figure. The figures retain the frontal eye despite their profile depictions.

The decorative details on the vase are bold and beautifully rendered. Large spirals serve to frame the composition in the centre. The figures also stand on a band of stylised grape leaves or lotus-buds.

Achilles and Ajax Playing Dice

This black-figure belly amphora, signed by Exekias as both potter and painter, shows Achilles and Ajax Playing Dice. It is considered to be one of the most refined pieces from the black-figure style, with, for example, the details and decoration of the clothing engraved with great care.

The two heroes are armed for battle, but instead of the tense battle-scenes we might expect, Exekias chooses to depict the men at a time of rest during the long seige of Troy. This depiction offers an alternative view of war to that we usually find, highlighting the seemingly endless waiting and boredom that would intersperse the violent battles.

The figures are accompanied by identification inscriptions. Both men sit on low supports, leaning towards a pedestal in the centre. They stretch out their hands to read the points gained in the game. The cartoon-like inscriptions emerging from their mouths suggest that Achilles, wearing his helmet and seated to the left of the scene, is winning 4 (tessera) to 3 (tria) over Ajax, seated to the right. The spears on which the two men lean, and their downward gaze, draw our attention towards the centre of the scene. Their shields stand discarded at the sides of the scene, again slanting towards the centre.

PRESCRIBED SOURCE

Achilles and Ajax Playing Dice

Date: *c.* 540–530 BC

Artist: Exekias

Vase type: belly amphora

Height: 61.1 cm

Provenance: Vulci, Etruria

Current location: the Vatican Museums, Vatican City, 16757

Significance: signed amphora from the height of the black-figure technique

FIGURE 2.93
Achilles and Ajax Playing Dice on the amphora by Exekias.

The reverse shows the Dioskouroi, Kastor and Pollux, returning home to their parents, Tyndareus and Leda. Kastor is shown leading his horse, while Pollux plays with a dog to the left of the scene.

Exekias is often considered to be the finest of the black-figure vase-painters. By choosing to paint an amphora, rather than the dinos or krater we have seen previously, Exekias presents a sizeable panel for decoration with a more gentle curve. The high quality of the potting, producing such a smooth surface, also enables him to show off his skills with incision to great effect. His use of colour is reserved, particularly in comparison to the earlier works discussed above, which only serves to enhance the effect of the red paint for the hair and the plumes of the helmets. The level of detail achieved in the patterns of the men's drapery is unsurpassed in black-figure, and, indeed, in a great deal of red-figure painting to come.

Dionysus sailing

The interior of this black-figure kylix, bearing the inscription 'Exekias epoese', or Exekias made it, shows Dionysus sailing in a ship surrounded by dolphins. The scene is

FIGURE 2.94
Dionysus sailing on the ocean on a kylix by Exekias. **PS**

PRESCRIBED SOURCE

Dionysus sailing on the ocean

Date: c. 540–530 BC

Artist: Exekias

Vase type: kylix

Height: 13.6 cm

Diameter of rim: 30.5 cm

Provenance: Vulci, Etruria

Current location:
Staatliche Antikensammlungen, Munich, 2044

Significance: kylix from the height of the black-figure technique reminiscent of the myth where pirates attempt to capture Dionysus, but he overpowers them by turning them into dolphins (see Ovid, *Metamorphoses*, 3.597–691).

Dionysus reclines in his ship as though he were at a symposium, or drinking party; he holds a rhyton, or drinking horn, in his right hand and leans back on his left arm. The white sail contrasts dramatically with both the red background and the black of the rest of the ship, drawing the viewer's gaze towards the centre of the scene. Although the ship itself is fairly small considering the available space, a grapevine with clusters of grapes fills the upper background of the scene. The prow of the ship is decorated with eyes, as was traditional for Greek vessels, and features two white dolphins, while the stern curves up into the shape of a swan's neck and head. Seven dolphins fill the rest of the scene, two of which appear to leap above what would be the water-line.

The scene occupies the whole of the interior space rather than being confined to a tondo as is more common in drinking cups of this sort. It is deliberately set at an angle to the handles of the cup. This is so that, as the wine is drunk and gradually reveals the image, the viewer is encouraged to turn the cup to view it, causing the wine to slosh in the cup and become the sea, completing the scene.

The exterior features a set of eyes on each side, similar to those seen on East Greek cups, with eyebrows and small noses. One suggestion about the interpretation of these eyes is that they are apotropaiac, that is they are supposed to offer protection, since they keep a watchful eye as the drinker's own are obscured by the vase. Another is that they enable the drinker to channel Dionysus and look through his eyes as they consume the wine within.

On either side of the handles we find battles over fallen warriors. On one side the warrior has been stripped of his armour, while this has yet to happen to the other.

THE TRANSITIONAL PERIOD

After the mastery of the black-figure technique by Exekias, in around 530 BC, painters began to experiment with alternative versions. The artist known as the Andokides Painter, thanks to his work with the potter Andokides, is thought to be the creator of the red-figure technique. Red-figure painting freed artists from the limitations of incision to indicate details on the figures. In the new techniques, these additions could be applied with a brush, allowing for much greater variation in the kinds of modelling available with more fluid lines of varying weight.

The strong contrast between the two areas, the background and the figures, which made vase-painting so successful was preserved in the new technique. The switch to the red-figure technique also led artists to experiment more with indications of mass and form, as the colour gave a greater sense of depth than black-figure had done previously.

Painters experimenting with this new technique, such as the Andokides Painter and Euthymides, are known collectively as the Pioneers.

Bi-lingual painters

Painters such as the Andokides Painter and the Lysippides Painter were known for their innovation and development of the red-figure technique. The term **bi-lingual** (literally,

> **bi-lingual** vases decorated with both black- and red-figure designs, which, though often similar, were not intended to be direct copies of one another and were occasionally painted by different artists

191

being able to speak two languages fluently) refers to the practice of replicating a black-figure scene on one side of a vase with a similar scene in red-figure on the reverse. While these scenes were not identical, the aim was to show off the intricacies made possible by the red-figure technique.

The Pioneers

The Pioneers, including Euphronios, Euthymides and the Dikaios Painter, worked in the Kerameikos of Athens around the start of the fifth century BC. There is no documentary evidence of the group; all information has been gleaned from their work itself. Their works make frequent reference to each other and suggest that a competitive spirit existed between them. For example, on Hector Arming/Three Men Carousing (see Figure 2.102), Euthymides boasts 'as never Euphronios'.

The work of the Pioneers is noted for the simple rendering of dress, bold handling of anatomy, including exploration of the depiction of both pose and mass, experimental use of foreshortening and a thematic preference for scenes of symposia, although the latter are only represented here by the Three Men Carousing.

The Mannerists

The Mannerists were another group of Attic vase-painters working in the red-figure technique. More than fifteen artists can be described as Mannerists, with the most important being the Pan Painter. They were active from *c.* 480 BC until the late fifth century BC and tended to paint column kraters, hydriai and pelikes.

The main characteristic of their work was to maintain some of the features of black-figure vase-painting, but in red-figure scenes. Figures appear elongated with small heads, garment folds are stiff and images are framed with ornamentation seen most commonly on black-figure vases. Figures were frequently depicted gesticulating, as if speaking a form of sign language, with the hands often seeming stiff and theatrical.

Dionysus/Herakles feasting in the presence of Athena

This bi-lingual amphora features Dionysus/Herakles feasting in the presence of Athena. Similar scenes are painted on both sides, one in black figure, the other in red figure. The vase is attributed to the Andokides Painter and the Lysippides Painter.

In both scenes the figure of Herakles or Dionysus reclines on a kline or couch. Herakles and Dionysus, both sons of Zeus by mortal women, were closely linked in ancient myth and in their artistic depictions. For example, in Aristophanes' *Frogs*, Dionysus dresses himself as Herakles wearing a lion-skin and carrying a club.

On the black-figure side, by the Lysippides Painter, Herakles reclines on a couch with elaborately carved legs, holding a kantharos. A table, intended to be seen as alongside rather than under the bed, is shown laid with a kylix, bread and other food. Athena, easily identified by her helmet, spear and aegis, stands at the end of the couch, holding out her hand to greet Herakles. Behind her stands Hermes, identified once again by his boots and travelling cap.

FIGURE 2.95
Herakles/Dionysus feasting in the presence of Athena on the amphora by the Lysippides Painter and the Andokides Painter.

PS

To the far right of the scene, a slave takes wine from a dinos on a stand. Herakles' quiver of arrows and his sword are suspended above him and vines fill the background space.

On the red-figure side, the figure appears to be Dionysus, as he wears a grapevine wreath around his head and no weapons are depicted. This figure is more upright than his black-figure counterpart. His left arm leans on a cushion and holds a kantharos; he rests his right on his knee. The couch again has richly decorated legs, and there is a table in front of the kline with meats, fruits and a kylix. To the left of the couch stands Athena, offering a rose to Dionysus. On this side, the figures of Athena and Dionysus appear more isolated in a scene that is calmer and more appropriate to a meeting between them.

The elaborate internal detail, particula[...] of Athena renders their clothing much richer in appearance on the red-fi[...] he depiction of form below the drapery, whi[...] us. Although not an entirely realistic render[...] par- ent, the depiction here shows the incre[...] t of the portrayal of the human form.

The Trojan War

This red-figure vase, known as the [...] attrib- uted to the Kleophrades Painter, s [...] of his career with the potter Kleophrade [...] Fall of Troy, as the city is sacked by the [...]

Next to the handle, Aeneas i [...] his son Ascanius runs along in front of [...] from the viewer, so that only his helm[...] ted onto Aeneas' shoulder, throwing hi[...] The bend in Aeneas' knees helps to dep[...] emotion- ally, as he attempts to flee the city with his family.

PRESCRIBED SOURCE

Dionysus/Herakles feasting in the presence of Athena

Artist: Lysippides Painter and Andokides Painter

Vase type: belly amphora

Date: *c.* 530–510 BC

Height: 53.5 cm

Provenance: Vulci, Etruria

Current location: Staatliche Antikensammlungen, Munich, 2301

Significance: bi-lingual amphora

FIGURE 2.96

Ajax attacks Cassandra in the Fall of Troy on a hydria by the Kleophrades Painter.

FIGURE 2.97

Priam at the altar in the Fall of Troy on a hydria by the Kleophrades Painter.

PRESCRIBED SOURCE

The Trojan War

Date: *c.* 490–480 BC

Artist: Kleophrades Painter

Vase type: hydria

Height: 42 cm

Provenance: Nola, Italy

Current location: Museo Nazionale Archeologico, Naples, 81669

Significance: red-figure hydria with experimental rear views

We then find the Lesser Ajax striding purposefully over the corpse of a fallen warrior, sword drawn, advancing on his prey, the prophetess, Cassandra. She is shown clinging to the statue of Athena, whose spear and shield are raised against Ajax to no avail. Cassandra reaches out her hand in supplication to her attacker as he grabs her hair with his left hand. She is pitifully nude apart from a cloak knotted around her neck. Another woman hides behind the statue, while a third sits nearby below a forlorn palm tree, lamenting their fate.

On the other side of the tree, Priam sits on the altar with the lifeless body of his grandson Astyanax lying limply over his knees. Neoptolemus lunges towards Priam, his huge sword drawn back above his head, ready to inflict the fatal blow. He stands in front of a fallen Trojan with his back to us. The artist's depiction of the rear view of Neoptolemus' right leg presents an interesting variation on the frontal and profile views we have become so accustomed to seeing.

Next we see a woman, tentatively identified as Andromache, defending herself against an attacking Greek soldier who has fallen to one knee to shelter below his shield. The identification is based on a similar scene by the Brygos Painter, housed in the Musée du Louvre, where the figure defending her son with a pestle is named as Andromache.

Finally, we find Aithra, an elderly woman held captive by the Trojans as one of Helen's maids. Here she is seated on a low slab and her grandsons Acamas and Demophon rush to her rescue. The two men offer their hands to their grandmother to help raise her to her feet. Thus, either side of the handle, we find the escapees, the glimmers of hope in these desparate scenes.

The composition is one of the desperation of war and its impact on civilians. Kleophrades was responding to the Persian invasion of Greece in 490 BC. Their return in 480–478 BC, which saw the Persians sack the Athenian Acropolis and raze its buildings to the ground, would have been either imminent or fresh in his mind at the time of painting. He demonstrates how vase-painters were using their new-found skills and mastery of the technique to present more emotionally responsive scenes.

Dionysus and the Maenads

This red-figure amphora by the Kleophrades Painter also shows Dionysus and the Maenads, but presents a very different scene, both in terms of style and composition,

PRESCRIBED SOURCE

Dionysus and the Maenads

Date: 500–490 BC

Artist: Kleophrades Painter

Vase type: pointed amphora

Height: 56 cm

Provenance: Vulci, Etruria

Current location: Staatliche Antikensammlungen, Munich, 8732

Significance: early example of a pointed amphora

FIGURE 2.98
Dionysus and the Maenads on an amphora by the Kleophrades Painter.

from that of the Amasis Painter discussed previously. This pointed amphora is one of the earliest known examples of this particular variant on the shape.

Here we again find a single band of decoration, which extends around both sides of the vase. Dionysus dominates the scene, holding his kantharos in his right hand and waving vines in his left. His head is once again wreathed in ivy. His chiton falls in numerous folds, almost like pleats, suggesting the fine nature of the material. It is in fact so transparent that his lower left leg remains visible through the cloth. He also wears a panther-skin tied around his neck, one of its paws visible at Dionysus' side. Dionysus moves towards the right while looking back towards the maenad behind him.

To the right of Dionysus is a maenad attempting to escape a **silen**. She holds a thyrsos in one hand and pushes the silen away with the other. He reaches for her hair with his right hand, while his left stretches down to the hem of her chiton.

To the left of the god is another maenad attempting to escape the amorous advances of a silen. She holds a thyrsos in one hand while a snake winds its way around the other. She wears a fawn skin over her chiton and mantle. The silen ducks under the handle of the vase to grab her thyrsos and reaches to touch her dress.

On the reverse we find a silen playing the aulos, or double-flute, in the centre, flanked by two ecstatic maenads. Each carries a thyrsos and the one on the left again has a snake wound around her wrist. The other looks upward with her mouth open as though singing to the music. Unlike their counterparts on the other side who wear bonnets, these maenads have their hair uncovered and, interestingly, one of the maenads is fair-haired.

The neck is decorated with athletes throwing javelins and discuses.

Kleophrades' use of a light-coloured slip on this vase is highly effective; he picks out the fawnskins, the snakes, the maenad's hair, Dionysus' kantharos and the vine leaves.

> **silen** named after Silenus, the elderly tutor of Dionysus, silens are mythological male followers of Dionysus, typically depicted with horse features and large phalluses; they inhabit the forests and amuse themselves with music, wine and women

---

PRESCRIBED SOURCE

Achilles and Hector/Memnon

Date: *c.* 490–460 BC

Artist: Berlin Painter

Vase type: volute krater

Height: 63 cm

Diameter of rim: 46 cm

Provenance: Caere, Italy

Current location: British Museum, London, GR 1848,0801.1

Significance: red-figure volute krater

THE CLASSICAL PERIOD

As in other areas of Greek art, the period following the Persian Wars saw changes in Greek vase-painting. Mythological scenes remained hugely popular as decoration. While the black-figure painting was almost obsolete in Athens by this point, the Mannerists revived some of the techniques and motifs in a sort of archaising manner.

Achilles and Hector/Memnon

This volute krater, attributed to the Berlin Painter, features duels between Achilles and Hector/Memnon. The majority of the vase is painted black, leaving the figures confined to a narrow frieze around the neck.

On one side, Achilles, son of Thetis, battles Memnon, the King of Ethiopia and son of Eos, goddess of the Dawn. Each is accompanied by his mother in support. The pair appear reasonably well matched as they both lunge towards the centre of the scene. As with earlier vases, the figures are accompanied with inscriptions identifying each. The

FIGURE 2.99
Achilles and Memnon
on a volute krater by
the Berlin Painter.

FIGURE 2.100
Achilles and Hector
on a volute krater by
the Berlin Painter.

> **Study question**
> Williams writes that
> 'the Berlin Painter's
> special talent lay in his
> ability to build small,
> elegant details into a
> graceful, living whole
> and then set his figure
> or group in perfect
> harmony with the vessel
> he was decorating'. To
> what extent do you
> agree?
>
> (Quote from Williams, D.
> 1999, *Greek Vases*, 2nd
> edn, London: British
> Museum Press, p. 80.)

strong diagonals of the frozen action draws the viewer's attention towards the centre of the scene and the imminent clash between the heroes.

On the other side, Achilles battles Hector. Athena looks on, offering encouragement while Apollo turns away, abandoning Hector to his fate. This scene is again composed of strong diagonals; Achilles' forward motion is reflected in Hector's spear and then in his own falling posture. This is then picked up in Apollo's arrow and back leg as he walks away. Athena's raised arm also causes her aegis to fall in such as way as to again provide this diagonal.

Hector's arms are stretched out helplessly as he loses blood from the wounds to his leg and torso. His body is open to attack from the approaching Achilles.

On each side the figures are widely spaced to fill the frieze without cluttering the scene with extra figures. However, these figures are not displayed in complete isolation; long spears are used to draw the viewer's attention in towards the centre of each scene.

Herakles and Antaios

This calyx krater by Euphronios depicts Herakles and Antaios. The combat in this scene is very different from the emotionally charged, yet relatively still, scene shown on the previous vase by the Berlin Painter. Here, the violent clash between the figures focuses on the depiction of action and anatomy. The other side depicts a young man with an aulos, surrounded by seated companions.

Here we see again the interest of the Pioneers in the depiction of emotion; the effort of the fight is easily apparent on Antaios' face. His mouth is shown in a grimace while his body is depicted in detail, revealing the immense struggle. In contrast, Herakles

EXPLORE FURTHER
Herakles and Antaios

On his way to the Garden of the Hesperides, Herakles encountered the giant Antaios. Antaios would challenge anyone who passed to a wrestling match. As long as he remained in contact with his mother, Gaia, Antaios was unbeatable. He therefore won all his bouts by pinning his opponents to the floor before killing them. During their match, Herakles realised this and raised the giant from the ground before overpowering him and squeezing him to death.

FIGURE 2.101
Herakles and Antaios on a calyx krater by Euphronios.

Study question
Compare the depictions of Herakles here with those on the metopes of Temple C at Selinus and on the Temple of Zeus at Olympia; how uniformly is the hero depicted in ancient art?

appears hardly affected by the fight. The usual contrast between civilisation and barbarism is also apparent in the ragged hair and beard of Antaios in comparison with the well-groomed appearance of the Greek hero. In the background we see women who are portrayed in a smaller scale, creating a novel sense of depth and perspective in the scene.

Hector Arming/Three Men Carousing

This belly amphora, attributed to Euthymides, shows Hector Arming and Three Men Carousing. At just over 60 cm, its size suggests this may have been created for its aesthetics, rather than as a functional piece of storage. It is particularly notable as being one of the first scenes to attempt **foreshortening** through the use of the three-quarter view.

On one side we see the three revellers, artistically nude to reveal their poses in an exploration of human anatomy. Their heads are wreathed in ivy added in red paint. Each appears entirely separate from the others. They have obviously been drinking as the left-most figure, named by inscription as Komarchos, holds a kantharos while the others dance merrily. The two outer figures are shown in dynamic, active stances with their legs and hands in motion. The central figure, named as Euedemos, stands with his back to the foreground but twists to look back over his shoulder towards the viewer. The right-most figure is named as Teles.

On the reverse, Hector stands in the centre of the scene arming himself for battle. He is already wearing his greaves and is fastening the corselet over his short tunic. To the left is his father Priam, and his mother Hecuba watches on the right, holding his helmet and spear. This side features the inscription 'Euthymides, son of Pollias, painted [me]'.

PRESCRIBED SOURCE

Hector Arming/Three Men Carousing

Date: *c.* 510 BC

Artist: Euthymides

Vase type: belly amphora

Height: 60.3 cm

Provenance: Vulci, Italy

Current location: Staatliche Antikensammlungen, Munich, 2307

Significance: red-figure belly amphora with attempts at foreshortening

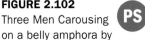

foreshortening creating a sense of three-dimensional perspective in a two-dimensional space

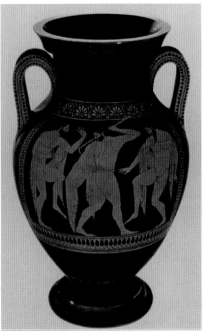

FIGURE 2.102 PS
Three Men Carousing on a belly amphora by Euthymides.

On both sides the figures appear to exist independently of each other. Euthymides seemingly created this piece as a study of the human figure in differing poses. The artist breaks away from the rigid frontal poses of contemporary statues and brings the figures closer together.

Although the foreshortening is primitive, its presence increases the naturalism of the whole composition. It is thought that this may be the reason for the inscription 'as never Euphronios'. The fine lettering used in the numerous inscriptions proclaim the lineage, cameraderie and literacy of Euthymides.

Herakles and the Amazons

PRESCRIBED SOURCE

Herakles and the Amazons

Date: *c.* 510 BC

Artist: Euphronios

Vase type: volute krater

Provenance: Arezzo, Italy

Current location: Museo Civico, Arezzo, 1465

This red-figure krater is attributed to Euphronios. On one side we find Herakles, identified by his lion-skin and club, battling against Amazons. On the reverse more Amazons run up to join the fray.

The composition on the body is rich and complicated. Herakles advances from the left (usually the position of victors in Greek art), striding forward against the Amazons. Three Amazons approach from the right. Two march in step with a shield raised for protection while a third aims her bow and arrow at Herakles. This third Amazon creeps forward, raising and twisting her foreshortened forward foot. Herakles is accompanied in his exploits by Telamon who crouches with his shield outstretched in front of him.

Here Euphronios offers a response to the challenge issued by Euthymides. The figures are no longer distinct from one another, but rather they overlap and even occupy the space beneath the legs of other figures.

The two fallen Amazons are mirror images of each other, apart from the differences in the positions of their arms, which add variety and realism to the scene. Each figure has her lower leg bent back and concealed behind her thigh in a bold development. The whole scene is vigorously active and full of foreshortenings, repetitions and mirrorings.

Study questions

1 Woodford notes that 'in terms of drawing and composition, [the painting] is masterly, but as decoration on the surface of a vase it is perhaps less satisfying that the primitive figures and simple patterns that were so sensitively arranged by the geometric vase-painter more than two hundred years before'. Which do you think is the more successful in terms of decoration? Give reasons for your answer.

2 How differently are Amazons depicted here to those on the Ionic frieze on the Temple of Apollo at Bassae? How can the similarties and differences be explained?

FIGURE 2.103
Herakles and the
Amazons on a volute
krater by Euphronios.

PS

PRESCRIBED SOURCE

Perseus and Medusa

Date: *c.* 460 BC

Artist: the Pan Painter

Vase type: hydria

Height: 34.3 cm

Provenance: Capua, Italy

Current location: British
  Museum, London,
  GR 1873,0820.352

Significance: red-figure
  hydria in the style of
  the Mannerists

Perseus and Medusa

On this red-figure hydria the Pan Painter depicts Perseus and Medusa. Perseus is shown fleeing to the left of the scene, having cut off the head of Medusa.

In the centre of the scene, Medusa falls, headless, to her knees. She wears a short, bordered chiton with sleeves. A stream of blood pours from her wounded neck. She has fallen to the left and supports herself on her finger-tips, her arms rigid.

To the left of the scene, Perseus flees with both arms extended in front of him. He looks back towards Medusa. He wears a chiton similar to that of Medusa, with no folds on the upper part, a winged hat and winged boots. A bag hangs from his right shoulder, across his body, in which the Gorgoneion (the head of Medusa) can be seen, her eyes closed. The harpe, a sickle-shaped knife, is visible in his left hand. His long hair is looped over his ears.

At the right of the scene, Athena runs towards the left, carrying a long spear over her right shoulder, and with her left hand, holds up her skirt. She wears a long, undertied sleeved chiton. The chiton has no folds but has a pattern of 'V's. She wears a dotted aegis fringed with snakes and her tall crested helmet.

The design is principally confined to the shoulder and extends very little below the level of the handles at the side of the vase. A strip of maeanders (Greek key design) frames the scene below. This scene lacks the drama of earlier depictions, such as that of the Gorgon Painter, creating instead an almost cheerful presentation of the myth.

FIGURE 2.104
Perseus and Medusa on a hydria by the Pan Painter.

Boreas and Oreithyia

This red-figure oinochoe by the Pan Painter shows Boreas and Oreithyia.

To the right of the scene, Boreas, god of the North wind, is bearded and winged. He wears a chiton and winged boots as he reaches for Oreithyia with both hands. Towards the centre of the scene, Oreithyia flees, looking back over her shoulder. She raises her arms in a gesture of alarm. Her woollen chiton is covered by a himation tied over her right shoulder. The lower folds of the chiton are grouped in regular sets of six to eight folds. Her hair is tied up in a fillet.

To the left of the scene, a nymph, possibly Herse, is also shown fleeing in a manner that mirrors Oreithyia. This figure has also been identified as another daughter of Erechtheus.

Erechtheus, Oreithyia's father, is seated on a rock to the far right of the scene. He wears a himation that covers his mouth and the lower part of his head. He looks down, striking his forehead with his right hand and resting his left on his staff. His fillet is indicated by a thin black line. His hair and beard are indicated only by outline. Here the focus is very much on the emotion of his character rather than his physicality.

FIGURE 2.105
Boreas and Oreithyia
on an oinochoe by the
Pan Painter.

FIGURE 2.106
Herse in Boreas and
Oreithyia by the Pan
Painter.

Study question
Woodford notes that in
his depiction of
Erechtheus' grief for his
daughter, the Pan Painter
'has produced one of
those powerful, sad,
muffled figures with
which Greek art opened
up a whole new, hitherto
unimaginable world of
feeling'. To what extent
do you agree?

(Quote from Woodford,
S., *Greek Art*, Bloomsbury
Academic, p. 109.)

TOPIC REVIEW

These questions should draw on your knowledge of the whole topic, so think carefully about the different things you have learned (check the Topic Overview on pp. 177–178).

1. What factors contributed to the increased naturalism of figures in vase-painting from the sixth to fifth centuries?
2. Who were more revolutionary in their advances, the Pioneers or the Mannerists?
3. Which is of greater interest to vase-painters, telling a story or portraying figures?

Further Reading

Clark, Andrew J., Elston, Maya and Hart, Mary Louise (2006) *Understanding Greek Vases: A Guide to Terms, Styles and Techniques*. Los Angeles, CA: Getty Publications
Williams, Dyfri (1999) *Greek Vases*, 2nd edn. London: British Museum Press, Chapter 1

Black-figure vase-painting
Boardman, John (1974) *Athenian Black-Figure Vases*. London: Thames and Hudson
Moignard, Elizabeth (2015) *Master of Attic Black-Figure Painting*. London: I.B. Tauris
Williams, Dyfri (1999) *Greek Vases*, 2nd edn. London: British Museum Press, Chapter 5
Woodford, Susan (1986) *An Introduction to Greek Art*. London: Duckworth, Chapters 1 and 2

Red-figure vase-painting
Boardman, John (1975) *Athenian Red-Figure Vases: The Archaic Period*. London: Thames and Hudson
Boardman, John (1989) *Athenian Red-Figure Vases: The Classical Period*. London: Thames and Hudson
Williams, Dyfri (1999) *Greek Vases*, 2nd edn. London: British Museum Press, Chapter 6
Woodford, Susan (1986) *An Introduction to Greek Art*. London: Duckworth, Chapters 5, 8 and 10

PRACTICE QUESTIONS

Source A: *A red-figure vase*

Source B: *A black-figure vase*

1. Who painted the scene shown in **Source A**? [1]
2. What does it depict? [2]
3. By comparing the content and composition of the scenes on **Source A** (Perseus and Medusa) and **Source B** (Gorgons Pursing Perseus), explain which scene you find more aesthetically pleasing. [10]
4. 'In vase-painting, the second half of the sixth century was a period of bold exploration and lively experimentation.' How far is this statement supported by the pots you have studied? [30]

2.5 Themes

Greek art tends to take one of two topics as its subject matter, either everyday life or mythological scenes. That said, the division of all the scenes considered earlier into just these two areas would be difficult. Consider, for example, the Ionic frieze on the Parthenon. The Panathenaic procession took place annually, and the Great Panathenaia only once every four years, so this can hardly be called an 'everyday' scene. We must therefore take the term more broadly to refer to those scenes that could take place every day. All others involve mythical gods, heroes and creatures, or divine intervention. Alternatively, we find examples of mythological subjects, such as Aphrodite of Knidos, where there is very little beyond exceptional beauty to distinguish her from a 'mere mortal'. She is simply a woman disturbed during the everyday act of bathing. Similarly, if we consider scenes such as the Wedding of Peleus and Thetis in comparison with depictions of mortal weddings, we find very few differences other than the divinities in attendance. Both mortal and mythical scenes feature chariots, processions, and grooms waiting in their homes to welcome new brides. It is evident that mythical scenes were designed to reflect the occurrences of daily life, albeit with the glossier sheen of divine characters.

While almost all pieces of Greek art can generally be divided into either everyday life or scenes of mythology, different themes and motifs were better suited to, and often more popular in, each of the three areas of the arts discussed.

FREE-STANDING SCULPTURE

Free-standing sculpture was generally limited to singular figures or, at most, very small groups. This made it difficult to depict scenes in the same way as we would find in architectural sculpture or vase-painting. Instead, free-standing sculpture tends to focus on individual gods or goddesses, or mortals. Where mortals are depicted, they tend to be in their idealised form, such as the ideal athletes of the Diskobolos of Myron, the Doryphoros of Polykleitos or the Apoxyomenos of Lysippos, none of whom are to be thought of as particular men, but rather the embodiment of what an athlete can be. Even when we consider the funerary figures of the Anavyssos Kouros or the Aristodikos Kouros, we still see stylised versions of the deceased. Not necessarily recognisable as depictions of those whose graves they marked, these stylised, nude figures again represent something more than just a portrait.

During the fourth century, once Greek artists had mastered the depiction of the human body, they moved on to explore ways in which to depict concepts rather than individuals. Considering the Eirene and Ploutos by Kephisodotos, we see the embodiment of peace and wealth. Here the artist's impression of bounteous Peace, both in terms of the cornucopia she holds in her hand and her ample curves, nurtures the young and vulnerable Wealth.

ARCHITECTURAL SCULPTURE

Architectural sculpture differs in that it includes multiple figures arranged in such a way as to depict a story or an event. While the sculptors of free-standing pieces developed an interest in the portrayal of mortals and deities, those working on architectural sculpture focused on particular myths that lent themselves to the confines of the decorative areas of buildings. Herakles made frequent appearances, as we have seen in the metope of Temple C, Selinus, and in the metopes of the Temple of Zeus at Olympia. He is easily recognisable due to his great strength and the popularity of the myths involving his character. His frequent depiction wearing a lion-skin also makes him easily identifiable. The need to be recognisable was all the more important in the semi-literate society in which these sculptures were produced. The number of his adventures enables sculptors to explore a variety of poses, making best use of the available spaces.

Battles were also popular motifs in architectural sculpture, thanks to the possibilities available in terms of the number of figures that could be included and the vast array of positions in which to arrange them: standing, kneeling, lunging, dying. All this adds to the realism and interest of the scenes. The Centauromachy was one of, if not the most popular, theme in architectural sculpture. Seen here in the metopes of the Parthenon, Athens, the Ionic frieze of the Temple of Apollo, Bassae, and the west pediment of the Temple of Zeus, Olympia, the Centauromachy created visual interest through the mix of human and horse-like figures, and was easily adaptable to fit all three areas of architectural sculpture. The other hugely popular battle for architectural sculpture was the Trojan War. This was probably due, at least in part, to the viewers' familiarity with the subject through its prominence in Greek literature. We find the Trojan War, or episodes from it, on the pediments of the Temple of Aphaia, Aegina, and the Ionic frieze of the Siphnian Treasury.

VASE-PAINTING

We also see the Trojan War as a popular theme in vase-painting, appearing prominently on vessels showing Achilles and Ajax Playing Dice by Exekias, Hector Arming by Euthymides, Achilles and Memnon/Hector by the Berlin Painter and the Trojan War by Kleophrades. Here we see its versatility as a topic for depiction; the number of figures in each scene ranges from two combatants to the epic battle scenes. Achilles is of particular interest to vase-painters. Not only do we see him as the great warrior in his duels against Hector and Memnon, but we also see a different side to him in his game against Ajax during a brief moment of calm.

Similarly, Athena appears in numerous guises in Greek vase-painting. We see her as a protector of Achilles and of Perseus in Perseus and Medusa by the Pan Painter, as the host to guests in Herakles/Dionysus feasting in the presence of Athena, and as a guest at the Wedding of Peleus and Thetis and on the François Vase. Again, it is her versatility, easily identifiable iconography and virtual omnipresence in Greek mythology that make her attractive to vase-painters.

Similarly, Dionysus and Herakles, with their particularly close relationship in Greek myth as half-brothers, also hold prominent positions in the Greek artist's array of stock motifs. The two occupy interesting positions, both being the sons of Zeus and mortal mothers. As such they are able to bridge the gap between the realm of the gods and the world of mortals. Hence we see them engaging in everyday activities, such as feasting or partaking in religious rituals, as in the vases showing Dionysus and the Maenads by the Amasis Painter and the Kleophrades Painter. Herakles' labours and adventures also provide an array of scenes with identifiable figures, easily adapted to fit a range of spaces and vessel shapes. Euphronios, in particular, uses Herakles' escapades to great effect, such as in his depictions of Herakles and Antaios using the two as the dominant figures in the scene, compared with his busier scene of Herakles and the Amazons, where he is outnumbered by the female warriors. Although on a much smaller scale than in his interaction with Antaios, he is still the central figure, commanding the viewer's attention.

TOPIC REVIEW

These questions should draw on your knowledge of the whole topic, so think carefully about the different things you have learned (check the Topic Overview on p. 205).

1. Was war the most important subject for Greek artists?
2. Why were depictions of Herakles so popular in Greek art?
3. What impact do the forms and functions of Greek art have on the scenes depicted?
4. What evidence is there for the popularity of certain scenes changing over time?

Further Reading

Barringer, Judith M. (2008) *Art, Myth and Ritual in Classical Greece*. Cambridge: Cambridge University Press

Carpenter, Thomas H. (1991) *Art and Myth in Ancient Greece*. London: Thames and Hudson, Chapters 1, 3, 6 and 9

Oakley, John H. (2013) *The Greek Vase: Art of the Storyteller*. London: British Museum Press

---

PRACTICE QUESTIONS

Source A: *Two metopes*

Source B: *A red-figure vase*

1. Evaluate how successfully painters and sculptors depicted Herakles. You may use **Sources A** (Metopes from the Temple of Zeus at Olympia) and **B** (Herakles and the Amazons) as a starting point.   [20]
2. Which presents the most varied depiction of Athena: vase-painting or architectural sculpture? You should support your answer with reference to the pieces you have studied.   [30]

What to Expect in the A Level Exam for Greek Art

This chapter aims to show you the types of questions you are likely to get in the written examination. It offers some advice on how to answer the questions and will help you avoid common errors.

THE EXAMINATION

This component of the A Level Classical Civilisation examination is designed to test your knowledge, understanding and evaluation of Greek art. The examination is worth 75 marks and lasts 1 hour and 45 minutes. This represents 30% of the total marks for the A Level.

There are two Assessment Objectives in your A Level, and questions will be designed to test these areas. These Assessment Objectives are outlined in the table below, together with the total number of marks available for each on the paper:

	Assessment Objective	Marks
AO1	Demonstrate knowledge and understanding of: • literature and visual/material culture • how sources and ideas reflect, and influence, their cultural contexts • possible interpretations of sources, perspectives and ideas by different audiences and individuals.	35
AO2	Critically analyse, interpret and evaluate literature and visual/ material culture, using evidence to make substantiated judgements and produce coherent and reasoned arguments.	40

EXAM STRUCTURE AND QUESTION TYPES

The exam is divided into two sections, A and B.

There are four question types in this exam:

- a number of short-answer questions (5 marks in total)
- 10-mark stimulus questions
- 20-mark shorter essay
- 30-mark essay

Try to plan your time well. The shorter essay question and the long essay question together make up 50 of the 75 marks available, and so you should aim to spend the majority of your time on these two questions.

Section A has the following format:

There will be two sets of prescribed visual/material sources on the paper.

- These two sources will be drawn from two different types of art you have studied; free-standing sculpture, architectural sculpture or vases.
- One or more short-answer questions relating to the sources (worth 2 or 3 marks in total, adding up to 5 marks over the two sets of sources). These questions will test AO1 only.
- You will then be asked a 10-mark stimulus question on each source.

The final question in Section A will be the 20-mark shorter essay question.

- You may use either or both sources as a starting point for your answer, as well as your own knowledge.

Section B has the following format:

- You will be given a choice of two essays, of which you should **only do one**. This is worth 30 marks.

SECTION A

Short-answer questions and visual/material-stimulus question

For example, you could be shown the following prescribed visual/material source.

Source A: *The Aphrodite from the Agora*

Short-answer question

An example of a short-answer question would be:

Question: What is the date of this sculpture? [1]
Answer: 420 BC [1].

This question is AO1 since it requires you to show knowledge and understanding, but there is no analysis or evaluation required.

Stimulus question

After the short-answer questions, you will be asked a 10-mark stimulus question. Of the 10 marks available, 5 are for AO1 and 5 for AO2. AO1 marks are awarded for the selection of material from the source, AO2 marks for the interpretation, analysis or evaluation of this material. These questions are marked according to a marking grid, which you can view on the OCR website.

For example, for the Aphrodite from the Agora, you might be asked a question such as this:

Question: Evaluate to what extent marble has been effectively used in the Aphrodite from the Agora. [10]

A key word here is 'evaluate'. You need to think about how far the use of marble is effective in this sculpture. As the marking grid indicates, it is more important to give clear and thoughtful analysis with good supporting evidence from the source. Two points you could make might be (you do not need to separate them in your answers):

Point 1: The smooth material enables the sculptor to show off the goddess' pure and radiant flesh, enhancing her alluring nature as the goddess of love and beauty.

Point 2: The marble does not so readily allow for the use of additional materials, as bronze would have. The sculptor could therefore not embellish the goddess with gold jewellery or enhance her facial features with materials such as copper for the lips or silver for eyelashes.

In each of these points, the evidence is drawn from the statue, AO1, and then this evidence is interpreted and analysed, AO2.

The 10-mark stimulus question could ask you to compare two pieces of artwork with each other.

Pot A

Pot B

Question: By comparing the content and composition of Pots A and B, explain which scene you find more aesthetically pleasing. [10]

Notice that in this instance you are not being asked to evaluate but to explain. You should aim to make a range of clear points, using evidence from both pots. If possible, refer closely to the pots. One example of one point that you might make is as follows:

Answer: In Pot B the figures of Perseus and Athena are arranged either side of Medusa. Their gaze, directed towards the fallen Gorgon draws the viewer's gaze towards the centre of the scene in a more aesthetically pleasing arrangement.

Here the analysis that drawing the viewer's attention towards the centre is aesthetically pleasing is AO2, while the evidence that supports this from the pot is AO1.

The shorter essay question

The final question in Section A will give you the opportunity to use one or both sources, as well as asking you to demonstrate your wider knowledge of the Greek Art topic. There are 20 marks available, 10 for AO1 and 10 for AO2. This question has its own tailored marking grid, which you can view on the OCR website.

An example of such a question might be as follows:

Question: To what extent do you think drapery is used more effectively for females in free-standing sculpture than in vases? You may use Sources A and B as a starting point.

When you **plan** your answer to this question, it might be a good idea to write down some key points of factual evidence, which you are going to use for AO1. You could start by noting the evidence from the two sources on the paper. Aphrodite from the Agora uses drapery to emphasise her sensuality and femininity in Source A. In Source B, Athena holds out her drapery with her left hand to show movement and she rushes towards the fallen Medusa in the centre of the pot. You might then list other examples and pieces of evidence from your wider studies. One example could be the Wedding of Peleus and Thetis where Artemis' peplos is decorated with a series of friezes, of repeated animals and shapes.

Think about some of the key words and phrases in the question. Firstly, note that the question specifies 'female' figures, so be sure to limit your discussion to this area. The phrase 'to what extent' gives you plenty of flexibility to examine both sides of the argument, and to agree to some extent but not fully. For example, you are not being asked to examine whether the use of drapery was effective at all, but whether it was more effective in free-standing sculpture in comparison to vases. There is no 'right' or 'wrong' answer to a question such as this – you simply need to back up your opinions with strong evidence from your studies.

SECTION B

The essay question

In Section B, you will be given a choice of two essays. **You should only do one essay.** The essay is worth 30 marks, with ten marks for AO1 and twenty marks for AO2 (this question also has its own tailored marking grid, which you can download from the OCR website). However, this does not mean that you should be aiming to give evidence and evaluation in exactly that ratio. A good essay is likely to have more evaluation than evidence in any case, and so you should just aim to write the best essay you can, where you back up your arguments with evidence from your studies. What you should avoid doing, however, is over-narrating: telling the examiner what is depicted in the piece rather than analysing it according to the question.

The first thing you need to do is to decide which question to choose. Make sure that you read both questions carefully and think about what is being asked. It is a common mistake for candidates to read the question as they want it to be, rather than as it is. For example, consider the following question:

'Greek sculptors were always bold and innovative.' How far is this statement supported by the free-standing sculpture you have studied? [30]

You should weigh up the extent to which different sculptors of free-standing figures were bold and innovative, rather than to simply discuss the appearance of the statues. However, notice that it would be possible to misread this question. A learner may previously have written a practice essay such as: 'To what extent was Praxiteles the boldest and most innovative sculptor?' If so, it would be very tempting to reproduce many of the arguments made in that essay. Be very careful not to do this. You must answer the question in front of you, which in this case is about whether free-standing sculpture was always bold and innovative. Therefore, when you make your choice about which essay to attempt, ensure that you have read each question carefully and are very sure about what each one is asking for. It may be that you think that you could answer both. This is a good problem to have! Make a clear decision one way or another and then stick with it.

Try to ensure that you give your essay a clear structure. Perhaps draw up a plan paragraph by paragraph or argument by argument. While it is a good idea to have a brief introduction and conclusion to the essay, try not to make these too long. Your introduction should simply briefly outline the key issues, and perhaps the line you are going to take, while the conclusion should be short and simply summarise the key points you have made to conclude your argument. To score good marks in AO1, make sure you choose a range of factual evidence from at least two of your pieces. To score good marks on AO2, make sure you examine the issue and weigh up your arguments carefully. You will want to make a variety of points, and again you may find that there are arguments on both sides. It is fine to have this, but you need to ensure that you come down on one side of the argument or another, and that you give clear reasons for why you have done this.

Modern scholarship

In this essay question, you are required to show knowledge of modern scholarship in your answer. This requirement of the exam is supported in the textbooks by 'Modern Scholarship' boxes. The OCR rubric says that 'Learners are expected to make use of scholarly views, academic approaches and sources to support their argument'. It is essential that you build in such material in order to do well on this question. How should you do this?

First of all, you of course need to read more widely about the topic. In this book, you have been given suggestions for articles and books to read on a variety of topics relating to Greek Art. Try to follow up as many as possible, and take notes about some of the key arguments that scholars make. It is especially interesting when two authors disagree with each other on a topic, such as what is depicted on the Parthenon's Ionic frieze. When referring to the view of a scholar, you need not quote them directly, although if you are able to remember a few words that they have written accurately, then that will be very impressive. However, it may be that you refer to a general argument that they put forward in a book, an article or a chapter.

Let us take an example relating to the question on page 214. One of your books for recommended reading is Stewart's *Greek Sculpture*. On p. 110, Stewart writes that 'it was perhaps the very lack of specificity of the kouros and kore that made them so popular'. This may well be a view worth exploring in your essay, since it suggests that the popularity of sculptures may have been based on different criteria for the ancient Greeks from those used today. It would also enable you to question to what extent the sculptures were merely copies of each other, or whether they bore individual traits, relevant to their context and function. Stewart's argument encourages you to consider the ancient purchaser of these sculptures and what they were looking for in their sculptures. You do not necessarily need to quote the details of where you read the ideas, it will be enough to mention the scholar's name and explain what they say.

Above all, make your use of secondary sources relevant to the question you are answering. To use a secondary source well you should think carefully about why it is supporting your argument or showing a different argument, and make it clear why you are including it. You might want to agree or disagree with the scholarly view, in which case you will need to explain why you do so. You may not remember everything about the secondary source you have read, but if you ensure the examiner understands what you are using and why, this will strengthen your argument. Using secondary sources in this way gives you a skill that is crucial at university level in many different subjects because engaging with what other people have thought about a particular topic enriches your own understanding.

GLOSSARY

Component-specific glossaries can be found on the companion website.

aegis this was often carried or worn by both Athena and Zeus, though its precise nature is unclear: it sometimes appears as a garment, worn around Athena's chest, or as a shield, and often has the head of a gorgon on it

Apadana (pl. **Apadanas**) large columned entrance hall where the king would receive his subjects. It featured porticoes (covered colonnades on two, three or four sides). There were towers on some or all of the corners

Archaic Period beginning around the start of the 6th century BC and ending between 490 and 480 BC, following the Persian invasions of Greece

aristocracy (pl. **aristocracies**) formed from 'aristos' meaning 'the best' and 'kratos' meaning 'power'. A system of government where the noble families in the city have the power. Their power is handed down through their families. In the Greek **poleis**, power was connected with ownerships of land

ate blindness that pushes those who display *hubris* into making poor decisions

barbaros (pl. **barbaroi**) Greek word referring to someone who makes the unintelligible sounds of a foreign language – 'bar-bar-bar'. The English language contains some comparable terms: 'jabber', 'mumble' or 'babble'

bi-lingual vases decorated with both black- and red-figure designs, which, though often similar, were not intended to be direct copies of one another and were occasionally painted by different artists

black-figure figures are depicted in black against the unpainted, and therefore red background

caryatid clothed female figures used to hold up architecture in place of columns

chiton a rectangular piece of linen clothing, worn by both men and women, sown at the shoulders or tied with buttons and frequently tied at the waist with a belt; in sculpture it is frequently worn by women, often as the thinner under layer to either a himation or a peplos

contrapposto literally, counter-pose: the figure's shoulders and hips are angled in different directions because its weight is on one foot

cult statue a statue that embodied and depicted a specific deity, and was situated within the main room of a temple

Delian League alliance of **poleis** set up in 477 BC. Under the leadership of the Athenians, **poleis** from the coastal regions and islands of the Aegean Sea joined together for mutual defence against the Persians

democracy (pl. **democracies**) formed from 'demos' meaning 'people' and 'kratos' meaning 'power'. It is a system of government where the freeborn men of the city voted on issues and elected officials

eros passion that can often accompany *hubris* and *ate*

foreshortening creating a sense of three-dimensional perspective in a two-dimensional space

free-standing sculpture not used to decorate architecture. Sculpture that stands alone, without a background or supporting unit

frieze (pl. **friezes**) a rectangular band of sculptural decoration that wraps around all four sides of a temple

himation a mantle or cloak; a thicker piece of clothing, that was often worn on top of the chiton or peplos

hoplite (pl. **hoplites**) a Greek soldier armed with a long spear and a large circular shield. They fought in a tight formation called a phalanx. Hoplite tactics were particularly effective against the Persians at Marathon in 490 BC

hubris mortal arrogance or defiance that is offensive to the gods

Immortals the name of the personal guard of the king, which was always made up to 1,000 soldiers. They were the elite soldiers of the Persian army and are represented on the walls of the royal palaces

in the round sculptures that are not attached to anything else, but are free-standing

kaolinite a clay that is free from iron-oxide and appears white. It was used to produce the background colour of white-ground vases

kore (pl. **korai**) literally, a maiden or unmarried girl, and a type of sculpture from the Archaic Period

kouros (pl. **kouroi**) literally, a male youth, and a type of sculpture from the Archaic Period

krater (Gk pl. **kratera**) a large bowl used for mixing wine and water

kylix (Gk pl. **kylikes**) a drinking cup used at a symposium

logos (Gk pl. **logoi**) 'tale' or 'story'. Herodotus includes **logoi** in his *Histories* to describe people, places and events. Words such as 'biology' and 'prologue' are derived from '**logos**'

medise a verb that means 'to go over to the Persian side'. The Persians are often called Medes in Herodotus. In every *polis* there will have been elements in the city who would have been keen to **medise**, particularly those who were not keen on popular **democracies**. The success of the Greeks against the Persians may have seemed unlikely to some

metope (pl. **metopes**) a square-shaped panel decorated with relief sculpture (where the sculpture remains attached to the background). These panels would decorate the space between the bottom of the roof and the tops of the columns of a Greek temple

motif either a recurring idea, scene or situation in artistic works (such as duelling warriors or the Master of the Animals), or a repeated pattern

oligarchy (pl. **oligarchies**) formed from 'oligos' meaning 'few' and 'archo' meaning 'rule'. It is a system of government where a small group of wealthy people rule the city

oxidation the process whereby oxygen interacts with other materials; on vases, the iron in the paint turned red

panhellenic literally means 'all' (pan) 'Greeks' (Hellenes). Panhellenic sanctuaries refer to those that were open to all Greeks

pediment (pl. **pediments**) the triangular-shaped gable end of the roof at the front and back of a Greek temple, usually facing east and west

peplos a rectangular piece of woollen clothing, without sleeves, that was belted and also tied or sown at the shoulder

polis (Gk pl. **poleis**) an independent state with a city at its heart. Each **polis** had an army made up of its own citizens and its own political system; in the 7th and 6th centuries BC, the governments in the Greek **poleis** varied between **aristocracies**, **oligarchies** and **tyrannies**. Each **polis** varied in size: Athens was the largest by population, Sparta became the largest by territory

red-figure figures are painted as silhouettes and details are then incised so that the red of the clay shows through

relief sculptures attached to a background surface; if in low relief, they project only slightly from this background surface, but if in high relief, they project at least half or more of their natural circumference from the background

rhyton (Gk pl. **rhyta**) a cone-shaped drinking vessel

satrapy (pl. **satrapies**) an administrative district governed by a *satrap* (pl. *satraps*). The *satrap* controlled only the civil government. As checks on the power of the *satrap*, the king also appointed a military commander, who was in charge of the army, and a finance officer, who controlled the treasury

Severe Style the transitionary period between the Archaic and Classical Periods, dating to roughly between 490 and 450 BC; the style is characterised by thick eyelids, heavy and simple drapery, and an increase in individual characterisation

silen named after Silenus, the elderly tutor of Dionysus, silens are mythological male followers of Dionysus, typically depicted with horse features and large phalluses; they inhabit the forests and amuse themselves with music, wine and women

symposium (Gk pl. **symposia**) a Greek drinking party

thoma (Gk pl. **thomata**) a wonder. Herodotus is particularly interested in the surprises offered both by nature and by different cultures

tondo (pl. **tondos**) a circular image painted on the inside of a **kylix**

topos (pl. **topoi**) a recurring feature of a writer's style

triglyph a series of three vertical grooves separating metopes

tyranny (pl. **tyrannies**) formed from 'tyrannos' meaning 'ruler'. It is a system of government where one person has overall control. Although it later came to be associated with cruelty, many Greek tyrants came to power after a revolt by the people of the city against wealthy land-owners

wet drapery technique used from the mid-fifth century BC onwards for female figures only particularly Aphrodite, minor goddesses or nymphs; the drapery is so thin that it clings tightly to the figure's body, as though wet, emphasising attractiveness and sexuality, or denoting movement or flight, as the wind forces the garment to cling to the body

white-ground figures are painted as on red-figure vases, but the slip is white

SOURCES OF QUOTATIONS

Inventing the Barbarian

All translations copyright OCR unless otherwise stated.

14 '"Greekness" . . .' Cartledge, *The Greeks* (Oxford University Press, 2002), p. 3; **15** 'They speak . . .' Herodotus, *Histories*, 7.9; **20** 'The Battle . . .' Cartledge, *Thermopylae* (Macmillan, 2006), p. xii; **21** 'Those who gave . . .' Herodotus, 7.138; **22** 'At this point . . .' Herodotus, 7.138; **22** '. . . to call . . .' Herodotus, 7.138; **23** 'Most of those. . .' Herodotus, 8.49; **24** 'We are well . . .' Herodotus, 8.143; **24** '. . . we are Greek . . .' Herodotus, 8.144; **24** 'In cold . . .' Cartledge, *The Greeks*, p. 54; **27** 'For the time . . .' Herodotus, 8.60; **27** 'Most of those . . .' Herodotus, 8.49; **29** 'a speaker of words and a doer of deeds' Homer, *Iliad*, 9.444; **31** 'My men . . .' Herodotus, 8.88; **34** 'emotional . . .' Hall, *Inventing the Barbarian* (Oxford University Press, 1989), p. 17; **35** 'Whenever Xerxes . . .' Herodotus, 8.90; **35** 'As soon . . .' Herodotus, 8.118; **36** 'A god . . .' Herodotus, 7.8; **37** 'The battle . . .' Lane Fox, *The Classical World* (Allen Lane, 2005), p. 107; **44** '. . . any Greek . . .' Mayor, *The Amazons* (Princeton University Press, 2014), p. 151; **53** 'The conventional . . .' Hall, *Greek Tragedy* (Oxford University Press, 2010), p. 128; **55** 'What now . . .' Euripides, *Medea*, 1316–1348, trans. J. Harrison, *Euripides: Medea* (Cambridge University Press, 1999); **61** '. . . it is beyond . . .' Hall, *Persians* (Aris and Phillips, 1996), p. 5; **61** 'In this play . . .' Hall, *Inventing the Barbarian*, p. 71; **64** 'This is the account . . .' Herodotus, 1.1; **64** 'If despotic . . .' Hartog, *The Mirror of Herodotus* (University of California Press, 1988), p. 130; **65** 'Since I came . . .' Herodotus, 8.8**65** 'The sun . . .' Herodotus, 7.8; **65** 'As much . . .' Herodotus, 7.18; **66** 'For we did not . . .' Herodotus, 8.109; **66** 'The first . . .' Herodotus, 8.53; **66** 'Even so . . .' Herodotus, 8.68; **67** 'This is not . . .' Herodotus, 7.16; **67** 'Even now that Xerxes . . .' Herodotus, 7.19; **67** 'When the envoys . . .' Herodotus, 7.142; **67–68** 'I have no way . . .' Herodotus, 8.77; **68** 'This is the account . . .' Herodotus, 1.1; **70** 'This dichotomy . . .' Flower, *Herodotus and Persia* (Cambridge University Press, 2006), p. 275; **73** 'This is the statue . . .' DSab, trans. Livius.org; **74** 'As I have learned . . .' Herodotus, 7.8; **75** '. . . he brought . . .' Cyrus Cylinder, lines 7, 8, trans. Finkel; **75** 'As for the . . .' Cyrus Cylinder, lines 25, 26, trans. Finkel; **76** 'There is nothing . . .' Herodotus, 8.98; **76** 'I am Cyrus . . .' Cyrus Cylinder, lines 20, 21, trans. Finkel; **81** 'The message . . .' Waters, *Ancient Persia* (Cambridge University Press, 2014), pp. 143–144; **83** 'Out of everybody . . .' Herodotus, 7.83; **85** 'I will punish . . .' Herodotus, 7.8; **85** 'Cyrus, Cambyses . . .' Herodotus, 7.8; **86** 'Look at the sculptures . . .' DNa, trans. Livius.org; **86** 'Darius . . .' DNa, trans. Livius.org; **87** 'So quickly! . . .' Aeschylus, *Persians*, 739–759, trans. P. Vellacott, *Prometheus Bound and Other Plays* (Penguin, 1961); **91** 'Medea! . . .' Euripides, *Medea*, 1323–1343, trans. J. Harrison.

Greek Art

109 'the Greek kouroi . . .' Osborne, *Archaic and Classical Greek Art* (Oxford University Press, 1998), pp. 78–79; **113** 'Stay . . .' IG I3 1240, trans. L. Jeffrey (1962) 'The inscribed gravestones of Archaic Attica', BSA 57: 115–153; **114** 'as grave . . .' Stewart, *Greek Sculpture* (Yale University Press, 1993), p. 110; **116** 'And if . . .' Thucydides, 2.46, trans. Lattimore *Thucydides, The Peloponnesian War* (Hackett Publishing Company, 1998); **117** 'it was perhaps . . .' Stewart, *Greek Sculpture*, p. 110; **121** 'He seems . . .' Pliny, *Natural Histories*, 34.57–58, trans. Stewart; **124** 'we no longer . . .' Osborne, *Archaic and Classical Greek Art*, p. 163; **127** 'among the sculptors . . .' Pliny, *Natural Histories*, 36.21, trans. Stewart; **127** 'masterfully . . .' Diodoros, 26.1, trans. Stewart; **128** 'she is . . .' Pseudo-Lucian, *Amores*, 13–14, trans. M.D. MacLeod, *Lucian Volume* VIII (Harvard University Press, 1967); **142** '. . . the Siphnians . . .' Herodotus III.57, trans. A. Godley, *Herodotus: The Persian Wars, Books 3–4* (Harvard University Press, 1921); **147** 'It produced . . .' Homer, *Iliad*, 4.17,. The Iliad. trans. Martin Hammond, *Homer: The Iliad* (London: Penguin, 1987); **151** 'dulce . . .' Horace, *Odes*, III.2.13; **154** '. . . one of . . .' Pollitt, *Art and Experience in Classical Greece* (Cambridge University Press, 1972), pp. 14ff; **154** 'The moment . . .' Osborne, *Archaic and Classical Greek Art*, pp. 171f; **197** 'the Berlin . . .' Williams, *Greek Vases* (British Museum Press, 1999, 2nd edn), p. 80; **202** 'quirky charm' Williams, *Greek Vases*, p. 88; **203** 'has produced . . .' Woodford, *Greek Art* (Bloomsbury Academic, 2015), p. 109.

SOURCES OF ILLUSTRATIONS

INDEX

Numbers in **bold** indicate figures.